SPACE, TIME
& MEDICINE

LARRY DOSSEY, M.D.

SPACE, TIME & MEDICINE

Foreword by Fritjof Capra

SHAMBHALA
BOULDER & LONDON 1982

Shambhala Publications, Inc.
1920 13th Street
Boulder, Colorado 80302

Distributed in the United States by Random House
and in Canada by Random House of Canada Ltd.
Distributed in the United Kingdom by Routledge & Kegan Paul Ltd.,
London and Henley-on-Thames.

Printed in the United States of America.

Library of Congress Cataloging in Publication Data
Dossey, Larry, 1940—
  Space, time, and medicine.

  Includes bibliographical references and index.
  1. Medicine—Philosophy. 2. Health. I. Title.
R723.D67   610'.1   81-84449
ISBN 0-87773-221-1   AACR2
ISBN 0-87773-224-8 (pbk.)
ISBN 0-394-52465-9 (Random House)
ISBN 0-394-71091-6 (Random House: pbk.)

Illustrations by George R. Holman, Dallas, Texas.

Contents

for Barbie
my wife
who knows these realms

FOREWORD

IN SPITE OF THE GREAT ADVANCES of modern medical science we are now witnessing a profound crisis in health care in Europe and North America. Many reasons are given for the widespread dissatisfaction with medical institutions—inaccessibility of services, lack of sympathy and care, malpractice—but the central theme of all criticism is the striking disproportion between the cost and effectiveness of modern medicine. Despite a staggering increase in health costs over the past three decades, and amid continuing claims of scientific and technological excellence by the medical profession, the health of the population does not seem to have improved significantly.

The causes of our health crisis are manifold and can be found both within or without medical science. Nevertheless, increasing numbers of people, both within and outside the medical field, perceive the shortcomings of the current health-care system as being rooted in the conceptual framework that supports medical theory and practice, and have come to believe that the crisis will persist unless this framework is modified.

The crisis in medicine, then, is essentially a crisis of perception, and hence it is inextricably linked to a much larger social and cultural crisis; a complex, multi-dimensional crisis whose facets touch every aspect of our lives. We can read about its numerous manifestations every day in the newspapers. We have high inflation and unemployment, we have an energy crisis, pollution and other environmental disasters, the threat of nuclear war, a rising wave of violence and crime, and so on. All these can be seen as different aspects of one and the same crisis, which derives from the fact that we are trying to apply the concepts of an outdated world view—the mechanistic world view of Cartesian-Newtonian science—to a reality that can no longer be understood in terms of these concepts. We live today in a globally interconnected world, in which biological, psychological, social, and environmental phenomena are all interdependent. To describe this world appropriately we need an ecological perspective, which the Cartesian world view does not offer.

What we need, then, is a new vision of reality; a fundamental change in our thoughts, perceptions, and values. The beginnings of this change, of the shift from the mechanistic to the holistic conception of reality, are already visible in all fields and are likely to dominate the entire decade. the present book is an eminent example of the movement from fragmentation to wholeness within medicine. Written by a practicing physician who illustrates his ideas with numerous examples from his clinical experience, *Space, Time and Medicine* presents compelling evidence for the conceptual crisis of current medical science and points to directions for change.

Current medical practice is firmly rooted in Cartesian thinking. Descartes based his view of nature on a fundamental division into two separate and independent realms: that of mind and that of matter. The material universe was a machine and nothing but a machine. Nature worked according to mechanical laws, and everything in the material world could be explained in terms of the arrangement and movement of its parts. Descartes extended this mechanistic view of matter to living organisms. Plants and animals were considered simply machines; human beings were inhabited by a rational soul, but the human body was indistinguishable from an animal-machine.

The conceptual framework created by Descartes was completed triumphantly by Newton who developed a consistent mathematical formulation of the mechanistic view of nature. The stage of the Newtonian universe, on which all physical phenomena took place, was the three-dimensional space of classical Euclidean geometry. It was an absolute space, an empty container that was independent of the physical phenomena occurring in it. All changes in the physical world were described in terms of a separate dimension, time, which again was absolute, having no connection with the material world and flowing smoothly from the past through the present to the future. The elements of the Newtonian world which moved in this absolute space and absolute time were material particles; small, solid and indestructible objects—the building blocks out of which all matter was made.

From the second half of the seventeenth century to the end of the nineteenth, the Newtonian model of the universe dominated all scientific thought. The natural sciences, as well as the humanities and social sciences, all accepted the mechanistic view of classical physics as the correct description of reality and modelled their own theories accordingly. Whenever physicians, psychologists, or sociologists wanted to be scientific, they naturally turned toward the basic concepts of Newtonian physics, and many of them hold on to these concepts even now that physicists have gone far beyond them.

In biomedical science the Cartesian view of living organisms as machines, constructed from separate parts, still provides the dominant conceptual framework. For Descartes, a healthy person was like a well-made clock in perfect mechanical condition, a sick person like a clock whose parts were not functioning properly. The principal characterisitics of modern medical theory, as well as many aspects of current medical practice, can be traced back to this Cartesian imagery. Follwing the Cartesian approach, medical science has limited itself to the attempt of understanding the biological mechanisms involved in injuries to various parts of the body and, in doing so, often loses sight of the patient as a human being. It has concentrated on smaller and smaller fragments of the body, shifting its perspective from the study of bodily organs and their functions to that of cells and, finally, to the study of molecules.

However, while biomedical scientists elaborated mechanistic models of health and illness, the conceptual basis of their science was shattered by dramatic developments in atomic and subatomic physics, which clearly revealed the limitations of the mechanistic world view and led to an organic and ecological conception of reality. In twentieth-century physics, the universe is no longer perceived as a machine, made up of a multitude of separate objects, but appears as a harmonious indivisible whole; a web of dynamic relationships that include the human observer and his or her consciousness in an essential way. Space and time are no longer absolute, nor are they separate dimensions. Both are intimately and inseparably connected and form a four-dimensional continuum called space-time. Subatomic particles are interconnections in a network of events, bundles of energy, or patterns of activity. When we observe them, we never see any material substance; what we observe are dynamic patterns continually changing into one another—a continuous dance of energy.

The conceptual revolution in modern physics foreshadows an imminent revolution in all the sciences and a profound transformation of our world view and values. The main fascination of Larry Dossey's book, for me, lies in the fact that the author discusses the dramatic shift in the conceptual basis of medicine and its relation to the new concepts of subatomic physics not from an abstract, theoretical point of view, but rather from the perspective of concrete clinical experience. In doing so, Dr. Dossey focuses particularly on the relation between our health and our perception of time. "Many illnesses, perhaps most," he writes, "may be caused either wholly or in part by our misperception of time."

As an alternative to the current medical model, Dr. Dossey develops the outlines of a "space-time model" of health that is in agreement with the view of reality suggested by modern physics. It is charcterized by the notion of the "biodance"—of human beings as essentially dynamic processes, not analyzable into separate parts and closey linked to their environment, and of health as the harmony of fluid movement. Dr. Dossey recognizes fully that this space-time model of health will require a profound reorientation of many of our basic concepts. In fact, he sees such a reorientation as a major aspect of any therapy:

> The spacetime view of health and disease tells us that a vital part of the goal of every therapist is to help the sick person toward a reordering of his world view. We must help him realize that he is a *process* in spacetime, not an isolated entity who is fragmented from the world of the healthy and who is adrift in flowing time, moving slowly toward extermination. To the extent that we accomplish this task we are healers.

Larry Dossey's book represents an important step in the reordering of our world view, which is not only intellectually stimulating but will also be therapeutic.

Berkeley, December 1981 Fritjof Capra

PREFACE

TAKING CARE OF SICK PERSONS can be heady business these days. I frequently hear that we physicians now know more and can do more than any of our predecessors; that our technological prowess is awesome; and that the remaining deficiencies in our skills will yield to a bit more basic research, funding, and manpower. It's just a matter of time. Sometimes I feel that an air of downright smugness has set it.

The eminent physicist Niels Bohr once remarked that a *great* truth was one whose opposite was also true. If Bohr was right, and if contemporary physicians are correct in their belief that medicine has never before been so powerful, then we physicians have laid hold of a monumentally great truth—for in many ways medicine has never been weaker. We are at once powerful and effete, good and bad, the best and worst.

It is hardly a revelation to hear that something is awry in medicine nowadays. Castigations are nothing new, neither from within nor without the profession, and most of us physicians are tired by now of the same worn criticisms. In spite of our periodic flights of enthusiasm about what we know and can do, most of us sense our weaknesses before we're reminded of them. Medicine isn't right, and we know it.

What is surely one of the greatest ironies in the history of medicine is being played out before us. Modern medicine has learned to look to the hard sciences as models, hoping to embody the precision and exactness demonstrated most notably by classical physics. Believing we have actually found that precision, we in medicine refuse to listen to the message that has come from physics for over half a century: *the exactness never really existed.* Today medicine is like a loser in a shell game: once we saw it, now we don't.

We have built a model of health and illness, birth and death, around an outmoded conceptual model of how the universe behaves, one which was fundamentally flawed from the beginning. While the physicists have been painfully eliminating the flaws from their own models, we have in medicine ignored those revisions totally. We find ourselves, thus, with a set of guiding beliefs that are as antiquated as are body humors, leeching, and bleeding.

This book is an examination of those flaws, and an exploration of new models. It is an attempt to correct the irony of "modern" medicine, believing that, surely, no medicine can be modern which does not square with the best of contemporary physical science.

There is an unmistakable sentiment outside of medicine that much of the cold, inhumane, and impersonal qualities of the health care system are a result of a reliance on science that is itself cold and uncaring. There is, thus, a widely held belief that the backwardness of an older medicine is preferable to the science of the new. Choices must be made: Are we to pursue a scientific but unfeeling modern medicine or return to a more humane and satisfying, yet clumsy, medicine of an earlier day?

These choices, I feel, are artificial constructs. They come about because of the flaws inherent in our outmoded medical models, and they vanish when we bring those models up to date. I am convinced that the only medical models that are truly salutary to the human spirit are those that are compatible with the best of science—but *best*, not *outmoded*.

The conceptual renovation long overdue in medicine, the trading of the old for the best, can give us what we so sorely need: a technologically advanced system characterized not by dehumanization and despair, but by brightness, hope, and life. Yes, we *can* have it both ways.

By training and temperament, I am a physician. I feel an unmistakable affinity with healers whatever the age or culture, whether shamans or my fellow internists. This book, therefore, is not the confession of an informant or disenchanted deserter from the ranks, but is quite the contrary—it is a thoughtful rumination of what it means to be born, to live and die; to suffer and grow old; to experience good health and bad, all from the perspective of a practicing physician who unapologetically considers the role of the healer still to be a lofty and legitimate calling.

I have not ceased to be awed by the ordinary and routine occurrences in medicine that constitute a part of my daily life. Recovery from pneumonia, acute appendicitis, an infected gallbladder, or diabetic ketoacidosis still seems miraculous to me. These events, ordinarily considered curable today, frequently were fatal in times past. And when I recall that I have in all my life never even seen an acute case of smallpox, plague, or polio, I *know* that we have done something in medicine that is very powerful and very right. I am proud to be a part of it.

It may seem paradoxical, therefore, that this book challenges almost every basic assumption of modern medicine, whose traditions and accomplishments I am glad to share. In explanation, to my fellow physicians I can offer that the history of our profession is the history of change; that we have always drawn from the advances of other disciplines; that as powerful as our models might be, they, like all scientific models, have always been imperfect; and that an insular, parochial defensiveness has always worked toward our impoverishment. And to the nonphysicians who might interpret this book as a strident, wholesale condemnation of modern medicine, I would invite you to use a finer scrutiny, for no condemnation is intended. What follows is not an attack on an honorable profession, but a sincere attempt to find new meanings and a better way.

I have taken great care to render several complex areas of science understandable to the nonscientist. To my fellow physicians who may be appalled at my purposeful simplification of disease processes, and to the physicists, chemists, and biologists who will look aghast at my uncomplicated, nontechnical descriptions of highly complex subjects, I can only reply that for the purposes of this book I can see nothing to be gained by being obscure. My goal throughout has been to be understood.

IN THE FORMULATION AND EXECUTION of this book I have incurred great debts. It should be said first that in many ways it is to one's patients that physicians owe everything. I am deeply indebted to those I have served.

It is impossible for me to express my gratitude to the greatest physician and internist who had a hand in my training, Seymour Eisenberg, M.D., my Chief of Medicine. Without his influence I likely would not now be a physician, even after becoming an M.D. Dr. Eisenberg embodies that ineffable amalgam of intellectual power, humaneness, personal strength, humor, and quiet compassion that typifies all healers who are worthy of the name. He exemplifies a nobility as a physician that was for me worth striving for.

I must also acknowledge my fellow physicians in the Dallas Diagnostic Association who collectively form the most skillful and compassionate group of physicians I know: Paul Anderson; Roger Camp; Don Crumbo; Joan Donley; Tom Hampton; Charles Harris; David Haymes; William Hensley; Lannie Hughes; Carlos Kier; C. Thomas Long, III; Jack Melton; J. Edward Rosenthal; Joe Sample; Jack Schwade; Charles Sledge; Rick Waldo; and Charles S. White, III—as well as Carl Ikard, our administrator and advisor. Their support was a major factor in the execution of this project.

Genuine thanks are due to Cathie Guzzetta, who first said this book must be written.

I must thank one whose words appear throughout this book, and who during its writing has consistently been looking on from a nearby place—Walt Whitman. Walt understood these concepts, and he set them down in his own way. He, too, cared for sick and dying persons as a nurse in the American Civil War, and those experiences surely helped to shape his vision. And in his own infirmity he was himself cared for by a great healer, Sir William Osler, the father of American medicine.

I owe a unique debt to Juan and Rosa Ortega for implementing the many pilgrimages to the mountains and deserts where much of this material was conceived and written.

I reserve eternal gratitude to my Mother and Father for the universal constant of love; to my sister, Bet, who never doubted; and to my brother, Garry, who shared with me a unique first knowledge of space and time through identicality and twinness in utero.

Finally, to one person all acknowledgments and thanks seem inadequate and hollow, frail and superfluous—Barbie, my wife, with whom I share a bond of unity and oneness that is a central theme of this book.

Larry Dossey, M.D.
Dallas, Texas

NOTE: The clinical cases which follow are taken from the author's practice of internal medicine. The names of the patients involved have been changed to preserve confidentiality.

I

Problem

Now I re-examine philosophies and
   religions,
They may prove well in lecture-rooms,
   yet not prove at all under the
   spacious clouds and along the
   landscape and flowing currents.

—WALT WHITMAN
LEAVES OF GRASS

HEXES AND MOLECULES

But the demons are immortals—fortunately for the sorcerers whose living depends on them. Next year the same rites must be performed all over again.
—ALEXANDRA DAVID-NEEL[1]

OUR SHADOWS DANCED ON THE WALLS of the small room, an examination area just off the nurses' station that we could lock from the inside. On the desk top in a metal ash tray the small white tablet burned with an eerie blue flame. It was a methenamine tablet, an antibiotic of low potency used to treat urinary tract infections. I had learned that it was flammable years ago. Always kept on hand on the hospital ward in the nurses' station, it was readily available for our "ceremony."

The old man sat stolid and wide-eyed. He had been admitted to the internal medicine service of the hospital two weeks before to Jim, my fellow intern and close friend. The man was dying. He was emaciated and had the look of death which, six months into our internship, we had learned to recognize. I watched the methenamine burn, not believing what we were doing.

For two weeks the wizened old man submitted to diagnostic studies—the usual barrage of x-rays and blood tests. Without exception they proved normal. His admitting diagnosis was cancer, a reasonable presumption in an elderly male with a fifty-pound weight loss in a six-month period. Jim patiently pursued the "workup" in spite of the chain of normal results with the faith that sooner or later he would find evidence of "real disease." And as the diagnostic workup proceeded, the old man worsened. By now he was profoundly weak, almost bedfast.

Then, two days ago, the evaluation was concluded. Jim had simply run out of tests to do. He was faced with the embarrassing dilemma of having a dying patient in his care and no explanation for his illness. As he made morning rounds he told the old man of the predicament. "You're dying and I don't know why." His patient replied, "That's all right, Doctor. I know I'm dying. And I know why, too." Jim stared at him, not believing what he had heard. The old man went on, "Doctor, I've been hexed."

He then related the astonishing account of how his health had begun to fail. Three months prior an enemy of his hired a local shaman to perpetrate a hex on him. (The reasons surrounding this event never came to light.) The shaman was successful in convincing his wife to clip a lock of the man's gray hair and to deliver it into her possession. Using this embodiment of the man, she worked a spell. At the proper time she let it be known to the old man and to his adversary that he had been "hexed," and that he would die.

Curiously, to us, from the start the old man never resisted this pronouncement. That the hex might not work never seemed to have occurred to him. It was as if he were already dead, delivered totally of his will to live. From the day he discovered he was hexed, he stopped eating. His weight loss was inexorable, and he came to the hospital to die.

Jim called me into an examination room and related the bizarre story. He was excited at this revelation. My own response to the new information about the hex was despairing—I felt sympathy for the patient's plight, but could not think of anything else to do. I felt he was right, that he *was* going to die.

Jim's attitude was different. "We have to cure him," was his parting comment as we agreed to meet later to discuss "therapy" for his patient.

Over the next twenty-four hours Jim developed a therapeutic strategy with little help from me. He threw himself into the task with an incredible energy. I now realize what I did not know then: I was witnessing an archetypal struggle—one shaman battling another shaman—a struggle over life itself. Although he didn't recognize it as such, Jim was pitting his medicine against his adversary's hex. And the stakes were the life or death of the old gray-haired man.

Jim had decided to wait until Saturday night for the "ceremony." Hospital activity was at a lull on the weekend, and there would be less chance of our being discovered. At midnight he went into the patient's room and assisted him into a wheelchair—by then he was too weak to walk. He then checked the corridor, making sure it was deserted, and scurried with his patient into the examining room across the hall where I was waiting, having lit the methenamine tablet already. As Jim entered with the old man I nervously locked the door behind him, feeling foolish and apprehensive about the prospect of being discovered. We were all three alone in silence and near-darkness.

Jim sat in a chair near the flame. After what seemed an eternity he arose, at perfect ease and in complete command of the situation. The old man and I followed his every move. He loomed larger than life in the strange light—I was witnessing a real shaman at work. He seemed absolutely serious about his task, aware that his patient's life depended on the skillful disposition of his power.

Jim produced from his pocket a pair of stainless steel surgical scissors he had "borrowed" for the occasion. In the faint blue light they gleamed as he moved toward the old man, who sat transfixed in his wheelchair, following every one of Jim's slow, deliberate moves. He walked to the wheelchair, raised the scissors, and grasping a lock of gray hair with his other hand began slowly to cut.

The old man seemed by then to have stopped breathing. With the lock of hair in his left hand Jim slowly retreated to the desk top, appearing massive as he stood over the dancing flame. Then he looked squarely at his rigid, wasted patient and said slowly in a calm, deep voice, "As the fire burns your hair, the hex in your body is destroyed." He lowered his hand, allowing the hair to fall into the flame. Then he added the whimsical caution, "But if you reveal this ceremony to anyone, the hex will return immediately, stronger than before!" (I was grateful that Jim was a shaman who was aware of potential professional humiliation!)

The ceremony was over. I unlocked the door as silently as possible, and Jim wheeled the mute old man across the deserted corridor to his room, assisting him to bed. He returned, but said little. For some strange reason an atmosphere of seriousness pervaded this zany occasion. Exhausted, we parted, after vowing eternal silence about this midnight caper.

The "de-hexing" was almost immediate in its onset. Jim's patient awoke with a voracious appetite! He ordered triple servings for breakfast, which was notoriously the hospital's most inedible meal of the day. He continued to order double helpings thereafter for every meal, seemingly oblivious to what was being served. His weight increased almost unbelievably.

True to the warning, he never mentioned the "de-hexing" ceremony, not even to Jim. His attitude was cheerful, almost ebullient,

from that time forward. He never waivered in his belief that he had
been truly rescued by Jim the Shaman.

Jim kept him in the hospital for several days, wanting to be certain
that his "de-hexing" had firmly taken. When he was finally sure
that his patient was cured, he discharged him. He left the hospital a
well man, leaving behind a fat hospital chart full of normal test
results—and an examination room which aggravatingly for days
reeked of burning hair. . . .

THE MOLECULAR MODEL

Jim and I ceased to discuss the incident. The issues of surviving a
hectic year of internship—hard work, little sleep, and subsistence
pay—were pressing; and as time passed I forgot about the event.

In retrospect it is interesting for me to recall how my own conscious processes dealt with the episode of Jim's gray-haired, hexed
patient. From start to finish the case was bizarre and unsettling. The
man's illness and cure didn't fit with anything I had learned in
medical school, where disease was considered to be the result of
deranged cellular processes. Disease, we were told, was caused by
a malfunction of the machine, the body. And the raison d'etre of
the physician was to localize the malady and exterminate it, where
possible.

But what of Jim's patient? It seemed clear that the *initial* break-
down was not in the "machine." Indeed, Jim's tests failed to find
anything wrong. According to the laboratory tests and x-rays, the
machine was functioning perfectly. But the old man was dying.

Now it seems clear why I relegated this experience to the status of
some quaint aberrant occurrence that had no real significance. To do
otherwise would have been to question my entire belief system
about disease causation. Now, years hence, the repressive efficiency
of my own consciousness is not so great, and that experience—and
hundreds similar to it that have occurred since—have transformed
my understanding of how humans become sick.

As an intern, and later as a resident physician in internal medicine, I prided myself in my expert mastery of the "medical model"—
that traditional set of guiding principles which show how individuals
fall ill. The emphasis began and ended with the body. The thrust
of the efforts of medical scientists results overwhelmingly in understanding disease processes at the level of the molecule. The molecule is to the bioscientist what the quark is for the particle physicist:

the fundamental unit, the derangement of which sets in motion a cascade of malfunction that we recognize as clinical disease. For this reason the modern medical model is called the molecular theory of disease causation.

The precision of biochemical analysis in probing to the molecular level has generated an enchantment that in our own time has become heretical to doubt. It is assumed that in any given disease, if our knowledge is complete, we shall be able to pinpoint how the molecule is misbehaving. That other explanations might exist simply is not ordinarily considered.

The evidence for the accuracy of the model was, until recently, never questioned in meaningful ways. Certain classical diseases demonstrated its explanatory power. For example, certain diseases of the blood could be traced to an abnormality in the synthesis of the hemoglobin molecule, where it was apparent that minor deviations from the normal arrangement of atoms within the molecule itself produced devastating consequences.

Every major disease is analyzed in this way. The central thrust in the most common cause of death in our society, arteriosclerotic heart disease, for example, is to understand why the cholesterol *molecule* is sequestered in the lining of blood vessels, forming obstructions we call atheromas. From the perspective of molecular medicine, all other approaches are shortsighted—diet, weight reduction, exercise, or even the spectacular intervention of coronary artery bypass surgery—because they merely skirt the *cause* of the problem, which (by definition) can only be understood by penetrating to the level of the molecule.

In the same way we approach the other major diseases of our day. What biochemical aberrations occur to cause high blood pressure? Are abnormal *molecules* elaborated within the body to drive the blood pressure up? Are too many sodium *molecules* reabsorbed by the kidney, producing high blood pressure? What kinds of *molecules*—called high blood pressure medication—can we ingest to lower the blood pressure? Molecular derangements lead to strategies of molecular intervention: molecule pitted against molecule in an attempt to correct the fundamental problem.

In cancer, we think in terms of abnormalities of the replication process of molecules. In diabetes, the insulin molecule is either in absolute or relative short supply, or is defective. Depression may be caused by biochemical imbalances—certain molecules, critical for normal emotional function, may be deficient.

All diseases find representation in the molecular pantheon. If there appear to be any exceptions, it is our data which is deficient, and not the theory itself. Eventually all diseases will yield to a molecular analysis, for which we shall design a molecular intervention. So the theory goes.

But what of Jim's patient? He and his hex lay for years in my memory as a nuisance. That kind of "data" simply did not fit. Ironically, it was as if, for me, the old man himself had hexed my model of molecular medicine, making *it* sick.

CHAPTER TWO

SCIENTISTS AND PATAGONIANS

. . . since we have come to the understanding that science is not a description of "reality" but a metaphorical ordering of experience, the new science does not impugn the old. It is not a question of which view is "true" in some ultimate sense. Rather, it is a matter of which picture is more useful in guiding human affairs.

WILLIS HARMAN[1]

SCIENCE: WHAT DO WE MEAN?

How exactly, does science work? How do scientists go about "doing" science?

Ordinarily we think science proceeds in a straight-forward way. Ideally scientists make observations, formulate hypotheses, and test those hypotheses by making further observations. When there is discrepancy between what is observed and what is predicted by the hypothesis, the hypothesis is revised. Science proceeds in this way, which is a gradual method of finding the best fit between observation and prediction.

But this idealized version of how one "does" science is naive. Although science demands proof that observations made by one observer be observable by other observers using the same methods, it is by no means clear that, even when confronted with identical phenomena, different observers will report identical observations. And it is most certain that, even if the same observations are made, the conclusions as to the meaning of the observations frequently differ. These variations in observation and in formulating ideas about what is observed are crucial to the studies dealing with human consciousness that follow.

9

The fact is that all of us, scientists included, see differently. Variations in human perception are well known and have been studied extensively.[2] Distortions in perception are frequently seen among observers, even though they may be in identical settings viewing identical phenomena.

A documented misperception from history can be found in the experience of Darwin. His ship, *Beagle*, after anchoring off the Patagonian coast, dispatched a landing party in small rowboats. Amazingly, the Patagonian natives watching from shore were blind to the *Beagle*, but could easily see the tiny rowboats! They had no prior experience of monstrous sailing ships, but canoes—small rowing vessels—were an everyday part of their life. Rowboats fit their model of the world and brigantines did not. Their model determined their perceptions.

Our idea that science proceeds on an utterly objective and straightforward basis ignores the distortions of reality imposed by our own perceptual apparatus. In many cases we see what we have been trained to see, what we are used to seeing. This is obvious from studies done in human visual perception. If a subject is fitted with special glasses that are designed to invert the visual field, at first the subject sees everything upside down. After a period of time, as the glasses continue to be worn, a correction is made by our perceptual mechanism and the image is flipped, so that the world once again appears erect.[3]

These observations suggest that the models we make of the world actually determine in some measure what we see, making the goal of scientific objectivity elusive indeed. Kuhn expresses this point:

> As for a pure observation-language, perhaps one will yet be devised. But three centuries after Descartes our hope for such an eventuality still depends exclusively upon a theory of perception and of the mind. And modern psychological experimentation is rapidly proliferating phenomena with which that theory can scarcely deal . . . . the inverting lenses show that two men with different retinal impressions can see the same thing.[4]

The problem now in medicine is that the fit of the medical model and the clinical observations that physicians actually make are so discrepant as to be beyond salvage. Later we shall look at this misfit, seeking clues for a better model. Unlike Darwin's Patagonians, we shall attempt to allow not only the miniscule rowboats to penetrate our perceptions, but the brigantines as well.

A model is merely a set of beliefs used to make sense of what we observe in the world. Thus, even though they may influence what we observe, models are in a strong sense *determined* by what we see. Prior to 1492, for example, one could easily count oneself learned and believe the earth to be flat. This belief was a perfectly coherent model for organizing personal experience. There was nothing in the experience of the average person to contradict it, and it fit well with the objective data of the day. But when it became possible to travel great distances, as did Columbus and Magellan, the data changed. And, consequently, the model of the earth's configuration had to be revised.

In medicine today we have taken Magellanic voyages. Our data has changed as a result. We no longer live on the level earth of the molecular model, which has heretofore served well in explaining a more limited data base. Just as the navigators and cartographers of the fifteenth century found the earth to be spherical and thus a more complex structure than the plane, today we are forced to recognize that human health is more complex than can be accounted for by molecular behavior.

In bioscience the Magellans have returned with news of strange lands, and the news that modern medical scientists are bringing back is no less revolutionary than that which the earliest circumnavigators announced. We have not had it quite right, they tell us. Our models dealt with limited information and were limited as a result.

What is the new information? It is this: *consciousness matters.*

CONSCIOUSNESS: THE NEGLECTED DIMENSION

In human health and disease, conscious processes are pivotal. The evidence supporting the importance of consciousness has emerged from the most unlikely place—modern bioscience, which has traditionally championed a strictly mechanistic view of man.

Consciousness, that long-abused term in modern science, is alive and well. Long the sustenance of countless mind-body philosophers, it has in our own time become the darling of the psychosomatic theorists, who have attempted in their own way to assert the importance of the mind in health. But the psychosomatic theories have never worked well for the reason that their working model of how humans are designed simply has not allowed for the *primacy* of consciousness. The emphasis on physicalism never really disappeared from psychosomatic concepts so that these ideas remained tied, hand in glove, to a molecular theory of disease causation. Psychosomatic theories never provided any meaningful explanation as to how mind affected body because they accepted a reductionistic explanation for mind in the first place.

They continued to see man as machine, albeit a complex one, and were thus solidly reductionistic. Reductionism—the notion that all events in the human body, including complex mental events, can be explained by the elemental electrochemical processes inside us—has dominated the thinking of most modern physicians who have paid lip service to the psychosomatic school of thought. This school has largely seen mind as derivative of body function; and although psychosomatic medicine has attempted to go beyond a stringent reductionism, the unmistakable physicalistic flavor remains. Thus, far from demonstrating a mind-body interaction, psychosomatic theories show us only more body-body transactions. For if the mind is merely body, as reductionism asserts, so-called mind-body theories are really only body-body theories, having no more intrinsic explanatory power than the molecular model itself.

THE BODY AS MACHINE: ORIGIN OF AN IDEA

In modern medicine we live with the idea that the body's processes are calculable, that they are in essence approachable with the same sort of logic we apply in attempting to understand any other natural phenomenon. There is nothing special that separates physiological processes from the physical processes we observe elsewhere in nature. We speak of "hard data" and "cold facts" when talking about physiological data, as naturally as if talking about theories of continental drift or the growth of crystals.

Where did this analytical emphasis originate, this idea that the living human body can be dissected with the same approach that is applied to any other naturally occurring process? Surely the roots of this idea are ancient; but as a major force in Western thought it assumed a powerful impetus at the hand of Descartes. Bronowski[5] states that prior to Descartes there was no widespread assumption in the Western world that natural processes in general had any intrinsic relation to numbers, to mathematics. True, numbers and mathematical reasoning had for centuries been used in describing certain events, such as the motion of heavenly bodies. And the Greek tradition was reflected by the statement of Pythagoras, "God ever geometrizes." But the idea of an intimate connection of numbers and nature was simply not then present as a strong force in the consciousness of the average person.

If we try, as Bronowski has done, to localize the beginning of that tradition at a single point in time, we might fix its birth to the night of November 10, 1619. On that night the young Descartes, still in his early twenties, underwent a mystical experience. For him this was a revelation of the deepest significance, and he was profoundly affected by the event for the rest of his life. It was revealed to him that the key to the universe lay in its logical order. He saw that if one were to comprehend this order, one's logic must be perfected for the task. Moreover, this logic could most powerfully be of a mathematical type; and he set about to invent new mathematical forms to express this logic of nature. Thus, in a powerful way Descartes was influential in harnessing numbers and nature.

What kind of universe emerged from this vision of nature? The model that followed was, above all, orderly. It was a universe perfectly assembled, moving in utter precision like a clock, just ticking away. In the generation following Descartes, the awesome genius of Isaac Newton mapped the workings of this clockwork universe. Newton elucidated laws that were elegant in their simplicity and powerful in their ability to predict natural events.

It was characteristic of the spectrum of Descartes' brilliance that he not only developed a model of the universe that was logical and orderly, he devised a model of human beings as well. It is not surprising that he invested humans with the same characteristics he saw in nature at large: qualities of precision and orderly function that could be comprehended rationally. This view gave rise to a physicalistic view of man, which virtually *demanded* a dualistic definition of how man is put together.

Descartes saw two parts to man, mind and body—*res cogitans* and *res extensa*. Although the body could affect the mind, no interaction was possible in the other direction. Mind simply did not affect the body. This formulation seems a perfect solution for an intellect that saw an order in nature, an order that had to be preserved by expunging from it all disorderly elements—such as the mind. (Thus, it is interesting to question whether Descartes may have himself "beat nature into line." Did he adopt a view of man that was designed to fit his mystically inspired, orderly model of the world? This conclusion seems plausible.*)

The Cartesian formulation led to the view that the body reflected the machine-like characteristics of the universe itself—machine-like bodies inhabiting a machine-like world. Disease thus arose as a disorder of mechanism. Something went awry in the machine.

As Frank has stated, this dualistic and reductionistic approach to human design was enormously fruitful to a seminal science.[7] Science was just awakening and was casting about for models and guiding principles. In the Cartesian approach it found the needed mandate of examining bodies, of actually invading them with anatomic dissection. Approbation for dissection of human bodies also came from the Church, as Rasmussen observes.[8] The mission of the Church was then, as now, to look after man's spiritual side. If the body and mind were separate as Descartes maintained, it was obvious that no harm would befall the soul if mere bodies were dissected. And they were dissected, and in great numbers. In Engel's view the Church's position was largely responsible for the emphasis in Western medicine that came to be placed on the anatomic and the structural.[9]

This proved to be the handiest of arrangements for an infant bioscience as well as for the Church. It gave scientists a green light to begin investigating bodies in earnest, searching for mechanisms of causation of disease; and the Church could take comfort that, in so doing, no violence would be done to the soul.

This model of human beings has fallen on hard times.[10] However well it may have served science in earlier times, it can only be maintained today by the most rigid and dogmatic inflexibility.

In forthcoming chapters we shall be looking at reasons for new visions of man. Radical reformulations of health, disease, birth, and death are at hand. Much of the new evidence cannot be understood in terms of the old models; it makes sense only through construction of new models of not only man himself, but of the universe he inhabits.

---

*The relationship of scientific observation and world view was the subject of an interchange between two of this century's eminent scientists, Albert Einstein and Werner Heisenberg. Heisenberg relates how he as a young scientist initially met Einstein. While discussing how the scientific endeavor proceeds and how scientists go about their work, Einstein discounted Heisenberg's view, which expressed the traditional belief that scientists observe, measure, and then form conclusions dispassionately from the data thus collected. Einstein contended that the *reverse* is true, that the scientist begins with a belief or model, and that this preconceived view determines to a major extent what is observed.[6]

Reformulations of reality, of the way things are, are wrenching. Yet there was never an age that did not find itself actually in the throes of change, or on the verge of change. Heraclitus was correct: the only permanent thing is change itself.

Disconcerting evidence has always stirred preference for the familiar, for the status quo. Yet resistance to change is unbecoming of true scientists, for the history of science is the record of change.

It was Leonardo who said, "Science comes by observation, not by authority," anticipating the disconcerting problems offered to all of us by change. And it helps little to appeal to the authority of an outmoded science in this dilemma—for Leonardo also warned, "Whoever in discussion adduces authority uses not his intellect but rather memory."

The new models which are to follow come by observation. They are an attempt to understand the problems that any physician encounters during the course of caring for sick patients. The author asks that the reader prove them not by adducing their authority—for none is intended—but through his own observations.

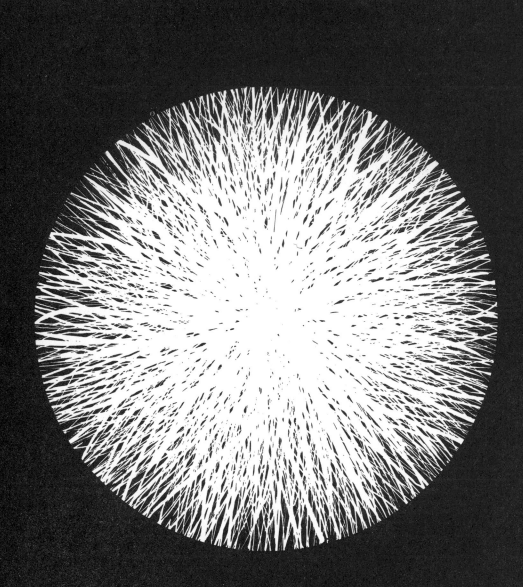

LINEAR BECOMING SPHERICAL

II

Time

I do not think seventy years is the time of a man or woman, nor that seventy millions of years is the time of man or woman, nor that years will ever stop the existence of me, or anyone else.

—WALT WHITMAN
LEAVES OF GRASS

THE LAKE OF TIME

A THIRTY-FIVE YEAR OLD PHYSICIAN came to me as a patient for biofeedback therapy. Since age thirteen he had suffered from severe
migraine headaches. During college and medical school these had
worsened, and at times were incapacitating. He perceived a clear
relationship of the headaches to stressful periods in his life. Partly
because of this reason he had taken up the practice of meditation on
a regular basis during his internship at age twenty-eight. He had
practiced meditation for seven years, and during this time his headaches began to abate. He came for biofeedback therapy because of
curiosity, because he had heard of the effectiveness of biofeedback
in treating migraine headaches, and because he felt that he might
add another dimension of skill to his meditation practice.

He proved adept at biofeedback. From the start he was extraordinarily capable of voluntarily lowering the electrical activity in his
muscles to extremely low levels, reducing his muscle tension on
occasion to the low levels seen in sleep. Although his initial ability
to increase the blood flow to his extremities was less impressive, he
nonetheless learned this skill thoroughly also.

I am always curious about the mental strategy that subjects employ
in voluntarily changing their physiology, especially when they are
unusually good at these tasks, as was the case with this physician.
When I asked him how he made these changes occur, he related the
following.

"I get deeply relaxed, just like when I meditate. After a while I
begin to think of time, which I visualize as a river. I see the river
from a great altitude, as if I were in an airplane. The river twists and
curves, and I can see it flowing. Floating on the surface of the river,
carried slowly by the current, is a giant orange T. This T is Time—
flowing in one direction, just as I ordinarily experience time flowing,

made of past, present, and future. I watch the River of Time flow gently for a while, having no particular thoughts about anything, just seeing the T carried along. Then something begins to happen. The river slowly starts to curve so much that it begins to flow back on itself, gradually forming a complete circle. It has transformed itself into a moving circular river, like none I have ever seen, still carrying the T along.

"Again the circular River of Time begins to change. It starts to flood its banks inwardly, overflowing toward the middle. The water flow is endless, it seems; and as it continues a giant lake is formed. The color of the water changes to a deep blue as the flow of water into the lake finally ceases. The surface becomes calm and still, reflective as a mirror. In the middle of the deep blue lake once again I see the orange T, floating motionlessly. The T, time itself, has ceased to flow. There is now no past, present, or future. Time is now boundless. It stands still.

"This timeless Lake of Time is indescribably serene, like a high alpine lake you encounter unexpectedly and never want to leave. It fills me with a sense of peace and I stay there feeling the stillness of the Lake of Time for as long as I wish."

Following his biofeedback training his headaches diminished dramatically. This patient had himself learned how to manipulate his sense of time to his clinical advantage. He had learned to experientially slow time and to stop it, and to express it in a most beautiful image. His headaches continued to diminish. As his physician I was elated because it seemed to me that his experience represented the maximal achievement in medical care: a methodology that was highly effective yet harmless to the patient, and that was executed by the patient himself in a way that was spiritually uplifting and aesthetically inspiring.

I was struck by the vast difference between the way this patient conceptualized time while engaged in biofeedback imagery, and the everyday, ordinary way of viewing time. For this physician-patient had "stopped" time. He saw events occur from a particular vantage point in a timeless space. Events did indeed enter his awareness sequentially, yet this process was entirely divorced from any sensation of a linearly flowing time. He had effectively dispensed experientially with past, present, and future.

When I first began to notice subjects in my medical practice adopting this kind of "time strategy," I regarded it as a curiosity. Then, as this observation became commonplace, I became increasingly intrigued. I began to realize that I was witnessing patients becoming healthier through acquiring a new experiential meaning of what time was all about.

My patients were learning a strategy that held serious consequences for the improvement of their health. My own curiosity about this phenomenon evolved into a serious concern. If, I thought, patients can *eradicate* certain illnesses through adopting a nonlinear view of time wherein past, present, and future merge into a timeless stillness, the obvious question was: do we make ourselves sick by conforming to an idea of a strict linear time composed of a rigid succession of future, past, and present?

I have come to have little doubt that this is the case. Many illnesses—perhaps most—may be caused either wholly or in part by our misperception of time. Just as the patient in the above example created bodily health through his vivid perception of a nonflowing time, I am convinced that we can destroy ourselves through the creation of illness by perceiving time in a linear, one-way flow.

One of the goals of this book is to examine the evidence for this assertion. We shall see that the emergence of both human health and disease is coupled to our perception of time.

Without a clear idea of the concept of time we cannot understand its impact on our health, nor can we appreciate how the sense of time can be manipulated in ways to make us healthier. In this Part we shall lay the groundwork for what is to follow by examining one of the thorniest issues with which philosophers and scientists have ever dealt: time.

For years I have had a fascination with differences between persons in their view of how time behaves. The ordinary view is, of course, that time flows, as does some fluid. But persons who believe this idea, as do most, disagree as to the *rate* of this flow. For some, time is a sluggish viscous fluid; for others it is fast-moving, like rushing water. Even in the same individual this perception is variable. The flow of time is not the same; it is a changing sensation, sometimes slowing, sometimes increasing in its rate of flow.

All of us at some moments sink deep into the linear way of viewing time. As an antidote to my own affliction with this problem, I have in my office two antique pendulum clocks whose tick-tocks are never in phase. They notoriously keep "bad time." One is always fast, the other slow. As part of my own private amusement about linear time I ask myself which one is more accurate. Surely one must be more correct than the other. Or can there exist two separate times in my office? Can I choose which time suits me best at this moment? Occasionally in the midst of a beleaguered day I sit at my desk fantasizing, as I listen to these asynchronous tick-tocks, about different layers of time, or about two rivers of time flowing parallel but at different rates. The whole exercise seems to defuse and humble the inexorable onrush of time which, in the process of hectic days, sooner or later begins to feel oppressive and defeating. When I sense myself busying about mechanically and maniacally as if time were running out, I sit down and listen to the sounds which are out of phase coming from the old clocks. I think to myself that the domination of time that we allow over our lives is not only arbitrary but downright absurd. Somehow this mental exercise comforts me.

WHAT IS TIME?

Time is nature's way of keeping everything from happening at once.

—signed J.C.

[graffiti in the men's room at the Strictly Tabu Club, Dallas, Texas]

WHAT EXACTLY DO WE MEAN BY TIME? "Many years ago a famous Church Father was troubled by the same question and confessed that if no one asked him, he knew, but if he tried to explain it to someone then he had to admit that he did not know."[1]

Time is not a single concept. The time of the physicist is not that of the poet. The time of the calendar is no help in knowing when to cook potatoes, although it can tell us when to plant them. The "time of my life" is not the same thing as the time to arrive at a party. The football official's "time out" is not the same as three-quarter waltz time. The time of the mystic is not the time of the scientific investigator.

We wander through varied sorts of time each day, giving little thought to the matter. We discard one concept of time in favor of another whenever it is convenient to do so. Yet we ordinarily maintain the illusion that time is a single concept, an entity that needs no explanation.

Here we are concerned with the time of *experience*, the kinds of time we actually *feel*. Where does our time experience come from? This has been a difficult question to resolve, as Nichols[2] implied in 1891:

> It [time] has been declared *a priori*, innate, intuitive, empirical, mechanical. It has been deduced from within and without, from heaven and from earth and from several things difficult to imagine as either.

As Ornstein makes clear, we experience at least four types of time; and the reason why the origin of our time sense has been confused is that the theories that purport to account for it are not always clear about which mode of time experience is being referred to.[3] The dimensions of time experience are:

1. The present, short-term time
   (a) The "perception" of short intervals
   (b) Rhythm or *timing*
2. Duration, the past; long-term memory
3. Temporal perspective—philosophical, social, cultural constructions of the world and their effects on the interpretation of time experience. "Becoming" the future.
4. Simultaneity and succession[4]

All of the different ways we utilize our time sense can be described by at least one of Ornstein's categories of time experience. There are, thus, many kinds of time experience.

This is obvious not only from the multiplicity of ways we experience time but from the various ways that have been used to measure it. The ancient Egyptians devised what Otto Neugebauer has described as "the only intelligent calendar which ever existed in human history."[5] They devised a way of recording time in which a year consisted of twelve months, each of thirty days, with five days added at the end of the year. This form of time-keeping is felt to have originated from continued observation and averaging of the time between successive arrivals of the Nile's flood at Cairo.

The observation of such successions in nature gave rise to the ancient idea of time as a cyclic phenomenon. The planets always returned at certain fixed periods. The sun and moon demonstrated unfailing periodicity, as did the seasons. Primitive man was surrounded by cyclic events in nature, and his concept of time mirrored this aspect of this world.

Even today primitive cultures generally hold to a cyclic notion of time. They have extremely vague ideas about clocks, as did most civilized cultures until about two or three hundred years ago.

The Hopi Indian language contains no words to refer to time in a linear fashion. Their verbs have no tenses. They live in a kind of continual present that contains everything that has ever happened.[6] Even though they make no explicit reference to past, present, or future, they are able to function effectively within their own time frame, a fact that comes with a certain astonishment to our clock-conscious culture.

Ingenious devices were used to measure cyclic time, such as sundials. These inventions had one thing in common: they functioned according to natural events, and thus reflected the idea that a cyclic time was intrinsic to nature. Even calendar time, constructed through the ages according to the average arrival date of floods or monsoons, did the same.

But eventually primitive man used other devices to designate time which measured man-made periodicity—such as the time required for a candle or a length of knotted rope to burn, or a pot of rice to boil. These artificial ways of demarcating time were crude, "and it was not until a successful pendulum clock was invented by the Dutch scientist Christiaan Huygens in the middle of the seventeenth century that man was at last provided with an accurate time-keeper that could tick away for years on end. This greatly influenced the modern concept of the homogeneity and continuity of time."[7]

With the development of accurate measurement devices, man became less and less observant of cyclical natural processes as a means of keeping track of time. He needed nature less in a world of clocks. Although Newton held to a cyclical view of time as intrinsic to nature, the linear view of time was increasingly popularized by such figures as Leibnitz, Barrow, and Locke. This view of time gathered momentum in the three hundred years following Huygens's invention of the pendulum clock, such that we now generally believe it to be intuitively obvious that time flows; that it is divisible into past, present, and future, and that once an event has happened, it will never occur again. Our lives are so chronometrically dominated that we not only have become unconscious of the cycles in nature, we have become inured to the cycles within ourselves. We no longer eat when hungry or sleep when sleepy, but follow the dictates of the clock.

This kind of clock dominance is viewed with bewilderment and absurdity by some, who find it unnatural and unnecessary. The story is told of a native American dancer who, in full regalia, was performing tribal dances for the tourists who had arrived at his pueblo. He had an alarm clock strapped to his leg, set to go off at periodic intervals. With each alarm he would interrupt his dance with "Now I sleep!" or "Now I eat!" This was his private parody on the time-conscious crowd who had gathered to watch the costumed dancing, who no doubt had little insight into its meaning.

Are we to say that the reason underlying primitive man's cyclical sense of time was that he had no sophisticated means of measuring time? Would he have held a linear instead of a cyclic view had he but had a dependable way of dividing time into bits—for example, if he had possessed a pendulum clock that could have provided a concept of seconds, minutes, and hours? Would he have then been struck with a sensation of an irreversible flow of time? Surely it is naive to suppose such a possibility. For primitive man *did* have ways of measuring time that were surprisingly accurate. Some primitive calendars compare in accuracy with our own. But although they were accurate, they simply never carried with them the modern axiom that *measured* time is *linear* time.

The time-measuring device is itself relatively unimportant. There is nothing intrinsic to the modern cesium clock that makes it a more powerful advocate for linear time than a burning candle or a sundial or the repeated arrival of the Nile flood at Cairo.

When we think about it, it seems rather strange that we should view clocks and watches as indicators of a strict linear time. For the hands of a clock always repeat themselves in their motion, always forming a repetitive tracking pattern, always making circles, always returning to a given point on the face of the instrument. It is the same for watches without hands. Even the numbers of a digital clock repeat themselves, recycling in monotonous repetition, forming circles with numbers.

How was it that this quality of repetition, this mechanical cycling, came to suggest a linear instead of a cyclic time? It is not the time device itself that is decisive in whether we see time as linear or cyclic. Given a sophisticated watch, a primitive man would not have been dissuaded from a cyclic view of time. We know that pre-modern societies such as the Hopi, even when afforded watches and clocks, continue to experience time as cyclical.

I unexpectedly experienced an insight into the way sophisticated means of time measurement dominated my function as a physician. When my watch stopped working several years ago I automatically had it repaired, only to have it stop again. I had assumed that I could not function properly without one. Of all the tools that I felt essential to the practice of medicine—such as stethoscopes, blood pressure cuffs, and telephones—I felt that a watch was perhaps the most indispensible. Without it I was sure I would be lost—unable, even, to take a pulse. But the repair of my watch for the second time was aggravating, and I found it easy to postpone having it fixed again. To my surprise I found I hardly missed it. The most notice-able difference was the pleasant sensation of the missing weight on my wrist. And I found that I could not escape time indicators. I discovered they were all around me, which I had never noticed before. On every floor in the hospital there were several wall clocks—in the central nursing stations, in family waiting areas, in hallways.

There were clocks in my auto, in my office, and at almost every patient's bedside. I found that my hospitalized patients not only wore a watch at all times, they brought their own clocks with them as well! I found that it was as simple to take a patient's pulse using his watch as my own.

To this day my watch lies defunct in a drawer, still awaiting repair. I have not worn a watch since and am occasionally reminded of the novelty of being watchless when I witness the surprised look of someone who has asked me the time, forcing me to admit that I have no way of knowing. The entire experience was revealing. I realized the degree to which, through the years, I had learned to see my function as a physician as utterly dependent on an accurate sense of linear time. I half expected my abilities as a doctor to stop with my watch. I am certain that we are all unwittingly addicted in different degrees to time.

CHAPTER THREE

PRIMITIVE TIME

IN HIS REMARKABLE BOOK, *The Myth of the Eternal Return*, Mircea Eliade states that primitive man believed that an object or act became real only insofar as it imitated or repeated an archetype.[1] Repetition or participation formed the sole basis for reality. Primitive man became real, therefore, only to the extent to which he became another. Only by ceasing to become himself could he achieve reality. Inherent in the imitation of archetypes and in the repetition of paradigmatic gestures is that, in this way, *time was abolished.*

> A sacrifice, for example, not only exactly reproduces the initial sacrifice revealed by a god *ab origine,* at the beginning of time, it also takes place at the same primordial mythical moment; in other words, every sacrifice repeats the original sacrifice and coincides with it. All sacrifices are performed at the same mythical instant of the beginning; through the paradox of rite, profane time and duration are suspended.
>   . . . . insofar as an act (or an object) acquires a certain reality through the repetition of certain paradigmatic gestures, and acquires it through that alone, there is an implicit abolition of profane time, of duration, of "history". . . .[2]

Obviously primitive man did not participate in the continual offering of sacrifices or in the continual repetition of archetypal behavior. These were special and were reserved for essential periods "when the individual is truly himself: on the occasion of rituals or of important acts (alimentation, generation, ceremonies, hunting, fishing, war, work). The rest of his life is passed in profane time, which is without meaning. . . ."[3]

What we discover in probing archaic rites and rituals is the willingness to devalue time. It is not man who is at the mercy of an external "real" time—it is time itself which is shaped by man. Eliade describes this attitude:

Carried to their extreme, all the rites and all the behavior patterns . . .
would be comprised in the following statement: "If we pay no attention to it, time does not exist; furthermore, where it becomes
perceptible—because of man's "sins," i.e., when man departs from
the archetype and falls into duration—time can be annulled."[4]

Unlike modern man, primitive man is not burdened with the
irreversibility of time. On the contrary this irreversible profane or
linear time is meaningless. Not only does the primitive become
himself most fully by participating in archetypal behavior, this realization occurs *only* in mythical time—that is, in a state where time is
abolished, where time is annulled.

The state of consciousness that recognizes a time of nonduration
is characteristic not only of primitive man. It would be a great
mistake to ascribe it only to the unenlightened or uncivilized. It is
characteristic of the mystic and of religious man in general, and is
confined to no particular epoch. And Eliade believes that the religious man and the mystic also may be said to be "primitive," in that
they live in a continual present.

". . . . he repeats the gestures of another and, through this repetition, lives always in an atemporal present."[5] Modern man presents
a pathetic contrast! Wedged between birth and death, most of us
sense the desperation that is engendered by a time that is playing
itself out. We flail about in our pitiful attempts to abolish time,
consuming vitamins, physical examinations, and facelifts with abandon, searching frantically for a temporary assurance that we will not
die—at least not this year.

If Gottlieb[6] is correct that the clock is the symbol of death, then we
all carry on our wrists constant little "death reminders": our watches.
We wear a watch with no conscious regard for the name we give it.
Yet it is well named, and regretfully so. Using it, we *watch*. We
watch time, we are fixated on it. It can even be said that most of us
are dominated by it. We do few things as well as we watch time.
Once you think about it, there seems to be something sinister going
on. Constantly watching, always watching, it is we who are in the
service of time—we, biological clocks ourselves with our internal
rhythms and cycles, constantly witnessing our own death, continuing to watch, watch, watch.

We find ourselves caught in a double bind: the more attentive we
try to be toward our health, the more acutely we become aware that
life—*all* life—is uniformly fatal. We cannot fool ourselves, and the
daily reminders come in the form of wrinkles, sagging flesh, aches

and pains, and medical bills—none of which we had in our youth. So we look backward in time, trying to re-create youth, sometimes imbuing it with a wonder and magic we never sensed, even while young.

We long for those spent days for the wrong reason. It is not lovely faces and lithe bodies that draw us to our youth, but an ability we never knew we had at the time, and that we have now forgotten how to use: the ability to abolish time.

It is partially for this reason that the child and the primitive have been compared. From our knowledge of surviving primitive races we have reason to believe that a great effort must have been necessary for man to overthrow his tendency to live in a nondurational time.[7] For example, although the children of Australian aborigines are of comparable intelligence to white children, they learn to tell time by the clock only with great difficulty. "It is surely significant that Rousseau, who extolled the noble savage, detested time and threw away his watch."[8] And one cannot but be struck by the canvases of Gauguin, who painted his natives with an unmistakable quality of childlike guilessness and innocence.

The child, the abolisher of time, has been lauded by most mystical and religious traditions that have left written records. Typical are the words of Jesus:

> Suffer little children, and forbid them not to come unto me: for of such is the kingdom of heaven (Matthew 19:14).

> And Jesus called a little child unto him, and set him in the midst of them, and said, "Verily I say unto you, Except ye . . . become as little children, ye shall not enter into the kingdom of heaven" (Matthew 18:2-3).

We visualize heaven as an eternal timeless state, and our religious traditions assert that it is the child who is its natural citizen. It is the child who is at home in a nonlinear time, and who fits the beatific visions of antiquity. In a way that goes unnoticed we conjoin the spiritual sense and the experience of time. Perhaps it is not surprising that most great religions have always prescribed methods such as prayer and meditation through which one can become as a child; for in practicing these disciplines one quickly discovers that the experience of time changes. It ceases to flow; and experientially one feels enveloped by the stillness of which all the great mystics have spoken.

CHAPTER FOUR

MODERN TIME

The flow of time is clearly an inappropriate concept for the description of the physical world that has no past, present and future. It just is.

—THOMAS GOLD[1]

NO DISCUSSION OF TIME PERCEPTION would be complete without an acknowledgement of the impact of modern physical theory on our ideas of time. At the heart of the special theory of relativity is the notion that it is not the external events themselves but their sense impressions that provide us with our conscious thoughts of how events are arranged in time. It takes time for light to travel from an external event to our eyes, so that it is impossible for us to perceive the instantaneous or exact moment anything happens in the universe. Relativity reminds us that we do not know things as they are; we must settle for our sensory impressions for our construction of "reality."

Yet we blithely ignore this feature of reality. We forget that "events throughout the universe are crudely located in our private time-sequence. Through this confusion the idea has arisen that the instants of which we are conscious extend so as to include external events, and are worldwide; and the enduring universe is supposed to consist of a succession of instantaneous states."[2]

Through a distorted view of time we have patched together a mangled view of the universe. We fail to see that an external reality does not exist as a given, that it is not "out there" conveniently waiting for us to sense it. The modern picture of reality is more like a tapestry in which sense impressions, consciousness, time, space, and light are the threads, combining in a delicately entangled way to form what we perceive as "event."

With our modern means of keeping time—digital watches, cesium clocks, etc.—we have developed the idea that our modern sense of

31

time is not only highly accurate but unique as well. Technology, modernity, and time-accuracy seem synonymous. But from one point of view this is hardly the case. If we compare ancient concepts of time with the view of time that has emerged from modern physics, we find striking similarities.

The time concepts of the primitive are described by Eliade:

> This eternal return reveals an ontology uncontaminated by time and becoming.
>
> In a certain sense, it is even possible to say that nothing new happens in the world. . . . this repetition constantly maintains the world in the same auroral instant of beginnings. Time makes possible the appearance and existence of things. It has no final influence upon their existence, since it is itself constantly regenerated.[3]

The description of time to be found in modern physics is surprisingly similar. In de Broglie's words,

> Space and time cease to possess an absolute nature. . . .
>
> In space-time, everything which for each of us constitutes the past, the present, and the future is given in block, and the entire collection of events, successive for us, which form the existence of a material particle is represented by a line, the world-line of the particle.
>
> Each observer, as his time passes, discovers, so to speak, new slices of space-time which appear to him as successive aspects of the material world, though in reality the ensemble of events constituting space-time exist prior to his knowledge of them.[4]

Thus, the idea of a linear time in which events occur in a nonending succession is rejected by both a primitive ontology and modern physics. Which, we may ask, is primitive and which is modern? The distinctions between the primitive and the modern physical view of time are hazy at best.

The concept of acts of re-creation occurring in time is not confined to primitive thinking. T. S. Eliot has maintained that it occurs in all artistic endeavors. He says,

> . . . . no poet, no artist of any art, has his complete meaning alone. . . ; what happens when a new work of art is created is something that happens simultaneously to all the works of art which preceded it.[5]

Yet the act of re-creation in time is counter to common sense. We know Eliot *must* be wrong; things just don't happen over and over. We can't go back in time. We cannot repeat past events, and that's that! Yet our lives are filled with events which suggest that we may indeed re-create the world.

There is a sense of the eternal return in every experience of deja vu. This phenomenon is probably universal. It embodies a recapitulation of bygone events, and experientially is an annulment of time.

We look at photographs and are easily caught up in reverie and fantasy. We allow ourselves to be transported to times and places captured on film. These experiences can be very vivid, evoking tears or laughter, and are in a sense a reenactment of previous events.

The same wonderment that Eliot attributes to the artist's effort also exists for the scientist. I recall my own awe in first peering clumsily into a microscope in a biology laboratory, thinking that in some measure I was participating in Leeuwenhoek's original experience. Was I re-creating an event? Experientially for me the principle of the eternal return had invaded the biology laboratory.

I remember also, while in the histology laboratory in medical school, my astonishment at the indescribable beauty of human tissue under the microscope. The complex architecture of the tissue was made visible by the application of chemicals, creating magnificent staining patterns. I was participating with the great histologist Ramon y Cajal, and with Virchow, the greatest pathologist of all time.

I was later to read Major's *Classic Descriptions of Disease*,[6] losing myself in Richard Bright's original description of the kidney disease that was to bear his name. When I first made a diagnosis of acute glomerulonephritis, or Bright's disease, in a ten year old boy, I recalled Bright's description, given during his work at Guy's Hospital in London. If Eliot awoke all past artists with each new artistic creation, then with my diagnosis perhaps I awoke Richard Bright.

I have long had a fascination—reverence is a better word—for human illness when present clinically in classical ways. I have only recently come to fathom why this reverence exists: perhaps it is a recalling of archetypes, a repetition of gestures, which involves an annulment of time.

For me this reverence is not limited to disease states. I vividly recall performing a physical examination on a very healthy patient one morning. As I routinely listened to the lungs, something extraordinary happened. I was captivated by the sound of flowing air—a sound that I had heard thousands of times before. But for some reason during this physical examination this act took on magical qualities. I could visualize the airways—the trachea, the bronchi and bronchioles, and even the tiniest units of the respiratory tree, the alveoli themselves. So acute was this sensation, I can only say that I *was* the lung, the air, the tissue itself. I feel now that I recreated with my stethoscope the same enchanting experience that must have occurred to ancient diagnosticians who first listened to human chests with crude blocks of wood pressed to their ears.

I am sure this event is not rare among physicians and scientists in general. In total immersion in a task, whether listening to lungs or weeding vegetable gardens, time is abolished. It stands still. Visualization and imagery are crucial in this process, and are perhaps the hallmark of participation in this timeless event.

The abolition of time can occur without our being aware of it. It can occur at times when we are most creative. The forms, images, and ideas that emerge in this timeless state remind us that no idea can be truly "new," for newness implies a linear time. When we "lose" ourselves in time, we escape the linearity of successive events, of past, present, and future. Time simply is; it does not happen.

Although speaking of the modern physical view of time, Russell describes this situation succinctly:

> A truer image of the world . . . is obtained by picturing things as entering into the stream of time from an eternal world outside, rather than from a view which regards time as the devouring tyrant of all that is.[7]

This concept of creativity as a feature of a timeless, eternal world is hard to swallow, especially if one wishes to see his creative act as a literal making of some new thing. But in the modern context of a nonlinear time, as de Broglie states, events exist prior to us in time. We create nothing, since all things exist already. We only discover what has hitherto been undiscovered. This process is reminiscent of Hegel's view that there is nothing new under the sun.

There is a marvelous sense in which this idea is affirmed by science. The goal of the scientific endeavor can be epitomized by a single word: *discovery*. Consider the dictionary description of this event:

> Discovery: to obtain for the first time sight or knowledge of, as of a thing *existing already*, but not perceived or known.[8]

Scientists, then, are discoverers of patterns and processes in nature that exist prior to them. Discovery is a process wherein certain manifestations of nature's ways "enter into the [scientist's] stream of time from an eternal world outside. . . ."[9]

It is true that we fix discoveries in time, as when we say that Roger Sperry was awarded the Nobel Prize in 1981 for his work dealing with the differential function of the brain's cerebral hemispheres. But in conferring dates and times on the scientific discovery, and in associating specific discoveries with specific scientists, we build history. We add Sperry's elucidation to the long list of Nobel Prizes, each of which was given to certain persons at specific times. These are the building blocks of history, and they are assembled in such a way as to confer a strong sense of linear time on the process of scientific discovery. It is obvious that a history of science *can* be assembled from such bits, but science is more than a historic process. Scientists themselves emphasize the historic aspects of their own work by stating, in their more humble moments, that their work rests on the contributions of countless workers who came before them. But this is an arbitrary view; for by emphasizing a historic quality of the scientific process it invokes a linear time, and ignores the modern physical view of the "eternal world outside"—the great timeless reservoir of natural pattern and process from which things filter into the stream of time of the individual scientist.

Discovery and creativity cannot be divorced from time—whether one prefers a linear, historic flavor or a timeless, anhistoric quality in these processes. And no matter how reasonable it seems to speak of scientific discovery as a historic process, this way of emphasizing the importance of a linear time in science begins inevitably to seem as mere window dressing—for it denies not only the "eternal world outside" (a description which itself is a discovery of science!), it ignores the timeless quality which is implicit in all creative experience of which Eliot spoke.

There are, then, many ways in which we abolish time in our daily rounds, some of which we never think about. It is natural to denigrate in our thinking many of these ways of annulling time—daydreaming, reverie, fantasizing—relegating these moments to "wasted" time. The premium is on linear time—the time of history, the time of getting things done, the time of goals and accomplishments and rewards. In linear time we *produce*, caught in a culture in which the only sin exceeding that of allowing capital to lie idle is that of allowing time to go unused.

We can begin, however, to reassess our capacity to abolish time. We have this ability and we use it every day without being conscious of it. It is a capacity which the primitive found natural, and which survives in us. And it is an ability which allows us experiential knowledge of the modern description of time, the "eternal world outside" of modern physics.

CHAPTER FIVE

HOW DO WE EXPERIENCE TIME?

HOW DO WE EXPERIENCE TIME? We often speak of a "sense of time," but this implies a special organ with which we actually sense time, as the eye senses light. No such organ has ever been identified. In spite of this, numerous biological or physiological theories have been suggested to account for our time sense. These theories rely generally on the notion that there are certain rhythmic cycles in the body, called circadian rhythms, which follow a predictable periodicity, such as the blood eosinophile count, the heart beat, the hydrocortisone level in the blood, body temperature, urine formation, the excretion of potassium and phosphate in the urine, and numerous other physiologic events.[1]* Theorists have attempted to show that these cycles, which can be plotted according to clock time, are responsible for our experience of time. It has not been possible to show, however, that *any* physiological process is responsible for our time sense. There are perhaps an infinity of body processes with cyclic characteristics; but as Ornstein says, "If every physiological process is judged a 'chronometer' then what is the usefulness of the term?"[3] And as Fisher has pointed out, these biological clocks do not run at the same rate. Which one would we choose as the biological clock?[4] Is the time sense a combination of all of their separate rates, or of a specific one? If so, how could we possibly decide which?

If we indeed had an organ with which we perceived time, this would imply that there is an external or "real" time that is being perceived. We almost intuitively take some type of clock time as this "real" time—either hours, minutes, or seconds. Astin[5] states that

---

*For the most complete account of the body's rhythmic cycles, see Gay Luce's *Biological Rhythms in Human and Animal Physiology.*[2]

our basic unit is the second, which we define as 9,192,631,770 cycles of the frequency associated with the transition between two energy levels of the isotope cesium 133. But all cultures are not so technically oriented as ours, as Nakamura notes,[6] and thus have different ideas of what a basic unit of "real" time might be—such as one Indian culture whose basic unit is the time required to boil rice.

Our clock time is no more "real" than the time required for a candle to burn. As Ornstein states, "It is a convenience, used as an arbitrary standard, useful for meeting and making arrangements. But it is not 'real time' any more than the 'time' of boiling rice is real or the cesium clock is 'real.' One may measure out one's life with coffee spoons as well as with a calendar, an hour glass, or with pots of boiling rice. A 'time basis' of duration experience founded on the interval at which experiential and clock times sometimes coincide is of no special significance."[7]

In approaching the relationship of time experience to health and disease and how modification of the time sense can be used as a positive health strategy, two points are crucial to keep in mind:

1. There is no rational basis for a "real" time; a basic unit for time is entirely arbitrary.
2. Because no sense receptor or a biological clock for time has been identified, it is unreasonable to say that the passage of physical time is the stimulus for perceived time, since nothing we know of is being stimulated.

Our sense of time changes with age. Prior to one year of age, infants show no sense of time, living in an eternal present.[8] By age two the use of the term "today" appears, and by two and one-half years the average baby begins to use "tomorrow." "Yesterday" emerges at age three. "Morning" and "afternoon" are used at age four, and by five years "days" arrive. With increasing age a gradual sophistication of the time sense occurs, with a major improvement occurring between the fifth and sixth grades. By the age of sixteen, maturity of time comprehension has occurred.[9]

Age is not the only factor affecting our time sense. Personality characteristics exert strong effects. According to Jaensch,[10] persons who are highly integrated are more susceptible to distortions in the way time is experienced. Depending on the content of the time interval, time consciousness undergoes modification in extroverted, but not in introverted, types.[11]

Parental dominance is associated with an over-estimation of time.[12]

Middle-class children demonstrate a more extended time sense than children from other social classes.[13]

Perception of time duration is strongly affected by the person's feeling toward the task in which he is engaged. A strong sense of purpose predisposes toward an overestimation of the duration of time.[14]

Even our body temperature exerts influences on our time perception. Hoagland, in 1935,[15] studied the effect of temperature in his wife, who had a fever. He related her body temperature and her "subjective minute" and concluded that time cognition was temperature dependent. Francois[16] also studied this effect and found that for each ten-degree rise in temperature of the environment, the time judged to be a one-second interval becomes 2.8-fold shorter.

Even the degree of illumination changes our experience of time.[17] The lower the illumination, the shorter a given time interval is judged to be.

There are marked differences in the way individuals relate to time. ". . . . Some neurotics exhibit claustrophobia in time. The patient feels cooped by his duties and oppressed by the shortness of time just as the claustrophobic feels hemmed in by the walls of space."[18] Fenichel[19] adds that others "are afraid of 'broadness in time'; they hasten from one activity to the next because empty time has for them the same significance as empty space for some agoraphobics."

The effects of drugs on our experience of time are variable. Some of those drugs that decrease the subjective estimation of time are cocaine, thyroxine, and caffeine. Other drugs increase time estimation, such as amphetamine, opium, mescal, hashish, *Cannabis indica*, marijuana, and psylocybin.[20]

Many other factors alter time perception which we have not discussed, and there are doubtless influences that have yet to be discovered. How can we possibly know which factors are operating at any given time? We cannot possibly gauge, for instance, just *how* absorbed we are in any given task from moment to moment, and thus what adjustment we ought to make in our time sense. And how much distortion in our time perception is being caused by the caffeine in this morning's coffee, or the tea we had at noon, or the alcohol in the dinner wine? Even if a real time existed, how would we know whose perception of it is most accurate? Are we to trust the judgment of some real-time interval of someone whose average body temperature is slightly higher or lower than our own?

The search for some external stimulus for our time sense, which we call real time, has failed not only because there seems to be no sense organ in the body to perceive it, but also because the myriad influences on time perception seem to render it unknowable. We cannot know what is influencing the knowing.

What, then, is Time? The most useful approach, as Ornstein suggests, is to discard the notion of an "inner clock" or a "real time" and to adopt a purely cognitive and experiential definition of time. When a cognitive approach is considered, "we find that one particular relationship [is] found: when an attempt is made to increase the amount of information processing in a given interval, the experience of that interval lengthens."[21] In considering the effect of any of the above influences on the experience of time—for example, marijuana—we can say that it increases the subjective appraisal of clock time because it increases the amount of information being processed in a given interval. Thus, the marijuana user may estimate that one hour of clock time *seems like* three hours, or one minute of clock time *feels like* five minutes.

We hypothesize that we can also reason backwards with this approach and say that when the time sense lengthens, more information *has been* processed. The Zen meditator for whom one hour of deep meditation seems as five minutes has processed less information than an individual who judges lapsed clock time correctly. Indeed, this is a goal of meditation—focusing, or "doing one thing well."[22]

Enormous semantic confusion enters when we talk about our experience of time. When we are totally absorbed in a task we may be surprised that so much clock time has lapsed. We may exclaim, "Time has flown!" Three hours of clock time may seem like one. We feel that our sense of time has expanded, that we have been "lost" in time, having forgotten the clock. But although our subjective sensation of time passage has become less acute, giving us a sense of forgetting about time, our actual time appraisal of *duration* has *diminished*.

It is important to keep these distinctions clear. If I am doing a job I despise, my sense of time becomes acute. I check my watch frequently. Time drags, time slows. My sense of time constricts; I feel enclosed by time; I can *feel* its closeness; I may feel oppressed by it. Five minutes seems like an hour. I *overestimate* time *duration*—so although my time sense constricts, my sense of time duration enlarges and expands, for I have tended to overestimate clock time. In discussing the subjective experience of time it is critical, therefore, to distinguish whether we are talking about the *felt* sense of time passage, or of the actual way we are estimating time *duration*. The following table illustrates this semantic comparison:

FELT SENSE OF TIME PASSAGE	ESTIMATION OF TIME DURATION
1. constricted, narrowed	1. enlarged, expanded
2. expanded, enlarged	2. diminished, shortened, contracted
3. acutely or uncomfortably aware of time passage	3. enlarged, expanded
4. unaware of time passage	4. contracted, shortened, diminished

The relationship of the estimation of time duration to the amount of information processed in a given time interval is illustrated as follows:

AMOUNT OF INFORMATION PROCESSED	ESTIMATION OF TIME DURATION
1. more	1. increase
2. less	2. decrease

CHAPTER SIX

TIME: WHAT IS REALLY GOING ON?

One windy day two monks were arguing about a flapping banner. The first said, "I say the banner is moving, not the wind." The second said, "I say the wind is moving, not the banner." A third monk passed by and said, "The wind is not moving. The banner is not moving. Your minds are moving."

—ZEN PARABLE[1]

THE VIEW OF TIME FROM MODERN PHYSICS tells us our ordinary notions of time are wrong. But the possibility that our ordinary concept of time is inaccurate is one of those emotional brick walls we run into in the night, which stops us painfully dead in our tracks, filling us with a momentary confusion bordering on dread and fear. How could we be so wrong about something so fundamental?

The modern physicist's description of time that we examined earlier is usually dismissed as a by-product of complex laboratory experiments that simply have no relevance to daily life. And the primitive's view of time, similar to the physicist's view as we have seen, evokes from us an even less serious consideration; for we assume, albeit incorrectly, that all of pre-modern man was generally unintelligent, and that primitiveness applied to his thought as well as to his culture. How could he possibly be correct about time?

For some persons, though, these descriptions of time are disturbing enough to stir impulses to look deeper, to discover *which* time, *whose* time, is "real." What is *really* going on? Surely there is a correct way of viewing time, if only we can apprehend what it really is. And someone *must* be wrong: the layman, the primitive, and the physicist cannot *all* be correct.

Thus go the logical machinations of almost everyone who stum-

41

bles onto the bizarre descriptions of reality that come to us from such diverse sources as anthropology and modern physical science. We demand the truth about how time *really* behaves, only to be met with warnings such as that given by Eddington, the great English physicist-astronomer:

> I am afraid of this word "reality," not constituting an ordinarily definable characteristic of the things it is applied to, but used as though it were some kind of celestial halo. I very much doubt if anyone of us has the faintest idea of what is meant by the reality or existence of anything but our own egos.[2]

It is a common, almost uniform, mistake to assume that science can resolve for us what is meant by "real." It is unsettling to discover that modern physical scientists no longer make any claim to reality, seeking instead to give only the best description of the world they can devise, and one that rests entirely on sense impressions. The quest for reality is an antiquated one in modern science, belonging to an era that ended with the advent of this century.

In our befuddlement in our attempts to resolve basic questions about how the world behaves, and about time in particular, it is of some comfort to recall that this confusion is not new. It was experienced by the scientists who crafted the new views in physics, which included the new vision of time. The physicist Pascual Jordan described the agony of the physicists in the early years of this century, when the world of physics was convulsing. He stated that it was as if the earth itself had started trembling, and one did not know when it might completely disappear from under one's feet.

What view of reality emerged? In the period following the publication of Einstein's special theory of relativity in 1905, extending through the late 1920s (by which time a comprehensive theory of the quantum had been formulated), physicists reshaped the concept of what is real from that of a static, external world existing apart from us, into one that could only be spoken of with an intimate regard for the human senses. In physics, the senses came to occupy a preeminent position. The physicist Ilse Rosenthal-Schneider said,

> Einstein states that the concept of the "real external world" of our everyday thinking rests exclusively on sense-impressions. . . .[3]

Planck, who discovered the quantum, the fundamental "packet" of energy, emphasized that

. . . there are no observables in the world picture. Observables belong to the world of sense-experiences. . . .[4]

And Einstein believed that

. . . all knowledge about reality begins with experience and terminates in it.[5]

These views of reality notwithstanding, we cling to the idea of a real time—a time that flows and is divisible into past, present, and future. Our belief in a linear real time underlies our basic assumptions of health and disease, of living and dying. But this kind of thinking is tied to an older science, which depended on an external reality, a reality independent of our senses. This view of the world has been discarded by modern physics. If we revise our idea of time in order to be consistent with the modern physical views, we must say of it what we have been forced to say of the external world: *time is bound to our senses*—it is part of us, it is not "out there." And our concepts of health and disease consequently must be revised, dependent as they are on our view of time.

Mortality, birth, death, longevity, illness, and health—we unconsciously construct these ideas, incorporating into them an *absolute* time, which we assume to be part of an *external* reality. But if Einstein was correct that all knowledge about reality begins and ends in experience, there is no external reality from which these events draw meaning. Our knowledge of health begins and ends with experience—i.e., health issues are quintessentially experiential; there is simply no other place to go for meanings of health, illness, life, and death than to our own senses. These events, thus, are not absolute.

The old ideas of health, illness, birth, and death give way to unsteadiness and uncertainty the instant we sense that we may have been wrong in fundamental ways about how the world behaves in general, and about what we mean by time in particular. We have arrived with the physicist Jordan at a place where the ground begins to shake.

In thinking about health, the mind must turn inward on itself. We begin to see that we have been thinking about *ourselves* all along. We have not confronted an external world in our ruminations about health, for there is no absolute external world existing apart from us. We have been seeing only a mirror, whose image is our own sense-impressions.

How, exactly, does a modern view of time change our concepts of health, disease, life, and death? The changes are far-ranging. We shall construct in later chapters new notions of health which are consistent with the modern view of the world. We shall see that the revised views are a liberating force, capable of freeing us from the "devouring tyrant," linear time. The oppression of disease and death is diminished with the new views, just as Newton's oppressive ironclad laws of nature gave way to the modern view in which mind and nature coexist in a more humane—yet mysterious—way in determining what for each of us is "real."

CHAPTER SEVEN

TIME AND PAIN

BEFORE LOOKING AT WAYS in which our idea of time enters into the course of specific diseases, let's consider how our time sense plays a role in perhaps the most ubiquitous symptom of all: pain. Before moving to actual illnesses, it will be well to note that even the most commonplace maladies such as pain contain hidden aspects of time as well as space. In other words, they demonstrate both temporal and spatial qualities.

The following simple formula can serve as a rough guide in thinking about the major determinants of pain:

Formula I
$$P = k \frac{S}{T}$$

We can read the formula as follows: The amount of pain (P) we experience is equal to some constant (k) multiplied by the actual degree of noxious stimulus (S) that causes the pain, and that is acting over some perceived period of time (T). Although we never conceptualize pain in this way, this is what we roughly mean when we say, for example "How bad does it hurt?" or "This fever blister has been really painful for a long time." If our pain were caused by a burn, the amount of pain we experience obviously depends on how hot the stimulus (S; a flame, for example) was, and for how long (T) we perceived it. (Note that we are talking about pain, which is a human perception, and *not* the actual burn that was produced by the flame, and that can be objectively measured.) If a *given amount* of heat (S) were applied over a long period of time (T), we might hardly noticed it (i.e., P would be small). On the other hand, if this same amount of energy were applied over a very short time period, it would be more intense—and, thus, more painful (P would be greater).

45

The actual degree of the burn (B) could be expressed as

Formula II

$$B = k(S\ T)$$

wherein we see that the longer (T) the heat stimulus (S) is applied, the greater is the burn (B) that results.

It should be clear, too, that pain perceptions also depend on our sense of space as well as our sense of time. The *area* over which a stimulus is applied is important. Returning to our example of a burn, if the heat of a tiny flame were diffused for a moment over the entire space, or surface area, of our body, we might hardly notice it. But if it were concentrated on a tiny area, it might well cause a third degree burn.

Formula I shows us how our perceptions of health events, such as pain, are tied to our perception of time, and how our perception of time influences the degree that we believe ourselves to be healthy. If our perception of time (T) is expanded (that is, if it is "large") the amount of pain (P) we experience is small (since P and T vary inversely). On the other hand, if our perception of time is contracted (that is, if it is "small"), we experience a larger degree of pain (P).

What is an expanded sense of time? It is something we are all familiar with. It is a state in which we "lose track" of time. The passage of time slips away from our awareness. Time stands still. It enlarges, it expands. For many of us these moments come unexpectedly, as when we become preoccupied with a certain task or when we participate in a pleasant diversion. In meditation, for instance, this sense of time can be entered routinely, by choice.

In contrast, we experience a contracted sense of time when our awareness of time passage is enhanced. In doing something unpleasant, moments may seem like hours. Time drags. The fear of having a tooth pulled or the anticipation of an uncertain outcome such as passing or failing an examination will constrict our sense of time.

The relativity of the sense of time was expressed by Einstein when he observed, "If you sit with a beautiful girl, two hours seem like two minutes. If you sit on a hot stove, two minutes seem like two hours. That's relativity."

Persons who experience pain ordinarily live in a contracted or constricted time sense. Minutes seem like hours when one is hurting. Because the time sense is constricted, pain is magnified—sometimes far beyond what seems appropriate. Are there ways to intervene in painful situations, ways to manipulate the sense of time by expanding it? Can we lessen pain by "stretching" the time sense?

Without realizing it we do it all the time as physicians. Almost all substances that we use to treat severe pain modify the patient's sense of time. Patients who receive these medications do not say, of course, that their time sense was altered, but they respond with statements such as "that medicine made me float!" or "I became really drowsy," or "I forgot where I was."

There simply is no good vocabulary to use in describing these events which occur hourly in every major hospital. What does a patient mean when, after receiving pain medication, he says, "I really lost track of things for a while," or "That medicine really 'zonked' me," or "That stuff 'bombed' me out?" Undoubtedly altered time perception is one of the hidden meanings in such statements.

Not only drugs but other techniques as well do much to alter the time sense and have become valuable adjuncts to controlling pain. Hypnosis is one such example, and is of incalculable value for some patients in pain control. Biofeedback, which relies heavily on imagery and visualization in achieving physiologic self-control, has a marked effect on modifying time perception. Meditation, autogenic therapy, and progressive relaxation have similar effects. In fact, *any* device or technique that expands one's sense of time can be used as an analgesic!

It is important to realize that when we experience a technique that diminishes pain through expanding our time sense, we are not merely exercising self-deception. We are not fooling ourselves into thinking the pain is not there. Evidence is solid that mental states can evoke actual changes in brain physiology, changes that alter pain perception. We now know that if subjects are given placebos, which are pills containing inert substances, and are told that pain will consequently be relieved, at least one-third of them will experience significant relief of pain. This response can, however, be blocked by the prior administration of naloxone, a chemical that is known to block the action in the brain of a class of naturally occurring chemicals called endorphins. Endorphins are the highly celebrated substances secreted by the brain, which have been synthesized and used clinically. They have potent pain-relieving properties, much like morphine, but differ from opiates by being exponentially more powerful.

What are we doing when we use techniques to expand the time sense in an effort to relieve pain? Are we setting in motion complex biochemical events in our bodies which we subjectively experience as both analgesia and time expansion? Almost certainly this is the

case. There are undoubtedly biochemical correlates to imagery, visualization, hypnosis, biofeedback, and meditation. Only through sys-
tematically investigating the mechanisms of these techniques can we
gain the knowledge necessary to maximize their effectiveness. But in
our investigations of these processes we must avoid the reductionistic trap of attributing our inherent capacity for analgesia and time
expansion to *mere* chemical events.

But more important, perhaps, than a knowledge of the actual
physiological events involved, is an appreciation of the *relativity* of
the felt experience itself. Pain, an inward index of health, is tied to
the time sense in our consciousness. And time, as we have learned
in this century, is a chimera. Through relativity we know that one
man's past is another man's present—and the future of yet another.
And in the same sense, health and disease, like space and time, are
relative concepts that are woven into the fabric of the perceptual
capacities of our consciousness. Health and disease, like space and
time, are not part of a fixed, external reality. As such, they are not to
be acquired so much as they are to be felt.

CHAPTER EIGHT

TIME AND DISEASE

Personal Electronics Inc., New York, has introduced a $100 watch with a "speak" button. If the alarm is set, the watch plays a minuet at the appointed hour. If the wearer does nothing, five minutes later the watch will play a shorter piece, and a synthesized voice will announce the time and say, "Please hurry."

—WALL STREET JOURNAL, MAY 15, 1981

PAVLOV, THE RUSSIAN PHYSIOLOGIST, conditioned dogs to salivate by ringing a bell while simultaneously presenting food to them. After a while they could be made to salivate by merely ringing the bell, irregardless of whether food was presented. Just as Pavlov's dogs learned to salivate inappropriately, we have learned to *hurry* inappropriately. Our sense of urgency is set off not by a real need to act quickly, but through learned cues. Our "bells" have become the watch, the alarm clock, the morning coffee, and the hundreds of self-inflicted expectations that we build into our daily routine. The subliminal message from the watch and the clock is: time is running out; life is winding down; please hurry.

Interestingly, the perceptions of passing time that we observe from our external clocks cause our *internal* clocks to run faster. (Anything that demonstrates periodicity can be viewed as a clock, such as many of our physiological functions.) Our sense of urgency results in a speeding of some of our body's rhythmical functions, such as the heart rate and respiratory rate. Exaggerated rises in the blood pressure may follow, along with increases in blood levels of specific hormones that are involved in the body's response to stress. Thus, our perceptions of speeding clocks and vanishing time cause our own biological clocks to speed. As we saw earlier, the end result is frequently some form of "hurry sickness"—expressed as heart disease, high blood pressure, or depression of our immune function, leading to an increased susceptibility to infection and cancer.

In later chapters we shall examine the revolutionary idea of modern physics that conscious human perceptions are tied in some way to the unfolding of what we call reality. There is reason to believe that we live in what physicist John A. Wheeler has called a "participatory universe." Modern physics has shown us that reality can no longer be conceived as existing solely apart from our perceiving minds.

The translation of our perception of a fleeting time into our own physiologic processes is an illustration of the participatory principle in action. We determine our own reality by mirroring our perceptions of a fleeting time in our body's function. Having convinced ourselves through the aid of clocks, watches, beeps, ticks, and a myriad of other cultural props that linear time is escaping, we generate maladies in our bodies that assure us of the same thing—for the ensuing heart disease, ulcers, and high blood pressure reinforce the message of the clock: *we* are running down, eventually to be swept away in the linear current of the river of time. For us, our perceptions have become our reality.

CARDIOVASCULAR DISEASE

Our sense of time is not only a major determinant in our awareness of pain, it affects our health by influencing the development and course of specific diseases. This is nowhere more obvious that in persons who have been called Type A individuals by Friedman and Rosenman.[1] Type A persons have "hurry sickness." Their lives are oriented around goals, deadlines, and objectives, which they seem to react to in a driven fashion. They are unable to approach a task in a healthy, balanced way, but in extreme cases seem almost consumed by a need to accomplish and achieve.

Not only do they have an *inward* sense of urgency, their *outward* behavior suggests the same quality. When sitting they may be in constant motion, not only with thoughts, but with body parts—hands, fingers, legs, feet. They are usually vocal, verbally expressing the products of a mind that cannot rest. This behavior frequently generates discomfort and tension in those around them.

It is as if Type A persons are "time sick." They resemble patients who are in chronic pain in that they have an acute sense of time. Only in this case, unlike the person experiencing pain, there is never enough of it.

Type A persons are usually ambitious and frequently are highly successful, having succeeded in harnessing their high motivation and sense of purpose. Yet for all the qualities for which they are admired—their vision, energy, and dedication—they possess, as a group, a characteristic that nobody envies: they have a high mortality rate from heart disease.

Time sickness is not merely a colorful appellation, it is an actual illness possessed by the group as a whole. It is not just that Type A persons may experience excessive anxiety, that they may be more nervous and discomfited than their Type B counterparts, in which case their hurry sickness might be counted only as a nuisance or a bother. The problem is worse than a nuisance: Type A individuals, as a group, *die earlier*. Their behavior puts them at risk for the most frequent cause of death in our society, coronary artery disease.

The importance of the exaggerated response to time, the sense of urgency displayed by Type A individuals, is that it is translated into physiologic effects. These effects are pervasive and are seen long before heart disease supervenes. These physiological events are so characteristic of time-sick persons, they could be called the time syndrome. Among them are increased heart rate and blood pressure at rest; elevation of certain blood hormones such as adrenalin, norepinephrine, insulin, growth hormone, and hydrocortisone, all of which are ordinarily secreted in an exaggerated way during times of urgency or stress; increased gastric acid secretion; increased blood cholesterol; an increased respiratory rate; increased secretory activity of sweat glands; and increased muscle tension throughout the body. The time syndrome is a body-mind process with effects on all major systems. It is not simply a conscious experience of unpleasant feelings.

The awareness that the time sense is awry in certain clinical disorders is enormously important, because this understanding can give us clues in treating these problems. We noted, for example, that the cholesterol level is frequently elevated in Type A persons. We can ask, therefore, if manipulating the sense of time in humans has any effect on the blood cholesterol level. The answer, interestingly, is yes. Cooper and Aygen have shown that if subjects are taught to meditate, which is an easily available method of "adjusting" the time sense toward the other end of the experiential spectrum than that which is felt by Type A persons, blood cholesterol levels fall by an average of twenty percent.[2] Moreover, other aspects of the time syndrome respond: blood pressure, heart and respiratory rate, as well as the blood levels of insulin, hydrocortisone, adrenalin, and norepinephrine are modified to more desirable levels.

The significance of these observations is inestimable: by taking thought in ways which "elongate" the time sense, time-sick individuals can alter many of the devastating effects of the time syndrome. The method involved is not critical, for as we have seen, many methods are effective, such as meditative disciplines, biofeedback, progressive relaxation, and autogenic therapy.

What is the value of emphasizing the temporal aspect of illness? Why not pick some other quality that is seen in most illnesses and focus on a means of altering it—for example, muscle tension or anxiety? Certainly there are other characteristics that are generalized across the spectrum of human disease. Why pick time? Why not insist that we are muscle tension sick, or anxiety sick, instead of time sick?

There is a primary reason for this: as the severity of a disease increases, the temporal aspects of being ill begin to influence our perceptions profoundly. The more severe an illness, the greater is the likelihood that we will be reminded of our mortality, of death. Serious illnesses are time-heavy for the same reason, therefore, as death. They force us to confront the end, the final state, the forever.

What words do we associate with death? Those that stir us most deeply are time related: final, always, forever. Indeed, these time-heavy words are practically an equivalent of death—for if we supposed death to be temporary, we shouldn't call it "death" at all.

Is it possible to capitalize on the time quality of serious illness in a positive way—for example, in the way we saw possible in time-conscious persons with elevated blood cholesterol levels? The question is worthwhile not because we wish to make death disappear anymore than we wish to eradicate all the cholesterol from the blood, but because our sense of time is *so* malleable, so manipulable. What might happen to our regard for death as we use methods to expand our sense of time, as we did in the hypercholesterolemic state?

As we learn to meditate, or when we become familiar with the states of consciousness that are peculiar to biofeedback, autogenic therapy, or to other techniques employing deep relaxation, we develop a familiarity with a new sense of time. We begin to experience time in new ways. We begin to feel at home with time as it expands. Phrases such as "the ever-present now" and "the eternal moment" become full with meaning. Above all, we develop a friendliness with time.

As this new regard for time evolves to deeper levels, new understanding unfolds. It becomes apparent that one of the motivating forces behind our old way of reacting toward the passage of time was fear—an indisputable feeling that took the form of busying ourselves in needless motion. This frenetic behavior begins to appear as a defense *against* time, a resistance that assumes its final form in our individual, silent protest against death itself.

All time-riven events such as illness and demise begin to appear less menacing. Events in our daily lives such as tragic happenings, which used to stir us reflexively to remorse, now evoke less painful responses. We see the world differently through a new time. And as we learn to see a friendlier face of time, the mask of death itself becomes transformed—if not into a smile, perhaps at least without a frown.

In some situations heightened time awareness can be fatal. In 1968, Cassem and Hackett[3] published their observations on a series of patients who were admitted to a coronary care unit in a major hospital following an acute myocardial infarction. One group was observed to be generally unruffled in comparison to another group of patients. Those patients who seemed intensely anxious and worried, even though these fears were appropriate, survived the coronary care unit in fewer numbers. Time awareness—expressed as fear of death, that time may run out—seemed to represent an increased risk of dying in the acute phase following a heart attack.

Why? What is there about an exaggerated time sense that predisposes one to death after an acute myocardial infarction? We know some of the reasons. In this situation a realistic attitude toward time requires that one entertain the possibility that one's time is limited. The confrontation of death for most of us generates either momentary or protracted fear which evokes typical and predictable body responses. In fear states or in states of high anxiety, the heart rate increases, so does the blood pressure. These events are coupled with an increase in the secretion of adrenalin, whose action is to drive the blood pressure and heart rate upward. Moreover, there are direct nerve connections from the hypothalamic area of the brain to the heart; and the hypothalamus, when stimulated, can produce a kind of electrical instability in the heart itself. The "fibrillatory threshold" in the heart muscle may be lowered, meaning that it is easier for the heart to fibrillate, or beat in a rapid, chaotic, and ineffective rhythm, resulting in sudden death. The increase in heart rate and blood pressure require the heart to do more work. In order to meet this task it requires more oxygen. But this cannot be supplied, for an oxygen lack is what caused the heart attack in the first place, brought about by an obstruction in one of the coronary arteries, the vessels that supply the heart with blood.

Time-related anxiety can kill. The increased fatality in time-conscious patients with acute myocardial infarctions is a grim reminder: time sickness can be fatal.

CANCER

A colleague of mine who is a skilled specialist in cancer therapy disarmed me one day with his remark, "I've just figured out why so many of my patients take up fishing after they are diagnosed as having cancer." His insight came while he himself was fishing the past weekend, and he had an uncomfortable sunburn to show for it. He continued, "If you're sitting in a boat doing nothing but waiting for a fish to bite, time drags. I can't think of any other way to make the days longer. It's a perfect recreation for someone who believes he's going to die and that his time is limited." I smiled. What a diversity of ways, I thought, to expand the sense of time: meditation, biofeedback, relaxation techniques—and now fishing!

My oncologist colleague had raised an important question. *Given* the presence of cancer, is there a relationship between time perception and length of survival? The question is far from settled, but there are clues to the answer.

Of all the predictable responses of patients who discover they have a terminal illness, panic is one of the most characteristic. Panic—a sudden, extreme, pervasive fear. "How much *time* do I have?" "How much *time* is left?" In the panic state the consideration of time is paramount. Time is running down, it is being played out. The time sense becomes heightened. Moments, heretofore unnoticed, are savored—but usually with a dread: soon they will be gone, and I with it.

"How much longer?" The exaggerated sense of the present is mingled with anticipation of the future, with the expectation of death. In this state the patient may turn inward—becoming unwilling or unable to externalize hostility and anger. The fixation on a constricted, diminishing time may thus be translated into the coping style of the patient who dies early from cancer. One can almost see patients living out their belief that "since my time is running out, I must turn my body off." This is no calm resignation, but the frequently painful acquiescence observed by West.[4]

The constricted time sense in the terminally ill[5] is apparently part of a psychological dynamic resulting in early death. It is associated with desperation, panic, and giving up. This coping style is a malignant path for the terminally ill. It should be dealt with as surely as we would employ drugs and surgery and irradiation in treating an underlying cancer.

Yet we persist in focusing on body problems almost exclusively. Is the patient maintaining his diet? Has the white blood cell count fallen too low to permit further treatment? Is the clotting mechanism intact, or should we defer chemotherapy for now? Body problems are real, and should be dealt with; but they are only part of the larger view, which includes the "time strategy" being used by the seriously and terminally ill.

How can we intervene in the time strategy being utilized by seriously ill patients? A great therapeutic reservoir of techniques exists for this purpose, most of which make use of the purposeful use of visualization, imagery, and relaxation. Entirely new disciplines such as biofeedback have arisen in the past two decades, which are known to be highly effective in modifying the time sense in sick patients.

The importance of these techniques should not be underestimated; for evidence suggests that they are potent factors in extending life in seriously ill patients.[6,7]

FOREST AND TREES

III

Unity

A vast similitude interlocks all,
All spheres, grown, ungrown, small, large, suns, moons,
*   planets,*
All distances of place however wide,
All distances of time, all inanimate forms,
All souls, all living bodies though they be ever so different,
*   or in different worlds,*
All gaseous, watery, vegetable, mineral processes, the fishes,
*   the brutes,*
All nations, colors, barbarisms, civilizations, languages,
All identities that have existed or may exist on this globe,
*   or any globe,*
All lives, and deaths, all of the past, present, future,
This vast similitude spans them, and always has spann'd,
And shall forever span them and compactly hold and enclose
*   them.*

—WALT WHITMAN
LEAVES OF GRASS

CHAPTER ONE

THE HUMAN FACTOR

"All real living is meeting. Meeting is not in time and space, but space and time in meeting."

—MARTIN BUBER[1]

PSYCHOLOGICAL FACTORS AND EMOTIONALLY CHARGED BEHAVIOR such as loving, touching, caring, sharing, and associating exert enormous effects on health. These patterns suggest an intrinsic mind-body unity that simply cannot be accounted for by the present biomedical framework, wherein all matters of health and disease are said to reflect either order or disorder originating at the level of the molecules in the body.

In this chapter we will look deeper into the biological world for evidence that unity in many forms is a seminal life quality. We will see the principle of unity expressed in surprising ways, such as the obliteration of the assumed boundaries that separate the organism from the world outside. We shall look at examples from the level of the gene to that of the person. We will see the principle of unity illuminated not only through the intrinsic oneness of mind and body, but in a much more powerful and general form: the unity of consciousness and the universe itself.

For a half century we have accepted almost without question the assumption that the primary threats to our health were "out there." The success of antibiotics in eradicating specific pathogenic bacteria and the effectiveness of immunizations in preventing disease are perhaps the major factors that historically led us to conceptualize disease as originating outside our bodies. Following this notion we have for generations formulated health strategies that are geared toward protecting us from malevolent external events.

Moreover, we have learned to insist on single causes for specific illnesses. We have a bias for straightforward causal relationships of how disease occurs. But the search for simple causal disease mechanisms has turned into a pipe dream. As Vaisrub has noted,

As various concepts of causality passed through the focusing prisms
of medical philosophers, they underwent further changes to accommodate the need for understanding and treating diseases. Such accom-
modations resulted in the addition, among others, of such causes as
macrocosm-microcosm, intrinsic, contributory, predisposing, and necessary. Newer cybernetic mechanisms have added further complexi-
ties to understanding causality in human physiology. Cause and effect
no longer bear a straight linear relationship to each other. Circular
mechanisms of positive and negative feedbacks have taken over in the
operational depths of homeostasis. The chain of causation is fast
dissolving before our eyes to be replaced by some form of invariable
association that does not lend itself readily to a graphic, mathematical,
or any other representation.[2]

Today it is impossible to think of *any* disease that is causally as
simple as we once supposed. Even in the infectious diseases, which
we once believed to be the result of a straightforward balance between
the aggressiveness of the microorganism and the defense capabilities
of the host, we have entered Vaisrub's "operational depths of homeostasis." We do not know with certainty, for example, why some
persons when challenged with a streptococcal infection contract
rheumatic fever, while others may develop "strep throat," or why
some may become an asymptomatic carrier of the bacterium, or why
others repel the organism completely.

The reasons, we supposed, were at least shrouded in the workings
of the cells of our bodies. We presumed that we could eventually
decipher all the factors involved—and even if we did not yet know *how*
to look for them, at least we knew *where* to look: in the body itself, or
in the bacterium. But, alas, even that presumption has proved illusory,
for we have discovered that we do not know precisely what it is we
mean by "body." For in investigating our resistance to infection, we
know now that the map of the body must include the mind.

In the main we have looked for disease causation in areas where
we knew *how* to look: the physiological, the realm of the flesh. Our
techniques of investigating physiological functioning far exceed our
facility in describing psychological phenomena, which in medicine
we have tended to ignore. Our strategy is reflected in a famous Sufi
story of Mulla Nasrudin, an enlightened fabled teacher. While on
his hands and knees, peering on the street for a lost key, he was
approached by a friend. "You lost the key here, Mulla?" his friend
inquired. "No," said Nasrudin, "I lost it in my house." "Then why
are you looking here?" asked the friend. "Because," said Nasrudin,
"the light is better here."[3]

In our efforts to explore human illness we have looked where the light is good. In some cases we have been fortunate enough to find valuable lost keys. Who can gainsay, for example, our capabilities to cure certain forms of Hodgkin's disease or pernicious anemia? But the problem in most diseases is that the key seems to be lost in many places at once, and the search leads us deeper into the dark where the chains of causation weaken and break.

Of all the frustrations in the search for disease causation, none has been keener than what we can call "the human factor." Why did medical students who had cold parental relations and who were able to externalize emotions poorly develop fatal cancer at an increased incidence?[4] Why do assertive, truculent, and irrascible patients with metastatic breast cancer live longer than their passive peers?[5] Why does the degree of job satisfaction rate as a major factor in the development of coronary heart disease?[6] Why do psychological coping styles in the face of a heart attack influence survival in the coronary care unit?[7]

This type of information has been a veritable irritant in biomedical research, where the premium has never been on answering these kinds of questions. The light has always been better elsewhere: in the world of molecular biology, where we had hoped that therapies would emerge whose effectiveness would be so great that the perplexing question of the human factor would simply not need answering.

This has not proved to be the case. While we maintain the hope of a pharmacologic cure for cancer, heart disease, hypertension, and infectious diseases, it is clear that human factors can no longer be regarded as peripheral to their causation. And in any consideration of *prevention* of these diseases, the human factor emerges with central importance.

What exactly do we mean by human factors in disease causation? In general we simply mean emotions and feelings, whether positive or negative. Joy and sorrow, as well as elation and depression, are human factors. So are grief, fear, anxiety, frustration, happiness, helplessness, hope, and satisfaction.

How do these diverse psychological traits influence disease processes? We shall examine several examples, beginning with a striking result found in an experiment at Ohio State University.[8]

A group of investigators were studying the effects of a diet high in fat and cholesterol in rabbits. At the end of a certain period the rabbits were sacrificed, and certain arteries in their bodies were examined for evidence of atherosclerosis. This process of cholesterol deposition forms obstructions and ulcerations in arteries, and in humans results in vascular disease of various types, such as heart attacks and stroke.

The results of the study should have been rather predictable, since it was known at the time from previous studies that a diet high in fat and cholesterol would regularly cause flagrant atherosclerotic changes in the arterial systems of rabbits. But when a certain group of the test rabbits demonstrated atherosclerotic changes which were 60 percent less than that of the overall group, the investigators were astonished!

There was no obvious explanation for this unexpected result. Finally an unplanned and unexpected variable in the experiment was discovered: the rabbits who were affected less severely were those who were fed and cared for by one of the investigators who, during the course of the experiment, regularly took them from their cages and petted, stroked, and talked to them.

Was this mere coincidence?* Many bioscientists would have considered laughable the possibility that such rabbit-human interchanges could play a role in atherosclerotic vascular disease and would have passed over this possibility. After all, atherosclerotic vascular disease is an *objective* affair rooted in molecular processes, and the battle against it should be fought on the battleground of the cell, not the psyche!—so the theory of molecular medicine goes.

In order to test this "coincidence," systematic controlled studies were designed in which two groups of rabbits were again fed the same diet and were treated identically except that one group was removed from their cages several times a day for petting, and were talked to each time by the same person. The results? The petted and talked-to group once again demonstrated a 60 percent lower incidence of atherosclerosis.

Not content with the possibility of two coincidences, the Ohio State investigators repeated the study. The results were the same. In an unexplained way, the human factor emerged. Touching, petting, handling, and gentle talking emerged as a crucial determinant in the disease process from which most of us will die: atherosclerosis.

There are sometimes marked differences between species of mammals as to how diseases occur. Some of these species differences are

---

*Had it not been for the keen insights of the experimenters, this would have been a perfect example of the wisdom in Philip Slater's comment: "A coincidence is a trend we've decided not to take seriously."[9]

known while some are unknown; therefore, to generalize the above study to humans may be reckless. Atherosclerosis in rabbits may not be so analogous to the human form of the disease as we might think. What reasons are there to assert that similar psychological factors operate on the human level?

One way of approaching the question is to simply note that the current *physiological* explanations of atherosclerosis in humans seem inadequate. With regard to heart disease, certain well-known risk factors are recognized: high blood cholesterol levels, diabetes mellitus, high blood pressure, and cigarette smoking. All tend to increase one's chances of contracting the disease. Yet in over *half* of the new cases of atherosclerotic heart disease, *none* of these risk factors are present.[10] Something else is going on. Could "human factors" be involved?

In 1973, a special task force in Massachusetts reported to the Secretary of H.E.W. their findings on the likelihood of survival from atherosclerotic heart disease. They found the most reliable factor in determining survival was not smoking, high blood pressure, diabetes mellitus, or high blood cholesterol levels, but *job satisfaction*. And the second overall best predictor was what the task force termed "overall happiness."[11]

In 1980, subjects with elevated blood cholesterol levels were taught the technique of transcendental meditation. Serial determinations of the blood cholesterol level were made. It was found that in subjects who practiced this technique the cholesterol level fell on the average of 20 percent. While this fall may seem modest, it should be noted that there are no drugs that are consistently more effective, safe, and inexpensive as this method of voluntary relaxation and mental quieting.[12]

These findings pose enormously complex questions. How do such human experiences as job satisfaction, happiness, and meditation "get into the cell"? How are the effects of the psyche translated into real physiological change, emerging as an increase in survival from atherosclerotic heart disease or a lowering of the blood cholesterol level?

Patches of light now exist, and we are no longer forced to search in complete darkness in trying to understand these mind-body interactions. For instance, we know that anxiety, stress, and tension stimulate a rise in the level of catecholamines in the blood—substances such as adrenalin and noradrenalin, which arise primarily from the adrenal gland. These chemicals exert profound changes on the way the body controls the levels of fat and cholesterol in the blood. When we are subjected to stress, cholesterol levels predictably rise— due in part, it is felt, to the increase in catecholamine levels in the blood.[13]

Yet we know that one way to reduce the level of catecholamines in the blood is to teach subjects to meditate.[14] Not only are adrenalin levels affected, but profound changes occur in the blood concentrations of other hormones such as cortisol (hydrocortisone).[15] As the concentrations of these substances are altered the physiological processes that they regulate are secondarily modified—including heart rate, blood pressure, regional blood flow, and blood levels of various other substances such as glucose, insulin, and glucagon. (The mechanisms of how psychological events are mediated into physiological changes are further discussed in Part II, Chapter 8.)

The human factor emerges not only when we pursue special techniques such as transcendental meditation, it exerts deep influences in quite ordinary situations. Angina pectoris is the term applied to the pain experienced by patients with atherosclerotic heart disease. It can be mild to severe in degree, even incapacitating. Medalie and Goldbourt followed 10,000 Israeli males aged forty years and older to determine the impact of risk factors on the frequency of angina. Most of the commonly known risk factors were correlated with angina, but so too were anxiety and severe psychosocial problems.

> Perhaps most surprising of all was the finding that, among men with severe anxiety, those who perceived their wives to be loving and supportive had half the rate of angina of those who felt unloved and unsupported.[16]

Petted rabbits and loved and supported husbands may not be distant analogies, after all.

Brown and his colleagues have conducted a series of studies in the United Kingdom, investigating the incidence and prevalence of psychiatric disorders. In a variety of settings (urban and rural) and among different social classes (working and middle class)

> . . . the most potent protective factor against psychiatric illness was the presence or absence of an intimate and confiding relationship with a husband or boyfriend; that is, one in which feelings could be shared, whether or not sexual intimacy occurred.[17]

As we shall see later on, Schleifer has recently found that bereavement following the death of a spouse engenders malfunction in the body's immune system.[18] But as early as twenty years ago Kraus and Lilienfeld [19] found that age-specific mortality ratios for widowed men and women were two to fourfold higher than for those who were married. And in 1963 Young[20] reported that in 5,000 British widowers there was a 40 percent excess mortality compared to the predicted rate in the six months following the wife's death.

The health-sustaining role of social support systems, or human factors, is strongly suggested from evidence from Alameda County, California.[21] 4,700 men and women were followed over a nine-year period, and mortality rates from all causes were examined. Mortality rates in men were significantly higher among the unmarried. Those men who chose fewer social contacts with friends and relatives, and those who were not church members, demonstrated a higher death rate. For women, marital status made no difference; but close friendship patterns, church membership, and membership in groups in general were associated with a lower mortality.

How does social support protect against death? What are the specific mind-body mechanisms involved? Work such as Schleifer's on the effect of bereavement on the immune system and the neuroendocrine effects we have already alluded to will undoubtedly prove important mechanisms. As Eisenberg states,

> It remains a task for future research to identify the psychophysiological mechanisms which mediate the impact of social factors on host resistance. Candidate physiological pathways include neural, hormonal, and immunologic control systems. . . .[22]

As every schoolboy knows, there is a physiology of loving and caring, ranging from the embarrassing facial blush to palpitations, sweating, and stammering. Feelings of love generate physical events. It may seem a distant transition from being in love in one's teens to being a confidant or a supportive spouse later in life, but physiologic changes are involved on *both* ends of the spectrum. These changes are not trivial. They can make the difference between life and death.

We affect the health of those about us. Human events such as touching and confiding exert profound consequences on health.

But if the health of one individual affects that of another, how does it do so? One of the mechanisms has been clarified by Steven J. Schleifer and his colleagues at the Mt. Sinai School of Medicine. It has long been felt that certain stressful life events such as bereavement could contribute to the development and course of a variety of illnesses. One of the most stressful events in life is the death of a husband or wife, and in 1967, Holmes and Rahe,[23] in assessing the relative stress imposed by various events, rated the death of a spouse as the single most stressful occurrence in life. Schleifer studied the function of the body's immune system in men before and after the death of their wives, all of whom suffered from advanced breast cancer.

The cells in the body that function to maintain our immunity are called lymphocytes. They are of two types, B and T lymphocytes, designations that refer to their origin in the body. B lymphocytes are concerned with antibody production which occurs, for example, when bacteria or viruses invade the body. The T cells, on the other hand, function primarily in affording us tissue immunity, a type of immunity which, it is felt, is particularly important in retarding the development and growth of cancer cells in the body.

Schleifer found that the total number of T and B cells did not change after bereavement. But the cells behaved differently. They could not be stimulated to perform their usual function. Both the T and B lymphocytes failed to respond appropriately when challenged by certain chemical agents, which ordinarily, in healthy persons, cause them to appear "turned on" to their task of providing immunity. It was as if the cells themselves were sick.

What happened? How did bereavement, a profoundly stressful event, produce changes in the body's immune system, compromising the defense against infection and cancer? The answer is not known, but Schleifer suggests that the causes are multiple, involving at least the complex chemistry of brain function.

Schleifer's work shows us that illness is a shared phenomenon, generating changes in the health of those about us. Even our own death, which the poets have long lamented as a lonely affair, is not private. It sets in motion a cascade of repercussions in those who love us, those who bereave our passing.

These views are dissonant with our traditional idea of health and disease as personal matters. And ironically it is science that is fueling this dissonance, validating the vision of John Donne, who knew of the rich connections which bind us together: "No man is an island."

John C. was a sixty-five-year-old patient of mine who was hospitalized in the coronary care unit. He had diffuse disease in the vessels in his body, with known obstructions in the arteries supplying blood to the legs, head, and heart. Two days prior he had suffered severe chest pain. His laboratory studies and electrocardiograms revealed an extensive myocardial infarction. He was gravely ill, a fact that was obvious to his healthy wife who came to visit him on the designated hours. On the third day I was summoned by an emergency call to the coronary care unit waiting room to attend someone who had suddenly developed shortness of breath. Running to the area, I was astonished to see *Mrs.* John C. lying on a couch, extremely pale and short of breath, by that time clutching her chest with pain. She was taken immediately to the same coronary care unit where her husband lay. Her condition stabilized, but the evidence revealed that she, too, had developed an acute myocardial infarction.

The sequential development of identical illnesses in spouses is by no means rare. Probably most physicians have observed this phenomenon. Mr. John C.'s heart attack extended beyond his own body. Such events occur in defiance of the orthodox concepts of molecular medicine, which would confine the effects of a heart attack to a single heart.

THE HUMAN FACTOR IN BIOLOGY

Social support systems, thus, are important for survival. Loving, caring, and confiding are crucial matters, matters of life and death. These human qualities may offend the molecular biologist who wishes to construct an utterly value-free description of disease, but we have seen how any complete theory of disease causation must include them.

The fact that medical scientists are shocked that these human factors can figure heavily in disease causation reflects a certain blindness toward basic characteristics of not only human life but of primitive life in general, life at its lowest levels of organization. But many biologists and geneticists—scientists, who, as a rule, are more familiar with the entire panorama of biological life than are medical scientists—find these ideas quite natural. For example, Dobzhansky has said,

> A solitary individual wholly independent of others is largely a fiction. In reality, most or even all living beings exist in more or less integrated communities, and the ability to maintain these associations entails some cooperation, or at least "proto-cooperation."[24]

(We must be careful, however, to attribute no more significance to words such as "cooperate," "solitary," and "association" than is justified. We mean no more than this: these qualities confer survival

value on the organism possessing them. As such, organisms possessing these qualities will be favored in terms of reproductive
success. We cannot say that primitive organisms "want" to cooperate or associate, but only that in so doing they have become generally more successful in the replication and survival of their genes.)

There are reasons to believe that our urge toward associating with
those of our own kind is rooted in our earliest beginnings. Montague
believes that "dependency and interdependency are the indispensible
conditions of life."[25] He constructs his argument with numerous
examples from biology, such as an early observation by Wilhelm
Roux in 1894. Roux shook apart the cells in a frog's egg early in the
course of its development and separated the cells at some distance
in water. The cells slowly began to approach each other, eventually
making contact.[26] Similar examples are plentiful. Separated from
their companions, individual amoebae begin immediately to find
their way back to the group,[27] and myxobacteria show a type of
social support in the remarkable division of labor that occurs in their
reproductive cycle. Individual bacteria generate slime (hence the
term "slime molds"), which holds them together in the form of a
nonreproductive stalk. At the top of the stalk numerous other bacteria combine in cyst-like forms to propagate themselves.[28]

There are endless examples in the plant and animal world that
social systems are important in the reproductive cycles and survival
of living organisms. Why is this pattern found? We do not know.
We can only guess why this arrangement was favored instead of
some other. However, it is pervasive and the exceptions, such as
spiders and certain fishes, are few.

The previous examples suggest that in associating with other
members of the species an individual achieves greater success in
reproducing his genes. This strategy has, therefore, a "biological
advantage" and is ubiquitous in the world of living organisms.

It is not surprising that a survival strategy such as association with
members of one's species might be allied with the quality of health—
for almost by definition health is itself a survival strategy. It is
practically axiomatic that sickly members of a species would be
relatively unsuccessful in perpetuating their genetic structure. Being
sick is a poor survival strategy, just so is isolation. If both being
healthy and being in association with one's kind confer survival
advantage, we might expect to see these qualities coupled in
individuals.

The healthy, associating individual—are his roots foreshadowed in the evolutionary history of primitive life forms? Should we be surprised to find that the presence of confidants and close relationships with a spouse emerge as statistically significant factors in modern mortality tables? Is it so astonishing that group membership correlates with survival from death of all causes? These facts seem to follow naturally from the pattern we have observed in nature.

To simply say that we are social organisms or to imply that we socialize as a result of mere personality patterns misses the point. Again, our primitive progenitors did not "want" to associate any more than to dissociate. It is simply that in the drift of evolution certain qualities are selected *only* for reasons that are of survival value to the genetic packet of the human individual organism concerned. We may place a human value on such a quality (which may be an attractive thing to do, especially if we possess that quality), but that is a different matter, and of no importance in the evolutionary process.

We can begin to see health in an evolutionary perspective. Surely the most ancient meaning of health was simply success in reduplicating and perpetuating one's genes. Health was the survival of one's own genetic material. Even today we do not regard members of our species as healthy who die prior to reproductive age. We have thus incorporated this ancient (if minimal) definition of health into our complex concepts of what it means to be healthy.

But if our health is coupled with the perpetuation of our genes, it is also tied to our association with members of our species. As Simpson has said,

> No animal or plant lives alone or is self-sustaining. All live in communities including other members of their own species and also a number, usually a large variety, of other sorts of animals and plants. The quest to be alone is indeed a futile one, never successfully followed in the history of life.[29]

We do not have to search for elaborate psychological explanations for why healthy persons seem to opt for socially supportive situations. The explanation is likely much simpler than can be found in theories of personality development. It is this: both the qualities of health and association with other members of our species lie deep in our genes. These are ancient associations, as primitive as life itself, and they are mirrored in simple as well as complex life forms.

The principle of association is found in the gene, we say. Can we go deeper than the gene? Perhaps. Is it odd that the DNA that comprises our genes is a *double* helix—*two* strands of complex chemical compounds entwined in an elaborate way? Is this design a signature within the gene itself of a principle of combination, of association?

I ask these questions half in anthropocentric amusement and half in seriousness. After all, we know of no solitary strands of DNA that have survived, finding only the double helical form in nature.

The skeptic should steel himself for the next logical question: are the combinatorial properties of the atoms within the DNA an indicator of the natural pattern for association we have been examining?

My goal is not to impart meaning in nature where there is none. Indeed, I agree with Dawkins that nature does not "want" or "wish" to have any specific qualities.[30] My point is to emphasize this position by showing that there exist patterns in life—such as our urge to associate with members of our own species—to which we ordinarily impart value, yet which are rooted in the value-free world of our own chemistry, the world of the gene. I also wish to search in a value-free fashion for further evidence of such patterns in the value-free world beyond the gene, the realm of the atom and molecule.

The irony of the search is that in the *value-free* world of the gene we find a mechanism for maintenance of the individual organism—that of association with members of the same species—which at the level of human consciousness seems *shot through with value.* It is not possible to consider association between human beings without invoking values of some sort. Human association free of emotion, feeling, and value would be a contradiction in terms. How are we to resolve the paradox that the value-free genetic mechanism generates life forms (of which humans are only one example) whose associative behavior seems bound to the world of values?

I believe this is a variation of what we have traditionally called the mind-body problem: how can the mindless electrochemical processes of our own bodies eventuate in something we perceive as consciousness? In asking how human values arise from processes rooted in the value-free domain inside the cell, we are faced with the analogous problem of how consciousness arises from the "stuff" of our bodies.

The physicist Schrödinger has examined this problem in detail.[31] He probes the mystery of all sensual qualities, noting, for example, that there is absolutely *nothing* inherent in yellow light—i.e., light that is defined by physicists to consist of electromagnetic waves of a wavelength of 590 millimicrons—that has anything whatsoever to do with the *sensation* of yellow. Schrödinger asks, "Where does the yellow come in?"; and where, as well, do the sensations of hot and cold, and smell and taste, arise?

Our question is similar: where do values come in when we trace our own survival mechanisms from their origins deep in our genetic structure? The resolution of the problem is likely to be that which Schrödinger described: "The observer's senses have to step in eventually. The most careful record, when not inspected, tells us nothing."[32] Whether we are inspecting wave lengths of 590 millimicrons or the associative behavior of living organisms, the observer's senses are brought into play. In the former instance the perception of yellow arises; in the latter, the perception of value results. This may be a property of our conscious mind, a property not found in the record itself. As surely as the physicist's wavelength of 590 millimicrons gives rise to the sensation of yellow, our inspection of our own genetic record may generate the concept to which we attach the term: value.

CHAPTER TWO

THE BIODANCE

"Every atom belonging to me as good belongs to you."

—WALT WHITMAN
"SONG OF MYSELF"

THE REASONS WHY SOCIAL BONDS are positive factors in human health may, then, be traceable to our fundamental reproductive units, the genes themselves.

The genes, we believe, are a kind of biological guarantee of our individuality. Except in the case of identical twins we know that the odds are infinitesimally high against anyone ever having our same genetic pattern. We have come to think, therefore, of genetic individuality.

But strange twists occur in our thinking about individuality at the genetic level: "individuality" or "uniqueness" frequently gives way to "specialness" (after all, it is *I* the genes have made!). And the sense that there is something special about our genetic self generates a sense that we stand apart from other genetic units, our fellow human beings. In our thinking we manipulate the quite correct idea of genetic individuality into the erroneous idea of genetic isolation and separateness, a phenomenon which in nature regularly spells doom.

We extend our own need for personal uniqueness to the notion of personal separateness, bending this concept into the misguided belief that our genes share this quality of separateness. Are they not us and no one else? How could they *not* be separate, since they are unique and individual?

Nothing could be farther from the truth. Nothing we know about genetic mechanisms even hints at any value of isolation at the level of the gene. Genes get around. They do not stay put. This is obvious, of course, in procreation, wherein with each succeeding generation following us our own contribution to the genetic packet of the offspring is halved. In our children our genes move over to share genetic authority with an equal number of genes from our sexual partner. This diluting process continues with each new generation. As our genetic input continues to be halved, by the time our great-great-great-great-grandchild is born our genes account for less than one percent of his genetic constitution.

Seen across generations the entire process of inheritance seems harsh to our idea of the preservation of our personal genetic individuality, as we see our genes diluted with each generation. We gradually dissolve genetically, generation after generation, so that finally the idea of genetic isolation and separateness is seen for what it is: an illusion with roots in our ego.

Even if our genes are diluted to the degree that we become genetically unrecognizable in our offspring, we can at least, we say, be assured that for *one single generation* they are fixed. At least we endure for a single lifetime as individuals, genetically different from our fellows for sixty, seventy, or eighty years. My genes, my biological blueprint which is I and no other, exists unchanged for *my* lifetime. Surely nothing could deny us that!

But our insistence on seeing ourselves as genetically unchanging individuals, even for our own lifetime, also turns out to be an illusion. For our genes are made of protein—DNA, the basic component of all genes—and the life span of protein molecules in the body is brief. A single DNA molecule is shortlived, existing only for a few months. Our proteinaceous genes are continually renewing themselves, exchanging bits and pieces for replacement parts. A continual streaming and shuffling goes on so that over a period of months our entire genetic structure is renewed. To put it another way, *nothing* in our genes today was present in them a year ago, having been totally renewed in the interval.

The *pattern* of the gene, of course, remains the same (barring certain accidents which we call mutations), and can remain the same for a hundred million years. But the stuff of the gene, the thousands of individual carbon, hydrogen, oxygen, and other atoms that comprise it are in constant exchange with the world outside.

Our persistent insistence toward some sort of individuality that endures across time becomes harder and harder to defend. Even our genes won't stay put for very long, with their dizzying exchange of parts with the world outside us. Even though our biologically individual genetic pattern remains the same for our lifetime, we are still frustrated in trying to hold onto a stable physical "I" that lasts even for that same duration.

This is an eerie quality of human life. In the constant dissolution of our genetic selves we somehow retain a sense of an unchanging physical I. Our dissolution is a silent flow occurring outside our awareness.

It is not only our genes that renew themselves. The entire body participates in this astonishing dynamism. Radioisotopic techniques allow us to trace the chemicals that enter and leave the body. Aebersold has concluded that 98 percent of the 10^{28} atoms of the body are replaced annually.[1] Some tissue, such as bone, is especially dynamic. Each body structure has its own rate of reformation: the lining of the stomach renews itself in a week; the skin is entirely replaced in a month; the liver is regenerated in six weeks. Some tissue is relatively resistant to the constant turnover, such as the supporting tissue called collagen and the iron in the blood's hemoglobin molecules. But even though these rates of replacement differ, after five years one can presume that the entire body is renewed, even to the very last atom.

We renew our physical body just as we regrow hair and nails. We are on the move. Five years ago we didn't exist, all our atoms having been replaced in the interval. Here today, completely gone in five years, renewed down to the last single atom, we endure only in the shape, form, and pattern that are assured by our genetic blueprint.

Our replacement parts come in constant flow from the earth itself. The carbon atoms in my body were once of the earth and shall be again, only to be exchanged for more of the same. After leaving my body they may re-enter me at a later time, unlikely though it may be. Or they may be fixed for a while in the body of someone else—or some*thing* else—in this unending round of "biodance," this dance of life.

Biodance—the endless exchange of the elements of living things with the earth itself—proceeds silently, giving us no hint that it is happening. It is a dervish dance, animated and purposeful and disciplined; and it is a dance in which every living organism participates.

These observations simply defy any definition of a static and fixed body. Even our genes, our claim to biologic individuality, constantly dissolve and are renewed. We are in a persistent equilibrium with the earth.

Yet the boundary of our body has to be extended even farther than the earth itself. We know that certain elements in our body, such as the phosphorus in our bones, were formed at an earlier stage in the evolution of our galaxy. Like many elements in the earth's crust, it was cycled through the lifetime of several stars before appearing terrestrially, eventually finding its way into our body.

A strictly bounded body does not exist. The concept of a physical I that is fixed in space and that endures in time is at odds with our knowledge that living structures are richly connected with the world around them. Our roots go deep; we are anchored in the stars.

Our connections with the world outside us are more elaborate still. Not only are atoms exchanged with the earth, entire *molecules* can be exchanged between distant organisms. For example, bacterial plasmids—rings of DNA—can be incorporated by plants, causing certain forms of plant tumors to develop. Even DNA, the building block for the genes, can therefore be shared between living organisms as dissimilar as bacteria and plants. Thus not only are boundaries between organisms and the outside world smudged and blurred, they dissolve between organisms that are radically dissimilar.

But how dissimilar are living organisms? Unexpected connections keep turning up. The Harvard biologist Bernard Davis proposes that viruses may turn out to have evolved primarily to transfer blocks of nucleic acid between organisms. Davis states,

> It is not inconceivable that all DNA in the living world may be part of an unbroken chain of low frequency contacts.[2]

Thus we see that viruses, the most primitive life forms we know, may be central participants in the living chain of connectedness that unites us with all living creatures.

Earlier we saw how human connections influence health. Those persons with close ties with other human beings not only lived longer, but experienced a lower incidence of specific symptoms such as angina pectoris. We also saw that association with members of one's own species was a pattern that pervaded the animal world in general from the simplest forms of life through the most complex. We asked whether this principle of connectedness was prefigured in our genetic structure. Now we can trace the pattern of connectedness and association beyond the level of the gene, seeing how the very atoms of our bodies connect with the world outside us in an endless flow, the biodance.

From atom to organism to person, the pattern that meets us in nature is that of connection and contact. In the world of living organisms, isolation is nowhere met.

The consequence to our health of this feature of the living world seems to be this: we cannot be our healthiest unless we allow the principle of connection to flower in relationships with other human beings. We need contact with our own kind, just as the atoms in our bodies need constant contact, communication, and exchange with the world outside our skin to maintain the living state. To confine our atoms within the bounds of our physical body is to violate a condition of life itself, that of contact with the world outside; and to confine ourselves to a position of isolation from others is to court ill health and death. At all levels, from atoms to persons, connection is a requirement for life.

Establishing connections with others is not merely a matter of participating in a particular pattern of personality. It is a matter of realizing our basic nature. If we adopt a style of aloneness in our relations with others, we contradict a fundamental life process: we defy the biodance, the ebbing and flowing pattern that connects, without which life would cease.

The biodance, the constant renewal of our body from the world outside, stands in playful contrast to our ordinary idea of death. We ordinarily presume that we are physically intact until we die. Scrapes and bruises and broken bones notwithstanding, we believe the physical integrity of the body is unchallenged until the time of death, at which point an irreversible decomposition begins. Eventually we are returned to the earth, we say, and the fulcrum of the process is the moment of death. But it is not so simple and abrupt. We do not wait on death, for we are constantly returning to the earth while *alive*. Every living moment a portion of the 10^{28} atoms in our body returns to the world outside. This constant streaming is so pronounced, so necessary for life, that the very notion of "boundary" begins to appear as an arbitrary idea rather than a physical reality.

The incessant flow of matter from living organisms forms endless chains of connections. Just as DNA can be endlessly transferred by viruses from one living creature to another, the atoms that leave our body may enter other bodies on leaving. Murchie has illustrated this fact in the act of breathing.

> Did you know the average breath you breathe contains about 10 sextillion atoms, a number which, as you remember, can be written in modern notation as 10^{22}? And, since the entire atmosphere of Earth is voluminous enough to hold about the same number of breaths, each breath turns out, like man himself, to be about midway in size between

an atom and the world—mathematically speaking, 10^{22} atoms in each of 10^{22} breaths multiplying to a total of 10^{44} atoms of air blowing around the planet. This means of course that each time you inhale you are drawing into yourself an average of about one atom from each of the breaths contained in the whole sky. Also every time you exhale you are sending back the same average of an atom to each of these breaths, as is every other living person, and this exchange, repeated twenty thousand times a day by some four billion people, has the surprising consequence that each breath you breathe must contain a quadrillion (10^{15}) atoms breathed by the rest of mankind within the past few weeks and more than a million atoms breathed personally sometime by each and any person on Earth.[3]

Thus, without exception, we are all partners in the biodance.

In Part I, Chapter 2 we examined the historical roots of our way of splitting man into a noninteracting body and mind. The body was seen as mere "stuff," while the mind was the thinking, the spiritual, the truly human part of man. The body was characterized as a patterned collection of chemicals enclosed in a bag of skin. This dual way of regarding man found acceptance not only by the common man, it became scientific dogma as well.

It is unthinkable that such a fixed, static, and adynamic view of the body would have arisen had Descartes, the most influential architect of this idea, had any presentiment of the astonishing life quality of the biodance. Dullness, fixity, and stasis are simply not body qualities. But Descartes could not have known it at the time, or he would likely never have propounded the mechanistic descriptions of man which have guided bioscience ever since:

> I wish you to consider, finally, that all the functions which I attribute to this machine, such as digestion . . . nutrition . . . respiration, waking and sleeping; the reception of light, sounds, odours . . . , the impression of ideas in the memory; the inferior movements of the appetites and passions; and finally the movements of all the external members . . . ; I desire, I say, that you consider that these functions occur naturally in this machine solely by the disposition of its organs, not less than the movements of a clock.
>
> —René Descartes
> *Traite de l'Homme*[4]

Today we know too much to formulate such a mechanical view of the human body. If the body *is* a machine it is a wondrous one, one whose parts are continually flying off in all directions, one which is not confined in time and space. It is a machine in constant dissolution, yet which is seldom in the repair shop. Like no clock, it is a machine whose every atom is renewed twice each decade.

Curious aspects of the biodance emerge. We saw that all breathing creatures share the same oxygen molecules, creating a low frequency chain of chemical contact between all living humans and with all humans past and present. Is there any significance to this contact at the level of human experience? Perhaps. For millennia there have existed statements of persons who claim to actually sense this contact. That diverse class of humans we call mystics have long claimed to have a direct sense of contact with others, an experiential knowledge of unity with all humans in all times. What are we to make of these claims? Are they conceivably valid?

Although we have exquisite sensing abilities, our nervous systems are ingeniously clever at screening out stimuli—for instance, we are seldom aware of our clothes touching our skin. When we elect to do so, however, we can call into consciousness certain perceptions that are normally unconscious. For example, at any given moment we haven't the slightest idea what the bottom of our right foot feels like, yet on concentrating we begin to receive signals that tell us something about that area of our body. *It is a matter of paying attention.*

Most of us learn to extinguish attention to external events. Aldous Huxley's "reducing valve" theory of consciousness still seems accurate: our consciousness, like an adjustable valve, is set to allow only a very small fraction of stimuli reaching us to register in our mind. Yet our actual powers of sense perception are astonishing. With regard to visual acuity, e.g., we know that the dark-adapted eye can detect a single photon! We are not sensorially so clumsy as we sometimes suppose.

But we do not all show the same sensing capacities. As Schrödinger has pointed out,

> Some twenty or thirty years ago chemists . . . discovered a curious compound, . . . a white powder, that is tasteless to some persons, but intensely bitter to others. . . . The quality of being a "taster" (for this particular substance) is inherited according to the Mendel laws in a way familiar from the inheritance of blood group characteristics.[5]

We differ enormously in what we can detect. Are mystics a special case? Are they able to "taste" the chemical connectedness that unites us all? Is there some chemical derivative of the biodance that is analogous to Schrödinger's curious white powder, to which certain gifted persons are sensitive? We do not know with certainty. But to deny that such capacities are plausible is analogous to a blind person's denying the possibility of vision.

Many chemical elements in our bodies originated in far-off parts of the universe. The earth's mantle is richly littered with elements that originally were formed in distant parts of space, and that eventually found their way into our bodies. We are the conceptus of the stars.

The biochemical machinery we have evolved owes its nature to the chemical elements that comprise it—elements which are stargifts. We are shaped by the stars, by distant events in the universe.

Modern cosmological theory has it that *all* events on Earth are influenced by distant parts of the universe. Astronomer Fred Hoyle has said,

> Present-day developments in cosmology are coming to suggest rather insistently that everyday conditions could not persist but for the distant parts of the Universe, that all our ideas of space and geometry would become entirely invalid if the distant parts of the Universe were taken away. Our everyday experience even down to the smallest details seem to be so closely integrated to the grand-scale features of the Universe that it is well-nigh impossible to contemplate the two being separated.[6]

We seem to be part of a basic oneness with the universe, not only concerning the origins of our constituent elements, the chemicals that comprise our bodies, but also with regard to the physical laws that govern us.

This idea—that the physical behavior of material objects on Earth is related to the universe as a whole—is not a new one. Physicist Ernst Mach held this view, which was enormously influential on Einstein's construction of his general theory of relativity.

Mach held that a material body had inertia—i.e., it resisted being accelerated—not because of any intrinsic property of its own, but as a result of its interaction with all the rest of the matter in the universe. Thus, to remove any of the matter in the universe would be to change the inertia of the matter that remained. This concept has become known as Mach's principle.

Einstein, in his general theory of relativity, developed Mach's idea into complex mathematical descriptions, which demonstrated the inseparability of distinct physical entities and their environment. His view of how the material universe works is *interactional*—i.e., the properties of all material objects can be understood only through a knowledge of how they interact with all other material objects in the world. Thus, all objects become inextricably linked to their environment in the view of modern physics.[7]

These concepts are conceptually revolutionary when contrasted with the classical ideas of Newton. Prior to the development of relativity theory, the universe was felt to demonstrate two fundamental features—matter and empty space. Einstein showed through general relativity that these concepts were inseparable. The physical features—the "geometry"—of empty space are shaped by physical bodies. This interaction between matter and the space surrounding it is so profound that the two must be visualized as mutual parts of a whole.

The unity between matter and its environment which appears at the macroscopic level is also present at the subatomic level. Capra describes this oneness:

> . . . .the classical contrast between the solid particles and the space surrounding them is completely overcome. The quantum field is seen as the fundamental physical entity; a continuous medium which is present everywhere in space. Particles are merely local condensations of the field; concentrations which come and go, thereby losing their individual character and dissolving into the underlying field.[8]

From the level of the electron to that of stars and galaxies, modern physics points to a unity of matter and its environment. This interaction is so intimate that matter and its surrounding environment cannot any longer be considered separate entities.

Man, in his in-between world, situated in size between the electrons and the galaxies, also cannot be considered separate from his environment. Our oneness with the universe is manifested in the biodance, the endless flow of chemical elements between the human body and its environment. And the views of Einstein and Mach that the inertia of material bodies in the universe is a function of the rest of the matter in the universe also fix us to our environment in an inseparable way. Furthermore, the quantum physical descriptions of the smallest level, the subatomic realm, have destroyed the idea of any separation of matter into distinct and separate particles, and have led to the conclusion that all "particles" are fundamentally connected to all other particles in the universe.

From electrons to human bodies to galaxies—from quantum physics to biodance to general relativity—parts form wholes with the environment. The physicist David Bohm describes this phenomenon:

> Parts are seen to be in immediate connection, in which their dynamical relationships depend, in an irreducible way, on the state of the whole system (and, indeed, on that of broader systems in which they

are contained, extending ultimately and in principle to the entire universe). Thus, one is led to a new notion of *unbroken wholeness* which denies the classical idea of analyzability of the world into separately independently existing parts. . . .[9]

CHAPTER THREE

DISSIPATIVE STRUCTURES

"NATURE IS PART OF US, as we are part of it. We can recognize ourselves in the description we give to it."[1] The words are those of Ilya Prigogine, the Belgium chemist who in 1977 was awarded the Nobel Prize for his theory of dissipative structures. Prigogine's work is a bombshell in science for it has, as the Nobel Committee said, "created theories to bridge the gap between biological and social scientific fields of inquiry." His theory states, in the language of chemistry and mathematics, the eternal message of the poet and mystic that we are one with the world; and he was indeed called "the poet of thermodynamics" by the Nobel Committee.

Man's search for unity with nature has gone beyond poetry and mysticism—or perhaps has fused to some degree with them—to form a vision that is unique for our time. This interweaving of science and mysticism is a new event in human history, and it places fresh demands on the scientist. These interconnections are so profound that it can safely be said that the scientist who does not perceive them not only does not understand mysticism, he does not understand his own science.

Prigogine's theory stands as a rebuttal to orthodox scientific views that hold that the worlds of physics and biology should forever be separate from the value-laden realm of human experience. He acknowledges that his "science of becoming" is "a human physics."[2] There is no hiatus between the microscopic world and our own.

The significance of Prigogine's achievement is that it breaks with the current views of biological determinism, such as those espoused by the late French molecular biologist Jacques Monod. Monod's great book *Chance and Necessity*[3] has stood as a veritable official proclamation of these ideas. His grim vision of man is that of "a gypsy on the margin of the universe that is deaf to his music, and as indifferent to his hopes as it is to his sufferings and crimes." Prigogine offers a counterpoint to Monod's deterministic idea that man is a victim of ironclad universal laws and that his highest and basest acts are equally valueless.

Prigogine says,

> We know we can interact with nature. That is the heart of the message I give. . . . Matter is not inert. It is alive and active. Life is always changing one way or another through its adaptation to non-equilibrium conditions. With the idea of a doomed determinist world view now gone, we can feel free to make our fate for good or ill. Classical science made us feel that we were helpless witnesses to Newton's clockwork world. Now, science allows us to feel at home in nature.[4]

The classical way of viewing the universe has embodied an attitude of hopelessness because it has seemed that everything was inexorably "running down." An irreversible degradation was going on, since any attempt to do useful work resulted in the loss of a certain amount of energy in the form of heat. This process was embodied in the famous Second Law of Thermodynamics, which predicted the "heat death" of the entire universe. Like a cup of hot coffee that cools and never becomes hot again, the universe itself is headed for a similar state of disorganized chaos. This end state is called "equilibrium" by physicists.

But obviously things are not so simple. The entire concern of the biological sciences, for example, is the study of *exceptions* to this irreversible trend. Biologists study *life*; and living processes embody a trend *away* from equilibrium. In a universe that is gradually running downhill, life processes are continually running uphill in defiance of the thermodynamicists' second law.

Prigogine has described through a series of complex mathematical equations how the second law can remain valid for the universe as a whole, yet fail in certain local parts. Chance fluctuations do occur, and at a distance sufficiently far from equilibrium their effects can be magnified enormously. In local defiance of the universal tendency toward disorganization, the fluctuations can give rise to forms of a new complexity. The resulting configurations in nature begin to behave like a "dissipative structure"—Prigogine's term—implying that they interact with the local environment by consuming energy from it, and by eliminating the byproducts of this energy utilization back into the environment.

Energy consumption and utilization within dissipative structures is not always a smoothly functioning process. Energy flow within the structure may cause perturbations, or fluctuations, within the system. If the perturbations are small, they are damped; but if they are great they may initiate severe changes within the structure. The more complex the structure, the greater is the energy flow required for its survival, and the greater the internal perturbation is likely to be if it occurs. In other words, increasing complexity generates a need for increasing energy consumption from the environment, which in turn gives rise to increasing fragility. But ironically *it is this feature of the dissipative structure that is the key to its further evolution toward greater complexity*. For if the internal perturbation is great enough the system may undergo a sudden reorganization, a kind of shuffling, and "escape to a higher order," organizing in a more complex way.

It is the quality of fragility, the capacity for being "shaken up," that paradoxically is the key to growth. Structures that are insulated from disturbance are protected from change. They are stagnant and never evolve toward a more complex form.

This concept at once resonates through disciplines beyond physics and chemistry, once we grasp the fundamental notion that susceptibility is the catalyst for change. Ferguson has expressed this situation clearly:

> At first the idea of creating new order by perturbation seems outrageous, like shaking up a box of words and pouring out a sentence. Yet our traditional wisdom contains parallel ideas. We know that stress often forces sudden new solutions; that crisis often alerts us to opportunity; that the creative process requires chaos before form emerges; that individuals are often strengthened by suffering and conflict; and that societies need a healthy airing of dissent.[5]

A recurring thesis in this book is that there are parallels between the reality of the microscopic realms of the universe and the level of ordinary human experience. Prigogine asserts that these parallels are built into nature. The components of a dissipative structure may act in a cooperative way to bring about a transformative restructuring of the whole—whether at the level of the molecule, or the level of human experience. In this transformation, as Prigogine has noted, even molecules do more than merely interact with contiguous molecules, "but also exhibit coherent behavior suited to the [needs of] the parent organism." The behavior of microscopic components reverberates to the macroscopic level. The meaning of the whole is traceable to the behavior of the part. But it goes beyond the behavior of the component part as new forms emerge, as the system evolves to a more highly complex and sophisticated structure in nature.

In the theory of dissipative structures is the haunting suggestion of order arising out of chaos—and that order could not arise *without* chaos. There is the hint of an ancient wisdom here.

> Consequently: he who wants to have right without wrong,
> Order without disorder,
> Does not understand the principles
> Of heaven and earth.
> He does not know how
> Things hang together.
>
> —Chuang Tzu[6]

The similarities in Prigogine's vision and those of Eastern philosophers have not gone unnoticed by him, and he has repeatedly drawn attention to them.

Prigogine's theory arose from the chemistry and physics governing the microworld, yet seems immediately applicable to the large-scale world of everyday life. This applicability is affirmed by Prigogine himself, as we have seen. An example that some of the principles of dissipative structure theory apply to the world of human experience can be found in the work of Barron. Before the work on dissipative structures was fully shaped, Barron made an intense study of creative individuals. His findings illustrate the applicability of Prigogine's concepts in human lives:

> . . . creative individuals are more at home with complexity and apparent disorder than other people are. . . . The creative individual in his generalized preference for apparent disorder, turns to the dimly realized life of the unconscious, and is likely to have more than the usual amount of respect for the forces of the irrational in himself and in others. . . . the creative individual not only respects the irrational in himself, but courts it as the most promising source of novelty in his own thought. He rejects the demand of society that he should shun in himself the primitive, the uncultured, the naive, the magical, the nonsensical; that he must be a "civilized" member of the community. When an individual thinks in ways which are customarily tabooed, his fellows may regard him as mentally unbalanced. In my view this kind of imbalance is more likely to be healthy than unhealthy. The truly creative individual stands ready to abandon old classifications and to acknowledge that life, particularly his own unique life, is rich with new possibilities. To him, disorder offers the potentiality of order.[7]

Barron's observations are in concert with those of Prigogine: order can arise from chaos.

As the Nobel Committee observed, Prigogine's theory bridges the biological and social-scientific fields of inquiry. These bridges, moreover, are not just the conclusions of his interpreters. Prigogine himself repeatedly uses everyday examples to illustrate his principles. Consider, he says, a town. It is a perfect example of a dissipative structure. It takes in energy from its environment, transforms it into useable products, and eliminates its wastes back into the world around it.

Dissipative structures are to be found at all levels in nature. The same ordering principles that operate at the microscopic levels of nature permeate our life at the social and cultural levels. There is a principle of connectedness here, implying a oneness between man and nature. Nature is part of us, and we are part of it, as Prigogine says. We *are* nature; and as such it is not surprising that we are discovering common principles that describe not only how *molecules* behave, but how *we* behave.

Some persons have decried these findings, fearing that, once again, humans are being devalued by science. We are reduced to descriptions of molecules; the theory of dissipative structures is reductionism in a new form. This attitude is a misunderstanding of the implications of Prigogine's work, which does not devalue life but elevates it to a position of primacy in a universe that we believed to be drifting to an inexorable, cold, entropic death, dragging us with it. Suddenly we face the dawning of a different prospect. With the recognition that the world of matter and life *can* be bridged, the future is brighter.

We are reminded of the position of the Nobel physicist Eugene Wigner, who asserted that physical objects and spiritual values share a similar kind of reality. Wigner contended that this was the only known position that was consistent with quantum mechanics. Now we can add: the union of physical objects and spiritual values is consistent also with the theory of dissipative structures.

Prigogine's theory evokes an attitude of disbelief from many persons who first encounter it. How can a theory that is so general be correct? The theory of dissipative structures has application to perhaps every domain of scientific and social endeavor. The broad applicability of the theory is seen by many, therefore, as its Achilles' heel. It appears too good to be true.

Yet we must remember that the goal of scientific theories is to bring together observations that have hitherto poorly fit together. Great theoretical advances *are* unifying. Maxwell's theory brought together electricity and magnetism. Einstein showed us the relationship between energy, matter, gravity, and light. If we have become inured to the explanatory power of these landmark observations, we have only to remember that in earlier times they too were seen as intellectual achievements of astonishing comprehensiveness, which themselves were "too good to be true" at the time they were enunciated.

Much of our difficulty in assimilating the comprehensiveness of Prigogine's theory of dissipative structures lies in our traditional assumption that the worlds of life and nonlife could not be bridged except in the experience of the poet and mystic. Now we are confronted with evidence to the contrary. We are asked to see in the microworld of nature what we see in ourselves. We are presented with a "human physics." We are asked to think in new ways.

We are asked to participate not in a new kind of science, but in a new vision of our place in the universe. This new world view goes beyond the idea of life as a "nothing but" process—nothing but the blind results of the electrochemical properties of specific molecular arrangements. The new view transcends this reduction of life to dead matter. It sees life *in* matter. As Prigogine says, we see in nature what we have always seen in ourselves.

THE THEORY OF DISSIPATIVE STRUCTURES APPLIED TO HEALTH

What consequences does the theory of dissipative structures hold for human health? If the theory provides a "human physics," we should expect to find implications about health and disease.

On the surface, Prigogine's ideas seem to challenge the accepted goal of medicine: to provide all persons with a disease-free life from beginning to end. The lengths to which we are willing to go to insure an illness-free state seem limitless. The worthiness of the goal is not questioned. Who would argue with the desirability of preventing disease and suffering?

Recall, however, a central concept of dissipative structures: only through perturbation can the system escape to a higher order of complexity. The key to growth is fragility. While mild disturbances are damped within the system, major ones are not; they have the possibility of stimulating a sudden change toward a more complex system.

How does this concept apply to human health? Disease is without question a perturbation, with repercussions in our entire psychophysical being. While we may damp mild intrusions—for example, a viral upper respiratory illness (the common cold) or a stubbed toe—we do not handle major illnesses with the same facility. Major illnesses "shake us up." They perturb us. If, for instance, I foolishly combine the use of alcohol and aspirin, I am very likely to develop ulceration or inflammation of the lining of my stomach, with the symptoms of indigestion, pain, and perhaps bleeding. However, I can use this disturbance in a positive way. I can "escape" to a higher level of awareness wherein I wisely forego the indiscreet concomitant use of aspirin and alcohol. I have experienced a perturbation from the outside environment (aspirin and alcohol); I have been disturbed internally (experienced pain, indigestion, bleeding); and I have organized a more complex approach to my personal health care as a result. As such, the internal richness of my own health care philosophy has grown.

Endless examples could follow. In matters of health we frequently see stress begetting strength. This is obviously true in the psychological realm where adversity may play a major role in increased insight and awareness.

But just as in the physical world all perturbations do not end in a successful reshuffling of a system toward a higher level of reorganization, in human beings the rule is the same: threats to our health are not always successfully dealt with by the body. Sometimes the system is not only shaken up, but shaken to pieces. Disease may result in chronic infirmity and death.

But evolution, says dissipative structure theory, is impossible *without* fragility. Perturbation and susceptibility to dissolution and death are the prices to be paid for the potential for growth and complexity.

In the 1800s the Hawaiian Islands were visited by an increasing stream of Americans who brought something new in the way of perturbation to the native islanders: measles. The measles virus was then endemic to America, where it was regarded, as in our time, as a nuisance. Only rarely did it cause more than the aggravating symptoms of rash, red eyes, transient fever, and malaise. But for the islanders it was deadly. The native population was decimated by the virus, for they were completely lacking in natural immunity to it. Following this event a degree of natural immunity to the disease developed, such that measles proved to be no more deadly in the Hawaiian population than in the American. The immune system of the native islander had changed as a result of a perturbation from the environment. It was "shaken up," but the population as a whole "escaped" to a new level of immune competence. A higher internal order of health had evolved.

We invoke the tenets of dissipative structure theory in many of our health care methodologies. Consider our practice of immunization. By artificially introducing altered microorganisms into the body, we cause a perturbation from the outside. In fact, we are creating a "mini-disease"—just enough to stimulate the body to produce antibodies to protect us from the same disease should we encounter it at a later date. Were our body to damp the effects of the innoculum completely, we would produce no antibody, and no immunization would result. We want to shake up the body's immune system just enough to stimulate resistance to the disease, but not enough to actually cause the illness. Through our practice of immunization we are producing an evolution toward biological complexity through intentionally perturbing the immune system.

If we were never perturbed by illness, could we *ever* be healthy? If we never knew illness we would likely lack a corresponding notion of health. But it is in more than an epistemological sense that we need to examine this problem. There is reason to believe that our body *feeds* on illness to create its health, just as dissipative structures "eat entropy," or disorganization, as Schrödinger maintained, in this evolution toward increasing complexity.

Our own body contains the wisdom derived from countless challenges to its integrity. From the skin that covers us to the white blood cells that engulf invading microorganisms, our body knows what to do. How did this information accumulate within us? By constant and repetitive perturbation in our evolutionary ascendency toward increasing complexity.

We have only to witness the failure of this feature of dissipative structures to recognize its importance. Occasionally there are children who are born with a spectrum of illnesses that are called immune deficiency states. These unfortunate children cannot make antibodies to bacteria, viruses, and fungi. They are helpless to combat infection, and usually die of overwhelming infectious problems young in life. They are the "bubble babies" who live in spacesuit-like sealed compartments or under impermeable canopies in an artificial sterile atmosphere.

Put in the language of dissipative structure theory, they cannot react to perturbations from the outside. They cannot effectively damp a challenge from the external environment. Because of their inability to respond, they cannot escape to a higher degree of immune complexity. Their primary hope is artificial isolation. We attempt to insulate them from external perturbations so that the "shake-ups" from microorganisms will not be fatal. They cannot respond to immunologic challenges. Because they cannot, early death is the rule.

We see here a subtle aspect of health: perturbation is bound up with shifts toward physiological complexity. Health is impossible without disturbances, although we traditionally think it is impossible *with* disturbances. These complementary processes generate health, one of the meanings of which is the ability to resist insults to our psychophysical integrity. We see in dissipative structure theory, and in observing how our own immune system works, that these processes are interwoven. The processes of health and perturbation form a complementary whole.

We can formulate an extremely general goal of health as follows: to do what can be done to facilitate the body's successful adaptation to perturbation. How differently we behave in our ordinary approaches to health! We strive to stand rock-solid against onslaughts to our health, battering at the perceived threats with a constantly changing array of injections, pills, and surgery. We move not *with* the perturbation, but *against* it. We try to avoid encounters with external challenges to our health; failing that, we struggle to resist them using any means at hand.

We must begin to question this general health strategy. If perturbations to the body's integrity had *never* occurred we would be truly defenseless against disease, for we would never have evolved the elaborate defense mechanisms which, on the whole, operate with silent efficiency. We would be like the immune-deficient children, helpless in a world of pathogens.

Perhaps we should adopt a strategy wherein we try to behave not like an immovable Gibralter but like bamboo, which in Oriental lore bends with the wind instead of resisting it, and is thus preserved. Like a bridge that has no flexibility and can thus be shaken to pieces in a wind, our heroic and inflexible stance to resist being moved by disease may doom us.

Our health strategy needs to incorporate flexibility as a primary goal—the adaptability and capacity to react to the periodic challenges to our body-mind integrity. What we do in the interval *between* illness also becomes crucial. I can, by conscious effort, sabotage my body's wisdom to resist perturbations. If I subject myself to negative health habits—smoking, obesity, unrelieved exposure to stress, chronic fatigue, failure to exercise, uninterrupted anxiety or depression—I limit my body's homeostatic capacity to react to external perturbations. I ask it to do what the bamboo in its wisdom never attempts: to remain rigid in the face of stressful and perturbing events.

Seen from this perspective, the *real* medicine is what we do *between* illness-events. All of the techniques of health care which we relegate to the second-class status of preventive medicine are of critical importance, for they help determine the body's capacity to successfully reorder itself to a higher degree of complexity when actually challenged by disease processes.

Conversely, the traditional approach of medicine and surgery should be viewed as a second line of defense. These methods should be used as a last resort, as a supplement to the body's wisdom. Too often they are used in an effort to shield the body from physical onslaught—as in the condemnable practice of prescribing antibiotics for a common cold, or using tranquilizers for the commonplace anxieties of daily living. For most assaults to its integrity the body needs no shielding. In any event, our efforts of this type result less frequently in *protecting* the body than in *meddling* in its affairs and frustrating its wisdom.

Sometimes a second line of defense *is* needed. (Perturbation is no *guarantee* of a higher reordering.) Even minor viral illness can eventuate in catastrophic problems, as when a mild case of chicken pox becomes complicated by pneumonia or encephalitis. Even stubbed toes can become infected, leading to life-threatening sepsis ("blood poisoning"). In these instances the body's wisdom may be overwhelmed, and exogenous help—drugs and/or surgery—are called for.

But these are unusual events. As Lewis Thomas[8] has pointed out, the body is almost unbelievably efficient at the business of health, extinguishing perturbations before we are even aware of them. For example, bacteria invade our blood stream with each vigorous brushing of our teeth, yet the life span of an individual bacterial invader is less than four minutes. Across our evolutionary history our body cultivated this high degree of complex efficiency through countless episodes of bacterial invasions. The wisdom remains, is astonishingly effective, and ordinarily needs no help from us.

Years ago when my attitudes about health and disease were rather typical of most medical school graduates, I found myself at a medical meeting embroiled in a heated discussion with an elderly psychologist about how to treat peptic ulcer disease. The psychologist was interested in the problem because many patients with peptic ulcers show strong patterns of stress in their lives. Their symptoms seem in some cases to correlate with their stress. I listened to the gentleman express his view about the importance of stress management in these patients, but soon became appalled at what I considered to be his very simplistic approach to the problem. Peptic ulcer development is a very complex event pathophysiologically, a fact that I realized the psychologist did not fully appreciate. When he began to decry drug treatment as an initial approach to the problem I became indignant, stating that were we to *withhold* the use of medications to control acid secretion by the stomach, we would thereby condemn several thousand patients to hemorrhage to death each year because of perforations of the ulcers into major blood vessels in the lining of the stomach and duodenum. The psychologist thought for a moment, then replied, "Yes, that's true. But the drugs don't do anything for the *person!*"

His words were lost on me at the time. We later became friends, however, and I developed an understanding of his position. His point was that although the drugs used could prevent pain from ulcers and death from the complication of bleeding, the patient learns little with that approach.

Neither he nor I had ever heard of dissipative structure theory at the time, but I now find it interesting to couch his reply in terms of Prigogine's ideas. When the drug is given (the drug under discussion was a newly released agent called cimetidine, about which the entire medical profession was enthusiastic), its effect is to block the cells in the stomach from being stimulated to produce acid. As this process is controlled the ulcer is given a better chance to heal. But the drug has its side effects, as do all drugs. It was expensive, moreover; and when the patient stopped taking it, the ulcer frequently recurred.

Even though the ulcer might heal, it is difficult to see how the body's wisdom increased after the use of the drug. Faced with a perturbation in the form of an ulcer, there was no escape toward a higher level of complexity whereby the body thereafter could resist future ulceration. The entire strategy was drug dependence, not body dependence.

On the other hand, if the patient had learned certain things about his disease—how diet affected its course or how psychological stress played a role in acid secretion—he was in a position to implement a new positive health strategy. It may or may not have been successful; but in the event that these "natural" methods did indeed work, we could say that the patient's mind and body had evolved to a higher level of sophistication following its perturbation by the peptic ulcer. It was reordered in a new way, more able to resist a recurrence of the same physical insult.

The lesson is: the best health strategies make us wiser. Insofar as any health intervention does not increase our psychophysical sophistication and our internal wisdom in dealing with perturbations to our health, it is an inferior therapy.

In my own private practice of internal medicine I had a vivid example of this principle in action. A patient whom I shall call Nancy came to see me for a problem of recurrent chest pain. She was twenty-nine years old, extremely intelligent, attractive, and very successful in her career. Periodically over the previous five years, however, she had become incapacitated with swelling, redness, and exquisite pain in the sternocostochondral areas—the regions in the front part of the chest where the ribs are joined to the breast bone, the sternum, by pieces of cartilage. This is a common ailment called costochondritis. It may be caused by a viral infection and, while it can be painful, it is usually transient, responding to minor analgesics, rest, and applications of heat.

Nancy's experience with costochondritis was different. This illness would strike suddenly, several times a year, and was incapacitating to her. She was unable to function because any motion of the arms increased the pain unbearably. The first time I saw her with this spectacular illness the involved areas alongside the sternum were grotesquely swollen and red. I immediately hospitalized her for diagnostic studies which, to my surprise, proved uniformly normal. Thinking I may have been incorrect in my assessment of the problem, I asked a rheumatology specialist to see her—to no avail. He had no other suggestions.

This episode subsided gradually, to be followed by four more similar ones during the first year I cared for her. Frustrated by the ailment, she visited a thoracic surgeon who feared she had a cancerous process in the enlarged, swollen cartilaginous areas. She refused his suggestion of surgically biopsying the regions, with surgery possibly to follow. She also saw a specialist in pain control who was affiliated with a very fine local medical school. A variety of techniques to control her pain were tried, all to no avail.

Two years later after multiple attacks she seemed no better than when I originally saw her. She came to my office one day and revealed what to me was an astonishing event. She had experienced the very early onset of a typical episode—a nagging pain in the chest at the border of the sternum. The thought that went through her mind was, "The problem still exists. Medical science can do nothing for me. I have to handle this myself." She went on to describe how she sat down in a relaxed, comfortable position and focused with all her mental intensity on the pain in her chest. She was unable to explain why she chose this strategy, but the pain gradually diminished and ultimately vanished. Over the next few hours as she pursued her ordinary activities she followed the same technique, focusing on the pain as intensely as possible while in a deeply relaxed state whenever it would begin to reappear. For the first time in many years the early symptoms of chest pain did not crescendo into a full-blown incapacitating episode of costochondritis.

I was immensely impressed. My own therapy had been an embarrassing failure for her. With her own devices she had accomplished what I had been attempting with my anti-inflammatory pills and potions. She became quite skilled at her technique, and developed an extreme sensitivity in detecting the earliest signals from her chest area that the problem was about to begin again. Each time she would abort the signals through her simple strategies. Five years hence, she has had no major recurrences.

Intrigued by her success, I asked her to participate in a biofeedback project I was just beginning, a suggestion which held great appeal for her. Biofeedback provides a means of bringing into one's conscious awareness events occurring in the body that usually are unconscious. Working with sophisticated instruments that monitor these bodily events, one can rapidly cultivate an exquisite sensitivity to such things as muscle tension, skin temperature, and galvanic skin resistance. I was convinced that Nancy had learned on her own to sense and abort certain body events that were critical in the early stages of the development of her costochondritis.

Not surprisingly, she was a gifted biofeedback subject. She threw her energies into the experience with a gusto, learning in a short time to refine her already enviable skills. Periodically in the ensuing five years she has come back to the biofeedback laboratory to test her abilities on the instruments. Her skills have not deteriorated, they have improved; and her symptoms remain controlled.

What does a single case of this sort mean? Anecdotal clinical cases are usually scorned in medicine ("Beware the series of one!"). But for any physician faced with the immediate necessity of caring for an intractable problem like Nancy's, it is impossible to remain unimpressed by the effectiveness of her health strategy.

If we try to dissect the events in this case in terms of dissipative structure theory, what pattern emerges? First, Nancy was recurrently perturbed by costochondritis. In spite of an array of medical treatments, her body's wisdom in handling future episodes seemed unchanged. No higher order, no increased degree of complexity resulted. Her periodic buffeting recurred, each episode similar to the previous one in duration and intensity.

With her new discovery this changed. Her psychophysical strategy was a sudden reordering of her health mechanisms, a new complexity which was utterly different in design from any of the measures that had been used before. Through the repetitive perturbations to her psychological and physical integrity, she escaped to a higher wisdom that made it possible thereafter for her to counter the challenges to her health.

Does Nancy's case illustrate a sheer coincidence? (The medical rebuttal when illnesses mysteriously improve is to ascribe the response to "the natural course of the disease." This explanation is no explanation at all, however, and says less about the natural course of disease than the natural state of our ignorance.) I am convinced it is not. In my own medical practice there are simply too many Nancys, too many illnesses that respond to her general approach.

My experience in utilizing biofeedback as a technique in controlling certain medical problems has been a fascinating personal journey. Frequently the patients who are most successful at implementing these techniques are like Nancy—medically they are at the end of their rope. They have run the gamut of the usual therapies, to no avail. Thus, they are somewhat desperate. Their encounter with uniformly unsuccessful medical techniques has left them disenchanted, skeptical, and fearful of another failure.

In many cases that respond to biofeedback techniques—such as when a patient with lifelong intractable migraine headache witnesses his headaches disappear—we have no adequate explanation physiologically why the improvement occurred. But it would require the most ardent skeptic to deny the effectiveness of these methods. In many good biofeedback laboratories, fully seventy-five percent of patients with classical migraine or tension headache can learn to rid themselves of their symptoms.

One of the most amazing results, however, is not the cessation of the headache, the costochondritis, etc.—it is the evidence of a *reordering* that involves not only the physiology of the patient, but that extends to the realm of his thought and feeling. This *is* more than conventional medication and surgery. As the psychologist with whom I petulantly disagreed said, it does something "for the person." Patients behave differently; they *feel* differently. Why?

In a very general way we can say that the therapies that evoke in a patient an awareness of his psychophysical oneness help facilitate the sudden reordering described by dissipative structure theory. This reordering is obvious not only clinically as physical symptoms disappear, but in changes in the patient's immediate felt experience, his very thought and behavior. These kinds of medical strategies do what ordinary pills and surgery never do: they facilitate an escape to a higher level of complexity, to a higher awareness of psychophysical oneness, to a higher health. And they provide a therapy in certain persons for specific illnesses of almost unbelievable effectiveness.

We are learning more about how these "reordering therapies" work. They will not supplant the marvelous accomplishments of current medicine and surgery, but beyond doubt their use will proliferate as we learn more about how to apply them. We are at an awkward stage in medicine, having stumbled onto effective therapies with no sure explanation of how they work. These explanations will emerge. In the meantime, dissipative structure theory provides a theoretical framework to guide us in their use.

A model of health care based on dissipative structure theory operates on a principle of oneness of body and mind. Reordering therapies work not only because the body becomes wiser, but because the changes that occur involve our complete psychophysical being. The current concept of molecular medicine, wherein therapeutic intervention seeks to aim at the level of the molecule to be effective, is an incomplete healing strategy. While its methods may be spectacularly effective in certain disease states, they ordinarily are implemented *after* problems have arisen (for example, an appendectomy for acute appendicitis). They are not designed to do more than that, on the whole. In the main, modern approaches to disease intervention work best after substantial problems have arisen. They are, after all, body therapies. As such, they are limited in scope.

As a physician and (as is everyone) a potential patient, I am grateful that contemporary medicine and surgery exist, that they can be brought to bear on me should I become ill. I am not disparaging of them; quite the contrary, they add to my confidence that I shall recover should I become sick. But we are asking in what ways contemporary methodologies must change to facilitate our psycho-physical reorganization to more complex levels, ways which increase our capacity to deal with external perturbations to our health.

The theory of dissipative structures does what orthodox science has long insisted should not be done: it identifies characteristics of behavior in nature that apply to distant organizational levels. It makes the audacious assertion that molecules and human beings behave in similar ways. Certain principles of behavior resonate equally forcefully in the domains of the atom and the person. Because these principles cut across such vast distances, Prigogine has asserted that we can now talk about "a human physics."

Dissipative structure theory puts us in intimate touch with the micro-world. It says that our nature is rooted in the fundamental processes that lie in the bone and marrow of the universe. We are no longer con-strained to devise tenuous and speculative philosophical arguments about how we as humans embody the organizing principles of nature. Dissipative structure theory hands us proof on a silver platter, gar-nished with elegant mathematical proofs, that the heart and soul of both humans and the microworld share certain identical characteristics.

A typical reaction to this observation is that it must be wrong. It may be a pursuit of philosophy to attempt the difficult task of uniting the microscopic world of atoms and molecules to the world of human behavior, but this is not a proper goal of science. Indeed, this belief has assumed the authority of dogma in science.

But we are now confronted with the theory of dissipative struc-tures, which accomplishes this heretofore impossible feat. Its math-ematical proofs have thus far been verified when put to the test by the world's largest computers, and the theory has been honored by a Nobel Prize in the process.

We must now face a fact that has heretofore been embodied in the presentiments of philosophers, yet rejected as a fit area of concern by science: *we are one with nature.* The realm of legitimate scientific inquiry is being extended. Another part of the philosopher's turf is being overtaken by the scientist. This is not cause for dismay, as all of us—philosopher and scientist alike—shall be enriched by these sudden shifts of boundaries.

CHAPTER FOUR

BELL'S THEOREM

"The physicist does not discover, he creates his universe."

—HENRY MARGENAU[1]

THE MYSTIC'S VISION OF A WORLD in which man participates in a seamless existence, indivisibly united with the universe around him, resonates through a discovery called Bell's theorem.[2] This discovery, first proposed in 1964 by the physicist John S. Bell, was first confirmed by experiment in 1972 by Professor John Clauser at Berkeley. It is an almost unbelievable result—unbelievable because the logical mind has great difficulty in comprehending how it can be true. Its impact on the physics community has been enormous. Professor Henry Stapp, a physicist at Berkeley and an authority on the implications of Bell's theorem, has called it the most important discovery in the history of science.

Although many verbal descriptions of the proof have appeared since its original description by Bell, perhaps the clearest is given by Stapp: *"If the statistical predictions of quantum theory are true, an objective universe is incompatible with the law of local causes."*[3]

Although formidable at first glance, Bell's theorem seems simpler once key terms are understood. First, an "objective universe" is simply one that exists apart from our consciousness. It has a legitimate, real existence in its own right, and is there even when we're not looking. Secondly, the "law of local causes" refers to the fact that events in the universe happen at a speed that does not exceed that of light. Things happen, in other words, always at the speed of light or less. This limitation is imposed by Einstein's theory of special relativity, and is a mainstay of modern physical theory.

In practice, physicists do not actually do experiments to prove or disprove the theorem itself. They conduct experiments to test whether or not the statistical predictions of quantum mechanics hold true. To be accurate, therefore, in actual experimental situations it is not Bell's theorem that is tested, but the predictions of quantum theory.

In order to understand the importance of Bell's theorem we must go back to 1935, a time when a consistent quantum theory had already been developed. The picture of the world had become one in which the principles of probability and statistics played a major role. Events could be predicted only when large numbers of individual subatomic occurrences were considered. But quantum physics could say nothing about *single* subatomic events. Even in principle, individual events were considered to be random. At this level of nature, cause and effect could not be identified.

Einstein, having contributed to the development of this picture of the world in major ways, became increasingly disgruntled with its probabilistic and statistical features. In 1935 he, together with Nathan Rosen and Boris Podolsky, devised an argument which he believed to be a reductio ad absurdum to the theory of quantum mechanics.[4] They proposed through flawless mathematical reasoning that if the quantum theory were correct, "then a change in the spin of one particle in a two-particle system would affect its twin simultaneously, even if the two had been widely separated in the meantime."[5]

This suggestion seemed preposterous. In the first place, how could one particle, separated from its twin, possibly "know" when its twin changed? Surely some kind of energetic signal had to pass between them, requiring some time to occur, thus ruling out the possibility of simultaneous change. And "simultaneous" is a dirty word in the theory of special relativity, which forbids the transmission of any signal faster than the speed of light. Obviously, a signal telling the particle "what to do" would have to travel faster than the speed of light if instantaneous changes were to occur between the two particles.

The dilemma into which Einstein, Rosen, and Podolsky dragged the quantum theory was a profound one, coming to be known as the ERP effect for the men who proposed it. By 1935 Einstein's special theory of relativity was quite properly regarded as one of the cornerstones of modern physics. Every time it had been put to an experimental test it had proved valid. No one was willing, therefore, to sacrifice one of its tenets, that nothing can exceed the speed of light, in order to salvage the quantum theory.

Einstein was delighted with this dilemma, believing that his argument pointed to an incompleteness in the theory of quantum mechanics.

But in 1964 Bell's theorem emerged as a proof that Einstein's impossible proposition did in fact hold true: instantaneous change in widely separated systems did occur. At the time Bell offered his proof it was technically not possible to rigorously confirm it experimentally. But in 1972, Clauser confirmed the statistical predictions of quantum mechanics, working with an elaborate system involving photons, calcite crystals, and photomultiplier tubes.[6] The experiment has since been run several times with the same consistent results: Bell's theorem stands solid.[7]

Even for the physicists involved, the implications of Bell's theorem are practically unthinkable. Once again, as has happened so often in this century, mathematics and experimentation have taken us where our logical mind cannot go. Imagine! Two particles, once in contact, separated even to the ends of the universe, change *instantaneously* when a change in one of them occurs!

Slowly new ideas are emerging to explain these unthinkable occurrences. One view is that, in some unexplainable way, the separated particles are still in contact although separated in space. This is the suggestion of the French physicist Bernard d'Espagnat. In 1979, writing about quantum reality, he said that the entire notion of an external, fixed, objective world now lies in conflict not only with quantum theory, but in facts drawn from actual experiments. D'Espagnat stated, "the violation of Einstein's assumptions seems to imply that in some sense all these objects constitute an indivisible whole."[8]

Physicist Jack Sarfatti of the Physics/Consciousness Research Group proposes that no actual energy-requiring signal is transmitted between the distant objects, but "information" is transmitted instead.[9] Thus, no violation of Einstein's special theory of relativity occurs. Exactly what this information is is unclear, and it is a strange thing which might travel instantly and require no energy to do so.

Nick Herbert, a physicist who heads the C-Life Institute, suggests that we have merely discovered an elemental oneness of the world. This oneness cannot be diminished by spatial separation. An invisible wholeness unites the objects that are given birth in the universe, and it is this wholeness that we have stumbled onto through modern experimental methods. Describing this quality of oneness, Herbert alludes to the words of the poet Charles Williams: "Separation without separateness, reality without rift."[10]

To be sure, there are other alternatives to these experimental results than to do away with the law of local causes, thus allowing for a seamless universe where events happen simultaneously through some invisible connecting principle. Alternatively, one may do away with the concept of an objective universe if one wishes to preserve the principle of local causes. And other options exist as well—each one of which forces radical revisions of our commonly accepted version of reality.[11]

Which outcome of Bell's astonishing theorem will eventually hold we now cannot say. But it would be a mistake to suppose that these effects operate only with relevance to the invisible world of the atom. Professor Henry Stapp states that the real importance of these findings is that they translate directly to our macroscopic existence. We are not concerned with merely trivial effects that are observable to only a handful of privileged physicists working with expensive equipment.

We are again reminded of Prigogine's "human physics"—so called because the ordering principles he describes operate throughout the universe, at the level of human beings as well as at the level of atoms. Stapp's implications are similar: the oneness that is implicit in Bell's theorem envelopes human beings and atoms alike.

CHAPTER FIVE

THE HOLOVERSE

Thus, if all actions are in the form of discrete quanta, the interactions between different entities (e.g., electrons) constitute a single structure of indivisible links, so that the entire universe has to be thought of as an unbroken whole. In this whole, each element that we can abstract in thought shows basic properties (wave or particle, etc.) that depend on its overall environment, in a way that is much more reminiscent of how the organs constituting living beings are related, than it is of how parts of a machine interact. Further, the non-local, non-causal nature of the relationships of elements distant from each other evidently violates the requirements of separateness and independence of fundamental constituents that is basic to any mechanistic approach.[1]

Ultimately, the entire universe (with all its "particles," including those constituting human beings, their laboratories, observing instruments, etc.) has to be understood as a single undivided whole, in which analysis into separately and independently existent parts has no fundamental status.[2]

—DAVID BOHM

CHINESE BOXES, EACH A REPLICA of the box enclosing it, and each containing an exact miniature of itself. . . .

Mirrors facing each other, reflecting an unending series of identical images which gradually diminish in size, eventually fading beyond our optical acuity. . . .

A giant oak tree producing an acorn that contains all the information to replicate itself, the succeeding oak tree continuing in the same pattern of producing its own acorns to reproduce itself, on and on. . . .

The pattern of each human being written into the genes of sperm and ova—miniaturized and concentrated information encased in the part, yet sufficient to reconstitute the whole. . . .

102

We live in a world of such examples: the part contains the whole. This is an ancient idea, but one which in the modern era has been given scientific legitimacy. Since the bespectacled Austrian monk Gregor Mendel established the notion of predictable patterns of inheritance we have come to accept as scientific orthodoxy that wholes *are* embodied in parts.

Mendel worked with peas in a monastery garden, and demonstrated that color patterns were transmitted in specific ratios with predictable regularity. His work provided the foundation for the modern science of genetics. Since Mendel, however, the scene has changed. The monk has become the physicist. Peas have given way to the universe as the object of scrutiny, and Mendel's vegetable garden has become the cosmos itself. His simple numerical ratios have become transformed into the complex mathematics of quantum theory. His description of ironclad deterministic patterns of inheritance have yielded to a language of probability and statistical likelihood.

Certain quantum physicists have expanded the principles underlying the Mendelian discoveries to an unbelievable scale: not only, they say, does the gene of Mendel's garden peas contain the information sufficient to reproduce the pea, each part of the *universe* contains all the information present in the entire cosmos itself!

This assertion is so audacious that it would be dismissed out of hand were it not for the scientific stature of its chief proponent, David Bohm. Bohm, a former associate of Einstein, is Professor of Theoretical Physics at Birkbeck College of the University of London. He must be regarded as one of the preeminent theoretical physicists alive today.

Bohm maintains that the information of the entire universe is contained in each of its parts. There is, he says, a stunning example of this principle in photography: the hologram (literally, "whole message"). A hologram is a specially constructed image which, when illuminated by a laser beam, seems eerily suspended in three-dimensional space. The most incredible feature of holograms is that any *piece* of it, if illuminated with coherent light, provides an image of the *entire* hologram. The information of the whole is contained in each part. This principle, says Bohm, extends to the universe at large.

Since Bohm frequently resorts to the holographic analogy, a brief description of the process will be given. The mathematical theory underlying holograms was developed initially in the 1940s by Nobel physicist Dennis Gabor. When Gabor initially proposed the possibility, holograms could not actually be constructed—this had to await the invention of the laser twenty years later.

Holograms are made using a kind of lensless photography. Coherent light—light whose waves are approximately of the same frequency—is required. This light, such as from a laser, is passed through a half-silvered mirror. The mirror allows the passage of some of it onto a photographic plate, but reflects part of it onto the object which is to be "photographed." The object also reflects the coherent light beam onto the photographic plate, at which point the reflected beam collides with the beam passing through the half-silvered mirror. When the two "wave fronts" of light meet, they "interfere" with each other, creating an "interference pattern." It is this pattern that is recorded on the photographic plate as a hologram.

Now the truly unique feature of holograms emerges. If a beam of coherent light is passed through the photographic plate, the observer on the far side of the plate sees a striking three-dimensional "picture" of the original object suspended in space. And what is also remarkable is that if any piece of the hologram is illuminated with coherent light, the same phenomenon occurs. To be sure, the smaller the piece the "fuzzier" the resulting image, and the larger the portion the more detailed the image becomes; but the entire representation of the original object is contained in each portion of the hologram.

Bohm proposes that the universe is constructed on the same principles as the hologram. His theory rests on concepts that flow from modern physics. In the modern physical view the world is not assembled from individual bits, but is seen as an indivisible whole. In modern physics the old classical view of "bit pieces and building blocks" has given way to the concept of pattern, process, and interrelatedness.

The aspect of the world that we ordinarily perceive *is* that of isolated parts, however. To us, things do seem disconnected and unrelated. Yet this is an illusion and a distortion of the underlying, behind-the-scene oneness and unity, which is an intrinsic quality of the world.

This unity, says Bohm, is "enfolded" into the universe. It is an expression of an implicit order—or, as Bohm says, an "implicate" order. How is this order enfolded into the world? In ways already described by physics: through electromagnetic waves, sound waves, electron beams, and in other numerous forms of movement. The behavior of all of these forms of movement constitute the implicate order in nature; and in order to emphasize its unbroken wholeness, Bohm states that what "carries" the implicate order is the "holomovement"—which is itself an undivided totality.

Scientists, of course, select certain facets of the holomovement for study: electrons, photons, sound, etc.

> . . . but more generally, all forms of the holomovement merge and are inseparable. Thus, in its totality, the holomovement is not limited in any specific way at all. It is not required to conform to any particular measure. Thus, the holomovement is undefinable and immeasurable.[3]

In order to illustrate how order can be hidden or enfolded, unapparent to the eye, Bohm uses a simple example. Imagine two concentric glass cylinders with a viscous fluid such as glycerin in the space between them. This apparatus can be rotated mechanically very slowly so that no diffusion in the glycerin occurs. Suppose you put a droplet of insoluble black ink into the glycerin and begin to rotate the system very slowly. Gradually the black droplet would be drawn out into a thin thread, eventually becoming invisible. Then if you begin to rotate the apparatus in the reverse direction, the droplet of black ink would gradually reconstitute itself, becoming visible again from the invisible black thread. The droplet of ink first became *enfolded*, invisible to the naked eye. It was not part of the *unfolded* reality that we could recognize. Yet it was still present in an *implicate* sense, and reversing the direction of rotation of the cylinder of glycerin rendered it *explicate*, visible to our senses.

For Bohm, order and unity are spread throughout the universe in a way which escapes our senses. They are part of an implicate order which, although hidden from us, constitutes a fundamental aspect of reality. In the same way that order and organization are spread throughout the hologram, each part of the universe contains enough information to reconstitute the whole. The form and structure of the entire world is enfolded within each part.

It is important to not underestimate the seriousness intended in Bohm's descriptions. For many working physicists these concepts are inescapable conclusions that flow from quantum mechanics and relativity. They are *not* mere poetic or metaphorical musings about how the world behaves.

It is crucial, too, to appreciate the scope of these implications. We frequently assume that quantum physics applies only to the diminutive realm of nature—electrons, protons, etc; and that relativity has only to do with massive objects of cosmic proportions—stars, galaxies, nebulae, etc. But Bohm's contention is that we are squarely in the middle of these phenomena:

> Ultimately, the entire universe (with all its "particles", including those constituting human beings, their laboratories, observing instruments, etc.) has to be understood as a single undivided whole, in which analysis into separately and independently existent parts has no fundamental status.[4]

Going farther, Bohm suggests that holograms may be ubiquitous in nature. Although they are constructed artificially from two interfering wave fronts of coherent light impinging on a photographic plate, it is possible that this general phenomenon could be recorded in other ways. After all, light is only one expression of wave phenomena. Waves are actually commonplace in nature, and Bohm's holomovement is alive with many types of them. Electron beams could make holograms, as could sound waves, or "any form of movement," including "movements known and unknown." The universe is permeated with wave forms; and it may be, implies Bohm, that we live in a holographic universe: the holoverse.

What are the implications of a holographic universe—a holoverse—wherein multitudes of wave forms collide and interfere and produce patterns of unending complexity? How could human beings comprehend such a chaotic panoply? First, we must understand that according to modern physics we are ourselves *part of* the processes of the universe. As Bohm says, the entire universe includes all particles: electrons as well as humans, their laboratories, and their observing instruments. If the universe is at heart chaotic, then it is likely that we, as constituent parts, share in the chaos. But it is patently clear to most of us that there is at least a limit to the chaos—i.e., we *can* make sense of things, we *do* comprehend. We obviously are capable of extracting knowable processes and patterns from the world. But how?

As part of the holoverse, do we have holographic features ourselves that allow us to comprehend a holographic universe? This question has been answered affirmatively by Stanford neurophysiologist Karl Pribram. In an attempt to account for key observations about brain function which for decades have puzzled brain physiologists, Pribram arrived at a radical proposal: the hologram is a model of brain function. In essense, the brain is the "photographic plate" on which information in the universe is encoded.

When the proposals of Bohm and Pribram are conceptually joined, a new model of man emerges: we use a brain that encodes information holographically; and it is a hologram that is a part of an even larger hologram—the universe itself.

Pribram's radical suggestions are founded on work that originated in the laboratory of one of the pioneers of modern neurophysiology, Karl Lashley. At a time when it was popularly believed that there were specific centers in the brain for practically every human function—such as speech, vision, appetite, sleep, etc.—Lashley demonstrated that this was apparently not true for memory. Working with animals, he found that even when the bulk of the cerebral cortex was surgically removed, leaving only a remnant intact, the memory of how to perform specific tasks remained. The rapidity and accuracy of the performance was frequently attenuated, but the knowledge was retained.

These findings fit poorly with existing theories about how information is stored in the brain. It was as if memory was spread everywhere in the cortex—but how? Pribram reasoned that the brain contained the memory in each of its parts. The analogy to a hologram was obvious. The entire memory pattern could be found throughout the cerebral cortex if the information had originally been encoded holographically.

Perhaps the greatest resistance to the idea of widespread information being stored throughout the brain comes from the stubborn insistence that specific brain regions control specific physiological and psychological functions. Yet there have always been flies in the ointment, most of which are conveniently ignored by neurologists and neurophysiologists. There is mounting evidence that the notion of brain centers may be an inadequate explanation of certain human functions.

In an article provocatively entitled "Is Your Brain Really Necessary?" a British neurologist, John Lorber, has questioned the idea that an intact cerebral cortex is even required for normal mentation.[5] It is possible to assess the thickness of the cortex of our brain using a technique called computerized axial tomography, popularly known as "CT scanning." Using this technique, Lorber has studied hundreds of patients with hydrocephalus, a condition in which the amount of cerebrospinal fluid in the brain is increased, replacing the normal cortical brain tissue. He discovered that many of his patients had normal or above-normal intellectual function even though most of the skull was filled with fluid. Normally, humans have a cerebral cortex measuring four and one-half centimeters in thickness, containing 15 to 20 billion neurons. In one patient, however, a college mathematics student who was referred to him because his physician suspected that his head was slightly enlarged, the brain scan revealed a cerebral cortex of only one *millimeter* in thickness. Functioning with only a tiny rim of cortical brain tissue of 1/45 normal thickness, this student proved to be gifted on standard IQ testing (he had an IQ of 126) and was normal not only intellectually but socially.

Lorber's query of whether the brain is even necessary suggests that a great deal of redundant information may be laid down in its tissue, so that normal function remains possible even after the destruction of large masses of brain substance.

In most right-handed persons, the left side of the brain is presumed to control the movements of the right side of the body. In instances where the left side of the brain is injured—for example, through a stroke or with trauma—paralysis or profound weakness of the right side of the body is the predictable result. A physician, Richard Restak, has reported a case, however, in a twenty-one year old female in which the entire left side of the brain was removed surgically in order to control epileptic seizures that were unmanageable with any other known form of therapy. The results of the surgery were astonishing. Although the seizures were stopped, within a few weeks the woman began to regain control of the right side of her body. She was able to return to work and to lead an active social life. Where did the right side of her body receive its motor information from with the left side of the brain in the surgeon's pail?[6]

In 1975 a similar case was reported by Smith and Sugar.[7] A six year old male underwent total removal of the left cerebral hemisphere because of intractable epileptic seizures. Conventional neurophysiological wisdom asserts that the left side of the cerebral cortex is responsible for our speech, mathematical reasoning, and logical thought in general, and that the right cerebral hemisphere controls our intuitive, nonrational, nonverbal forms of thought. Yet this young man grew up to become a gifted student, proficient in verbal reasoning and language abilities—testing even into the gifted range on standard intelligence tests. Again the idea of narrow specialization in the function of specific brain areas seems specious.

Pribram's theory that the brain functions as a hologram is a clever alternative explanation—too clever, according to some neurophysiologists. Yet many specialists in brain function are attracted to the idea, if for no other reason than the glaring inadequacies of the present orthodox views.[8]

How could the brain encode information holographically? Until recently it was believed that the neurons in the brain functioned in an on-off, binary mode. They either fired or they did not. Between firing, the synapse—the space between the neuronal endings—was electrochemically "silent." This picture, however, has been revised. It is now known that even between moments of activation the synapse is the site of "slow wave potentials"—ongoing electrochemical activity at low ebb. The synaptic cleft, the junction between neurons, is never quiet. It is like the proverbial wind in Texas: there is nowhere it does not blow.

The synaptic cleft, we now know, is approximately 200 Angstroms wide—a minute range of distance in which quantum phenomenon are known to operate. Given the existence of ceaseless electrochemical activity acting across such a distance in 15 to 20 billion neurons, some of which are capable of firing 20 times per second, the possibility has been raised that complex wave forms could be generated with inevitable patterns of interference—which is one of the requirements for the production of holographically encodable information. Acting throughout the cortex, this wave activity could result in the diffuse storage of information, providing, conceivably, an explanation of the clinical examples given above, as well as the widespread nature of memory function in man.

There is no general agreement among neuroscientists as to the validity of these possibilities. There is enormous resistance to them in some quarters: holistic theories of brain function are hardly cherished by orthodox specialists in brain physiology. Hologrammatic brains interpreting a hologrammatic universe—these ideas are dismissed by most mainstream scientists as fanciful, mystical nonsense. Others, however, see in them fertile possibilities to account for actual clinical data that has never been adequately accommodated by traditional theories of how the human brain operates.

The central quality of the universe is a kind of oneness: the whole is contained in the part. The parts, however, are not, strictly speaking, particulate. They form a whole, and Bohm states that this unbroken wholeness can be described quantum mechanically. And although we can select in our thinking certain features of the universe such as electrons and protons and ascribe to them specific features such as particle or wave aspects, we should be wrong if we fail to capture the overriding feature of this multifaceted reality: it is a "single structure of indivisible links."

This indivisibility also applies fundamentally to space and time. Relativity has shown that they are inextricably linked, and cannot be teased apart.

THE HOLOVERSE AND HEALTH

We conceive ordinarily that during the course of a lifetime health and illness alternate like undulating waves. They are events that occur across time and apply to physical bodies occupying a specific position in space. The body, fixed in space and existing across time, is either healthy or not. True, fine gradations may occur in the transitions between health and disease, but we fundamentally think of them as either-or phenomena.

But, as Bohm says, quantum theory implies that elements that are separated in space are generally noncausally and nonlocally connected. These conclusions follow in part from the arguments of Einstein, Rosen, and Podolsky, as well as from Bell's theorem. If space and time are inseparable in the modern description of the world, we must consider that *moments separated in time are also noncausally and nonlocally related.*

Recall one of the possibilities embodied in Bell's theorem involving nonlocal features of the universe: objects once in contact, though separated spatially—even if placed at distant ends of the universe— are somehow in inseparable contact, since any change in one immediately and unmitigatedly causes change in the other. This is a nonlocal occurrence, meaning that any information passing between the two objects would have to travel faster than the speed of light to cause such instantaneous change. Since it is impossible for the speed of light to be exceeded, according to the special theory of relativity, this event is said to be noncausal—i.e., not caused by the transfer of any conceivable kind of energy passing between the distant objects.

Although these nonlocal and noncausal descriptions are worked out for objects separated in *space*, Bohm states that the implications of quantum theory, as we observed above, also apply to moments separated in *time*.

> What is crucial . . . is that, according to the theory of relativity, a sharp distinction between space and time can not be maintained. . . .

Thus, since the quantum theory implies that elements that are separated in space are generally non-causally and non-locally related projections of a higher-dimensional reality, it follows that moments separated in time are also such projections of this reality.[9]

Human bodies, we say, are spatially separated objects; and health and illness are processes which occupy a collection of moments. As such, they are temporally extended events. The problem we stumble headlong into is this: if Bohm's contention is correct, that the entire universe and everything in it can only be understood as an inseparable entity describable by quantum theory, how can we possibly retain our ordinary ideas of what bodies, health, and disease actually mean? Human bodies, spatially separated, seem to be noncausally and nonlocally inseparable in a modern physical view; and health and disease, as collected moments in time, also take on a noncausal and nonlocal oneness.

Separateness of bodies, and absolute distinctions between health and disease cannot be maintained in a context of quantum wholeness. This is not to say that the notion of bodies, health, and disease cannot be abstracted as apparently discrete features of reality. We can speak of them as aspects of the world just as physicists speak of the wave and particle features of electrons. But in so doing we must bear in mind the underlying unbroken wholeness that envelopes all manifestations of the entire universe.

If we cannot dissociate space and time in the modern universe, we cannot make separate distinctions between bodies and health and disease. Just as electrons are not things, as Niels Bohr constantly insisted, so too are bodies not things. Just as electrons do not "have" particality or waviness, so too our bodies do not "have" health or disease; they *are* these very qualities, which are more precisely described as unending, unbroken processes connected nonlocally and noncausally in both space and time.

Our habitual way of describing isolated healthy bodies as being recurrently besieged by spells of poor health from birth to the grave has to be reevaluated in any modern description of the world. If moments in time are inseparable, then so are health and disease. If elements in space are inseparable, then so are our bodies. And if time and space are inseparable, then our bodies are one with the health and disease that we traditionally presume they "possess" in some alternating sequence.

We arrive at a view which suggests that bodies, health, and disease come together in much the same way as the sky and its hues coalesce. Although we speak of different skies, the sky is a seamless, inseparable entity. It is a whole. It does not "have" blueness or redness or any coloration, for it *is* that blueness and redness. Temporally, as well as spatially, the sky does not end. It does not die. It is an unbroken whole in both space and time. So it is with human bodies, health, and disease.

How can we translate these visions of space and time and health into practice? Two clinical examples follow, showing that when our focus is toward a principle of relatedness and oneness, and away from fragmentation and isolation, health ensues.

In a study in which biofeedback was to be used to treat chronic recurrent headaches, the subjects involved were asked to keep a diary prior to actually starting biofeedback therapy. The object of such a log was to document the frequency and severity of the headache so as to judge the eventual success of biofeedback as a specific form of treatment. Amazingly, most of the subjects found that when they began to keep the diary, their headaches disappeared.[10]

What happened? Ordinarily we think of illness—whether headaches or pneumonia or heart attacks—as originating external to us. We are "attacked" by ailments. They come from without. Keeping a diary wherein one is asked not only to describe the frequency and severity of the actual symptom, but the circumstances and events surrounding the ailment, forces a shift away from this perspective. Disease is seen in a *context*—a milieu of behavior, diet, sleep and exercise patterns, and various other relationships with the world at large. Patterns of events emerge that redirect the headache sufferer's attention. The headache no longer is seen as an intruding disease originating elsewhere, but as part of a process of living which can accurately be described as an unbroken whole. With such a perspective, spatial separations break down. And as we shall see in a later chapter, time distinctions are also transformed; for in the visualization and imaging process that is employed in "seeing" wholes, the shift is away from a fragmented time of past, present, and future toward a felt time of all-at-once wherein individual moments lose their separateness.

In another experiment a group of epileptic children were video tape-recorded while interacting with their family groups. During several such sessions there arose periods that were emotionally charged. These moments were frequently followed by actual seizures, which were recorded by the video monitor. Then the experimenters replayed the tape sessions for the epileptic patients. After

watching the sessions and seeing the relationship between emotional events and actual seizures, they became almost seizure-free![11]

These epileptic patients, like the headache patients in the preceding example, experienced a new view of their body, their health,
and their disease. The video record allowed a contextual perspective
in which the allegedly independently acting epilepsy was seen *in
relationship* to the world at large. This relationship accentuated connectedness of thought, feeling, and emotion between persons. The
epileptic attacks were seen as derivative of an unbroken wholeness
that included the entire family. It lost its independent, malevolent,
and external features. A spatial fusion of persons and bodies occurred
experientially and interpretively on viewing the replay of the video
tapes. The temporal disconnections into past, present, and future
which are part of an ordinary linear time experience were attenuated
in the period of reflection after the viewing, and moments ceased to
be separated in time. With this shift toward spatiotemporal unity,
the seizures ceased. A heightened degree of health followed.

The problem with all clinical examples, however, is that language
and "word pictures" must be used to describe events that fundamentally cannot be reduced to verbal description. This disjunction
between thought and language is not a new problem in science. The
physicists who developed the quantum theory early in this century
were well aware of this difficulty. For example, it began to be
appreciated that the very attempt to conjure a mental picture of an
individual electron automatically involved one in error. For an electron was quintessentially not something discrete and individual,
since it demonstrated properties that showed that it was connected
to all other existing particles. This interconnectedness was such a
prominent feature that the very meaning of the word "particle" was
in doubt. How could one describe this quality? The problems of
language here were profound, and Niels Bohr suggested that many
of the new concepts could best be described metaphorically and in
the language of poetry.

We face the same problems in citing clinical examples of spacetime
concepts. The word "patient" is as misleading as the word "particle." All mental images of human beings as isolated, fundamental,
clinical units are bound to be as wrong as the notions of subatomic
particles as spatially separated particulate bits. Although we will
continue to use clinical analogies through the book, the reader must
keep in mind that when we refer to patients or to bodies, these
concepts carry with them new meanings: human beings are essen-

tially dynamic processes and patterns that are fundamentally not analyzable into separate parts—either within or between each other. Like health and disease, they are spread through space and time, and it is their interrelatedness and oneness, not their isolation and separation, which is most important.

The possibility that we are each a holographic mind interpreting a holographic universe is a tantalizing concept. It provides at once an explanation for the universal experience of unity and oneness, an emotion which pervades the written legacy of all cultures. It may be the answer to Whitman's query:

> Locations and times—what is it in me that meets them all, whenever and wherever, and makes me at home?[12]

CHAPTER SIX

PARTICLES, PERSONS, PLANETS: WHY COMPARE?

In the modern concept . . . there is no possibility of a detached, self-contained existence.

—A.N. WHITEHEAD[1]

ONENESS AND UNITY ARE QUALITIES of our universe. Our tendency to think of the world in terms of noninteracting parts violates the most accurate descriptions of the world we have, those of modern physics. These descriptions of the universe tell us that the "parts" are illusions, understandable only in relation to all other parts. Subatomic particles are comprehended only through their relationships with all other subatomic particles, and the same can be said for massive bodies—planets, stars, galaxies.

But what of human beings? Earlier we examined the principle of association with one's kind, looking at this characteristic of living organisms from several perspectives—from the level of the gene to the large-scale realm of everyday life. We saw that association with one's own kind was a ubiquitous quality of living forms from the primitive to the complex. In humans this characteristic is a critical factor in health. We saw that the human body might itself demonstrate this principle of interrelatedness through the constant exchange of its component parts with the environment—the physical body associating with a physical earth, inseparably linked to all around it.

But is the interrelatedness of material bodies in the universe, which can be described mathematically, analogous to the interrelatedness of human beings, which cannot be so described? It would surely be a mistake to apply in wholesale fashion a principle that had been developed for one aspect of the physical world to an unrelated facet of physical reality. But the problem is that there is no way of knowing that human thought and behavior are *not* related to

115

events with which physical science deals. We do not wish to press the concepts of physical science into services for which they were never intended. But how are we to know when the violations occur?

We are back to old problems. Common sense tells us that principles of interrelations between physical bodies in the universe, such as atoms and planets, are categorically unrelated to interrelations among human beings. The world of matter, where physical law prevails, has nothing to do with the world of human association where emotions and feelings come into play.

But common sense can be misleading. Consider the case of the petted rabbits in the Ohio State experiment (pp. 61–62). The effect of emotions *did* translate into verifiable physical changes. And what of the effects of interrelations among humans on mortality, on death from *all causes* (p. 65). Clearly, the world of emotions and feelings *are* related to the physical world because they generate changes that any scientist can measure.

The interrelation of human consciousness and the observed world is also obvious in Bell's theorem (p. 98). In Bell's theorem we run headlong into another interactional aspect of reality: human consciousness and the physical world cannot be regarded as distinct, separate entities. What we call physical reality, the external world, is shaped—to some extent—by human thought. Again, the attempts to define reality in terms of noninteracting parts—physical matter and human consciousness—fails.

The lesson is clear: We cannot separate our own existence from that of the world outside. We are intimately associated not only with the earth we inhabit, but with the farthest reaches of the cosmos.

MAN IN THE COSMOS: AT HOME OR AT ODDS?

It has long been argued from primarily religious points of view that the cosmos was created as a place *for* us. It was designed as a comfortable home for life itself. This idea has given comfort through the ages to multitudes. It is perhaps the most ancient explanation of man's relation to the universe he inhabits.

An alternative view, however, asserts that the universe and human life are indissolubly entertwined. We are the way we are because it is the way it is. In this view it makes no sense to separate man *from* the universe, attempting to analyze him as we might an insect extracted from its environment and pinned to a dissecting board in a biology laboratory.

An example by Davies may make clear this relationship.[2] We know that the universe is not static in size. Modern cosmological theory tells us that it is expanding, a process that originated at the time of the "big bang," that moment when the concentrated stuff of the universe exploded. The universe, therefore, has an age which dates from that moment, reckoned at about 14 billion years.

Although this magnitude of time is well-nigh incomprehensible, it is crucial to our own existence. Our very life structure is dependent on carbon that was synthesized not on earth but in distant stars. The life span of these stars was several billion years. They then exploded, dispersing their material into the universe, part of which found its way to earth.

Life on earth, of course, did not arise fully flowered, but required again several billion years to evolve from the basic elemental prerequisites. Evolution is exceedingly slow, its history written in the geologic formations of the earth's crust. These fossilized records can be dated with considerable accuracy using radioactive carbon techniques. They tell us we were a long time in the making.

It follows that if the universe were considerably younger than it is, life on earth could not exist. There would have been no starting material to begin with, nor enough time for the infinite number of false starts required by evolutionary progress to eventuate in conscious life on earth.

Thus, the age of the universe is linked to the fact that we are here to observe it in the first place. Davies proposes also that since the universe is expanding, not only its age but its size is linked to human life. He points out other qualities of the universe, such as temperature, which are also bound to the fact of human existence. Should the age, the size, and the temperature of the universe be other than it is, we would not exist.

It is a curious property of human thought which insists that something special is happening at our local level on earth. We must insure our own importance. This is the echo of many civilizations: we are here and the universe is out there. Either it was designed for us (the view that has been religiously most palatable) or we are some capricious anomaly adrift in a godless expanse. It is no wonder that the latter view has found little currency in recorded history.

There has seemed to be little middle ground on this issue through the ages. But now modern cosmology suggests that the characteristics of human life and the properties of the cosmos are bonded. We have always thought that such an association was demeaning to human life, rendering it cold, meaningless, purposeless. Now we can invert the reasoning: if we are indeed special, then so is the universe, so entwined are we in an interdependent existence.

Gregory Bateson affirmed this view:

> Insofar as we are a mental process, to that same extent we must expect the natural world to show similar characteristics of mentality.[3]

But we keep insisting on not seeing who we really are. The human mind appears bedeviled in realizing its true affinities with the universe in which it finds itself. We cannot easily comprehend our indissoluble oneness with the cosmos. In an attempt to contribute to this understanding, Alan Watts continually used analogy in his typically concise, oriental way, stating that mountains are not made up *of* stone, they *are* stone; rivers are not made *of* water, they *are* water. Perhaps modern cosmology can point in a similar way to a fact that is exceedingly simple yet profound: we are not made up of fragments *of* the universe, we *are* that universe.

THE PARADOX OF PERCEPTION:
DIFFERENCE IS ONENESS

Our inseparability with the world around us is manifested in other ways we seldom notice. Evidence of this oneness comes from the basic act of perceiving.

We ordinarily believe that our perceptions are about *something*. We perceive events that are out there, happenings that are external to us. This dissociation between the perceiver and the perceived is characteristic of our Western attitude toward knowledge: knowledge is something to be gained, acquired, and taken in from an outside source. Somehow our perceptual apparatus stands apart from the world.

This view of the relationship between our conscious perceiving selves and the world we occupy has been challenged by the developmental biologist Davenport. He observes that we are only capable of perceiving something when *differences* arise—differences being contrasts occurring in the world around us. If contrasts were absent, perception would never occur. Davenport states,

> If we examine the experiences from which our knowledge of the world arises, we can see that they consist of various types of differences. Without difference, there can be no experience. The experience of difference is basic to our notion of existence, the latter being derived

from the Latin *ex sistere,* which means "to stand apart," i.e., to be different. . . . The foundation of any valid epistemology must be the recognition that, since all properties must be experienced as difference, the physical world exists for us only in terms of relationships. . . . Recognition of the nature of the experience that underlies our knowledge is important for the realization that physical reality does not exist before us as an object of study but *emerges from our consciousness during our changing experience within nature.*[4]

The visual apparatus of certain species of frogs demonstrates this phenomenon clearly. Sitting quietly, looking at a still, unmoving environment, the frog's visual stimuli tell him little. It is only when movement—i.e., contrast—occurs that he is visually excited. The motion of a moving fly or insect is detected with surprising accuracy and speed by the frog, who may turn this "contrast" into a meal.

This process lies at the core of all sense perception. Contrast in the world about us is the substrate of all perceptual knowledge. Bertrand Russell intimated this situation by observing that, although we have no idea who discovered water, we can be certain it was not a fish. If insufficient contrast exists in our environment, we, like fish, are simply blind to the world.

What are we to say about the relationship of our own consciousness and the world it perceives? Certainly the concept of consciousness is tied to our notion of perception—i.e., it is difficult if not impossible to postulate consciousness devoid of content. We have to be conscious of *something,* it seems, in order to be conscious at all. But these perceptions are tied to the world, as we have seen, since they cannot occur without contrast in the world itself.

Our consciousness, thus, seems bound to the world so tightly that it may not be possible to conceptually tease it apart from it. It isn't that our consciousness *is* the world outside, nor that the world itself is conscious, but that all such attempts to lend independent status to either consciousness *or* the world are wrong.

Our consciousness, its very meaning dependent on perception, is inseparable from the world in which perception-giving contrasts occur. We are indissolubly united with the universe around us in the most quintessential human quality, consciousness itself.

Yet we frequently refer to certain qualities such as consciousness as being "peculiarly human." We talk about these characteristics as if they somehow exist in human brains alone, unshared with other species and even isolated from the world outside. We must reconsider whether any quality is peculiarly human, since all human perception is tied to contrasts occurring in the world around us. Our conscious perceptions do not stand alone; thus, we would be just as accurate in saying that human consciousness is as "peculiarly world-ly" as "peculiarly human."

THE PERCEPTUAL UNIT

It is engrained in our thinking that our perceptual apparatus, our brain, acquires knowledge as if it were an amoeba engulfing a particle of food. This reflects our basic subject-object orientation of how we see ourselves in the world. However, this view is inconsistent with the intrinsic oneness between the perceiver and the perceived, a relationship we examined above.

We must go beyond the dichotomous thinking that insists on subject and object if we are to accommodate a concept of oneness with the world. This is a difficult task. The notion that we stand totally apart from what we perceive in the world around us is an extraordinarily stubborn illusion.

One way of starting to think in a new manner, however, is to consider the "perceptual unit"—the combination of both the per-ceiving faculty and what is perceived. The perceptual unit is the conglomeration of "us and it." The *unit*—implying oneness—cannot be sundered. The perceptual unit is consciousness and the world around it, standing in a fundamental, irreducible relationship.

PATTERN VS. PURITY IN SCIENCE

Throughout the preceding chapters we have repeatedly drawn comparisons between events occurring in nature and the world of everyday human experience. We have drawn analogies between the interrelatedness of all subatomic particles and the interconnections of human beings, and between the oneness that is implicit in the smallest realms of nature and the oneness of man with the cosmos of which he is a part.

These comparisons may be blatantly offensive to scientific "hard-liners." They will argue that there are no known rules of reason allowing one to join the lifeless subatomic world to that of human experience. Atoms are atoms and humans are humans and they differ as day to night, as life to nonlife. We have committed the cardinal sin of mixing the value-free descriptions of science with the world of human experience which, by its very nature, is permeated with value.

I believe this traditional and predictable criticism is wrong. For in making these comparisons we are not joining value to nonvalue so much as we are seeking to identify patterns in nature. We are asking: is there a regularity in nature that can be identified across many levels of organization? Can we discover a general principle of oneness and unity? Surely nature does not always conform to the preconceived notions of scientific tidiness; and to insist that principles of oneness do not exist at the level of human experience, just as they exist at the level of the atom, is to insist that nature should follow our biases.

Indeed, in the history of modern science it has been extraordinarily fruitful to look for parallels between certain qualities of human experience and the behavior of nature. The very search for regularity, pattern, and sequence led Mendeleev to discover the periodic table of the elements. Should it be discarded because it is contaminated with the human quality of repetition, of pattern and regularity?

The fact is, we cannot keep human qualities out of our science. They keep turning up in nature. And scientists—even the best of scientists—frequently insert descriptions into their picture of the physical world that remind us of qualities present in ordinary human activity.

This is nowhere more obvious than in the particle physicists' search for quarks. In 1964 physicist Murray Gell-Mann proposed the term "quark" for the hypothesized smallest subunit of matter. "Hunting the quark" became a passionate endeavor in particle physics laboratories all over the world. As the existence of these hypothetical particles began to appear more certain, a nomenclature arose for them. They were not named Quark I, II, III, or Quark A, B, or C. Instead, the most audacious terms were applied: up, down, strange,* charm, and beauty. (Most physicists believe there should be a sixth quark to complete the symmetry of a third pair. When it is found, it will be the partner of beauty, and will be called *truth*.)

These terms, like "quark" itself, seem downright playful. There are those in and out of the physics community who applaud the brazen use of these terms, even though they mischievously insert human qualities (especially *charm*!) where they perhaps do not belong.

Of course, if pushed the physicist would deny that there is anything serious intended here. Any fool knows we do not really think

*from Sir Francis Bacon's "There is no excellent beauty that hath not some *strangeness* in the proportions."

the subatomic world is akin to the realm of human qualities, he would say. But I am not so sure. Certainly nothing prevented the choice of neutral designations that have heretofore been employed in describing subatomic particles: electrons, protons, neutrons, or alpha, beta, or gamma particles. But charm, beauty, and truth!

I am not suggesting that I have special insight into what physicists really think about these matters. I do suggest, however, that all of us—scientist and nonscientist alike—experience feelings of oneness with the world about us. These feelings are manifested when physicists find it acceptable to give subatomic particles names suggesting human qualities. They are manifested through the urge of scientists to find patterns and symmetries in nature—an urge that is fundamental to the entire scientific endeavor.

THE TRADITIONAL MYTH OF TRADITIONAL SCIENCE: DETACHMENT AND DISPASSION

Still, to suggest that the oneness of subatomic particles is similar in kind to the oneness that may unite human beings rankles most scientists. It is a kind of selling out. It subverts the meaning of scientific objectivity. It is shameless anthropomorphism. It lets the gate down—in addition to seeing oneness in the physical world we shall soon be seeing ghosts and goblins.

I believe these objections are inevitably bound to fail, and that eventually we must admit that our descriptions of nature must bear the ineradicable stamp of our consciousness. Although we may be successful in filtering from our world picture the grossest dregs of conscious thought—such as ghosts and goblins, or angels pulling levers to make the world run—we shall never purge it to the depth expected by traditional science. We shall never attain what has been demanded by scientific orthodoxy—a clear, value-free, dispassionate, pure description of nature. This lesson has surfaced most clearly in quantum physics, and is expressed by Heisenberg:

> The laws of nature which we formulate mathematically in quantum theory deal no longer with the particles themselves but with our knowledge of the elementary particles.

And:

> The conception of objective reality . . . evaporated into the. . . mathematics that represents no longer the behavior of elementary particles but rather than knowledge of this behavior.[5]

Since we cannot lay hands directly on nature but are forced, as Heisenberg says, to deal with our abstractions *of* nature, the question is not whether we are justified in making comparisons between an objective realm (atoms and subatomic particles) and a subjective one (human thought and feeling). Modern science has shown us that a stringent objectivity has evaporated, since the world *does not exist for us as an object*. Pure objectivity, unadulterated by human values, is an illusion. This position has been poignantly advanced by the Nobel physicist Eugene Wigner, who asserts, even, that physical objects and spiritual values have a similar kind of reality.[6]

Do these nonobjective characteristics of nature apply only to the microscopic quantum realm? Probably not; for as Wigner has pointed out there is no evidence that the accuracy of quantum mechanics begins to fade as the size of the system increases, "and the dividing line between microscopic and macroscopic systems is surely not very sharp."[7]

QUANTUM BIOLOGY

Yet there is strong reluctance on the part of bioscientists to apply concepts drawn from modern physics to biological systems. The feeling runs deep in biology, physiology, and medicine that modern physics describes phenomena that are relevant only to subatomic events and that are essentially inapplicable to the macroscopic world inhabited by living things. One may apply quantum concepts to neutrinos, protons, and quarks but not to dogs, cats, and human beings. The giant macromolecules inside us, such as enormously complex enzymes, are describable in the language of chemistry, not physics.

As Capra has pointed out, this is a greatly distorted view. It is not generally appreciated that quantum phenomena are widely relevant to ordinary, day-to-day events.

> For example, the solidity of matter, the fact that you cannot walk through doors or walls, is a direct consequence of the quantum reality. It is something that comes from a certain resistance of atoms against compression which cannot be explained in terms of classical physics.[8]

In the biological sciences we have assumed for too long that there are two worlds existing in parallel—that of living things, describable only in terms of chemistry; and the nonliving microworld of atoms and their components, describable in the language of quantum physics. It is not generally appreciated by bioscientists that the potential application of quantum physical concepts to the biological world was glimpsed almost from the time quantum theory was spawned. Heisenberg, a central figure in this development, quoted Bohr in this regard:

> The eventual addition of biological concepts to quantum mechanics is a foregone conclusion. . . . Perhaps the wealth of mathematical forms hidden in quantum mechanics is large enough to embrace biological forms.[9]*

The embrace which Bohr predicted has been slow in coming. The modern concepts of how the most basic events in the body occur are not quantum physical, but resoundingly mechanistic, in flavor. Many biological activities are explained through the concept of receptor sites—specific locations in a tissue that recognize a passing molecule and bind to it, initiating a specific physiologic effect. For example, certain cells in the stomach, the parietal cells, have receptor sites designated as H_2 receptors. These loci are specific in their affinity for histamine. When a histamine molecule attaches to an H_2 receptor site, a complex series of biochemical events is triggered, resulting eventually in the secretion of hydrochloric acid by the parietal cell.

Most interactions of molecules in the body, we now know, occur in this general way—one molecule fitting into a specific locus, setting off a chain of biochemical events. We have receptor sites not only for histamine but for a myriad of other substances such as insulin, various digestive hormones, adrenalin, etc. Like a key opening a lock, the incalculably complex chemistry of the body is set in motion through these interactions.

This general model has seemed all the more powerful because it has led to the development of specific drugs that have proved to be effective in certain disease processes. Pharmacologists have been able to synthesize chemicals that resemble certain "keys," but that "jam" the locks, the receptor sites. They thus prevent the attachment of the actual messenger molecule. The widely used drug cimetidine, for example, resembles the histamine molecule and is capable of attaching to and blocking the receptor sites for histamine in the parietal cells in the stomach, leading to a diminution in the

---

*As an example of the current beginnings of the interpenetration of quantum mechanics and biology, in June 1980, Jack Peter Green and Harel Weinstein, two scientists in the department of pharmacology at the Mount Sinai School of Medicine of the City University of New York, organized a conference on quantum chemistry in the biomedical sciences. The proceedings of the meeting were published as volume 367 in *The Annals of the New York Academy of Sciences.*

secretion of hydrochloric acid. This drug has been a boon to sufferers of peptic ulcer disease, and is only one example of many similar achievements of modern pharmacologists.

In the early development of modern pharmacology it was believed that the *shape* of the messenger molecule and the molecules constituting the receptor site was crucial. The lock and key concept demanded *geometry* as its explanatory principle. Only spatial arrangements were felt to be important when one molecule met another. Molecules were conceived as rigid conglomerations of atoms with frozen angles and bond lengths that could fit here and there throughout the body into specific niches designed for their peculiar spatial configurations. Once again the concept of mechanism was paramount—only this time the machine resembled a simple child's toy, where round holes would accommodate only spherical objects and never triangles or squares.

How can quantum mechanical concepts conceivably apply to this physiological domain? Quantum physicists are not concerned with shapes, but with *fields*. In quantum mechanics molecules are not stick-and-ball entities with rigid angulations, but entities whose electrons generate more or less a force in one area, similar to a magnet. It is the composition and conformation of these variegated fields of force within and around molecules that determine whether attraction or repulsion will occur when two molecules meet. This force-field quality is obviously quite different than the square-block-in-square-hole conception based on geometrical considerations only. And in the quantum concept the electrons in one molecule exert a force that distorts the electrons—and thus the force field—of another molecule, and vice versa. Whether they come together, then, is determined by this mutual distortion of electron distributions.[10]

So, then, is quantum physics relevant to living systems? If we can go beyond our habitual lock-and-key, ball-and-stick conceptions of how our bodies work, the answer seems to be yes. As Green and Weinstein state,

> Although the detailed information we have about these giant [enzyme] molecules comes from a variety of experimental sources—spectroscopic, physicochemical, biochemical, and kinetic studies—all this highly specific and variegated data can be formulated in quantum mechanical terms, allowing us to understand the principles that underlie the behavior of millions of different interactions.[11]

There is more at stake in the question of the applicability of quantum mechanics to living organisms than simply a new theory of drug and receptor site interaction. We are confronted with an entirely new conceptualization of our inner being which is radically different than our traditional notions of body-as-machine. The quantum theory overturned Newton's clockwork, deterministic universe and its billiard-ball-like elements, and erected in its place a cosmos with different complexions of space, time, mass, and causation. If quantum physics wrought such a revolution in our concept of the nature of the entire physical universe, we can expect it to wreak astonishing transformations in our views of our psychophysical self, an expression *of* that very universe.

Perhaps we should not be surprised that quantum physics is making incursions into biology and physiology. Quantum physics is the most accurate description we have ever discovered of the physical world—and, after all, there is only *one* world, and we are of it. Perhaps we should never have presumed that the best description of this world would have spared us.

AESTHETICS AND VALUES IN SCIENCE

In science we do not live in two worlds, the objective and the nonobjective. Although the charm of the quark may not be the same as the charm of one's lover, there are patterns and regularities that do seem to span both worlds.

We have been reluctant for too long in searching out these patterns. In so doing it is likely that we have deprived ourselves of a deep comforting wisdom. We *need* to make comparisons between physical objects and the realm of human thought and feeling, because the failure to do so may result in our spiritual impoverishment. To underscore this point, Wigner's comment is emphasized:

> The recognition that physical objects and spiritual values have a very similar kind of reality has contributed in some measure to my mental peace. . . . At any rate, it is the only known point of view which is consistent with quantum mechanics.[12]

There is an area in which scientists of the highest caliber have consistently allowed human value to mingle with the content of a presumedly objective science: that of aesthetics. The notion that rational thought is intrinsically lovely and not unlovely is surely ancient; and in the age of modern science this general agreement among scientists has approached unanimity. Acceptable scientific theory is expected to embody the aesthetic ideal of simplicity. Pattern, regularity, and symmetry in nature are part of the aesthetic of science. Unnecessary complexity and tortuosity in scientific description is eschewed. In the event that descriptions of nature do not meet this ideal, they are suspected of being flawed.

The history of this notion is at least traceable to the Greeks. Over two thousand years ago Pythagoras announced, "God ever geometrizes." While modern mathematicians would hardly go as far, they have shown no reluctance in joining mathematics and values. For example, the French mathematician Poincare was adamant that the allure of mathematics lay in its inherent beauty.

Einstein also was firm in his belief that the universe bore the signature of the creator. His view of the inherent harmony of the natural world led him, he said, to his revelations. Indeed, it was because the quantum theory came to insist on a random, probabilistic, and statistical feature of the universe that Einstein took issue with it, believing to his death that the theory was somehow flawed and incomplete. His objections are epitomized in his famous statement that God does not play dice. It seems that he, like many great scientists before him, felt at ease in drawing comparisons between human and divine thought, and in expecting to find evidence of these likenesses in the way the world behaved. He saw no shoddy anthropomorphism here. For him this approach to understanding nature was entirely legitimate—*so* legitimate that he seemed willing to place scientific theory in the service of aesthetics and values, and not vice versa, as is the habit of orthodox science.

THE ARGUMENT ACCORDING TO SIZE

Nothing could be more absurd, so this argument goes, than in making extrapolations from the behavior of subatomic particles to the behavior of humans, so fantastically distant are they in size. The world of the atom is a phantom, unknowable without instrumentation.

But obviously the behavior of subatomic particles has *something* to do with human behavior (neglecting for the moment the most obvious association, that our bodies are made up of them). Consider the situation wherein a human subject is confined to a completely darkened room. He is given the instruction: when you see light, press this button. After several hours he will become dark adapted, and his ability to perceive light signals will be heightened to a maximum. The physiological changes that occur in this adaptive mechanism are highly complex and efficient, such that after several hours in total darkness our subject will be able to perceive a *single* photon, the basic element of light.

From an experimental device in the dark room a single photon is emitted. It is aimed at the subject's eye, "shining" on his retina where it initiates a series of elaborate electrochemical events. Eventually the neurological pathways connecting the retina and the visual cortex are activated, the area of the brain where light impressions are perceived consciously. The end result of these events is likely a thought such as "I see light." This simple thought might then be used by the subject as the basis for action—for a change in his behavior—which in this instance is to press the button as instructed.

In this simple illustration it is clear that the behavior of a single subatomic particle, a photon, is tied to human behavior. Because of *its* behavior, the behavior of the subject in the experiment changed. Moreover, the *conscious thought* of the subject ("I see light") is tied to the behavior of an individual particle.

It is not difficult to extend these analogies. Oxygen atoms, without which the human brain begins to die after four minutes, fuel our bodies and our brains. Not only is the *behavior* of humans tied to that of the oxygen atom, life itself would not be possible without it.

Iron—the symbol of dead, inert matter—is also crucial to human life. If we are depleted of iron our body ceases to synthesize hemoglobin molecules. Without hemoglobin, the oxygen carrier of the body, all the biochemical events in the body that are oxygen-dependent fail. This deficiency not only results in changes in our behavior, it results eventually in our death as well. The human body, thus, behaves as it does because the iron atom behaves the way it does.

Examples of this sort are endless. They tell us that in spite of our unimaginable separation in size, the behavior of human beings and subatomic particles is inextricably linked.

In spite of these associations between human physiology and the chemistry of the elements, there is a curious resistance to what seems to me the obvious. This resistance takes an unexpected form, one which seems profoundly inconsistent. It is common to hear the most sensitive and humane individuals, those given to the highest hopes for our race and for our planet, embrace concepts of unity and oneness between human beings, and between human beings and the cosmos, but at the same time repudiate any notion of oneness with what they take to be a dead, inert world—such as iron atoms. Oneness and connectedness between humans, and between humans and larger cosmic bodies such as stars and galaxies are acceptable;

but unity between humans and the smallest things in the universe is not. There seems to be a *spectrum* of respectability operating here: the sense of unity is directly related to size. Gigantic heavenly bodies evoke lofty feelings of unity, while microscopic entities do not. It is as if we cannot love what we cannot see.

This attitude of playing favorites according to cosmic size is widespread among the most devout humanists. Why? I think part of the explanation lies in the fear of reductionism—that we must resist, at all costs, the efforts of orthodox science to reduce all human qualities to the mere function of dead atoms. Living in the shadow of reductionism, it has become unacceptable to identify emotionally with the smallest realms of nature. To do so would somehow be playing into the reductionists' hands. No matter that the stars and galaxies and cosmos that evoke feelings of unity and transcendence are made up of these same subatomic particles!

It is valid, according to this view, to identify only with the large-scale features of the cosmos and with our own kind. By some curious twist of logic we legitimize our loftiest emotions according to the size of things. I believe this is a misguided notion, based neither on reason nor the capacity for transcendence, but on a squeamish resistance to the perceived evil of reductionistic science.

There are other ways that are seldom noticed in which the behavior of the smallest elements of the world connect with human behavior. An illustration from the history of modern science will perhaps make it clear how science accepts without questioning the implicit relationship between the realm of human behavior and the world of the very small, in spite of its protestations to the contrary.

In 1945 the Scottish bacteriologist Sir Alexander Fleming was awarded the Nobel prize for his discovery of penicillin. Fleming's achievement is one of those astonishing events in science that stand alone not only for their scientific merit but for their importance to the human race as a whole. Like many such stories, this discovery began in an almost ignominiously simple way—as a laboratory accident. Fleming noticed that a container used to grow bacteria had become contaminated by a greenish mold. The mold was itself surrounded by a growth of a bacterial organism; but, curiously, there was a zone around the mold that was clear, almost as if there were a barrier to the growth of the surrounding microorganism. Fleming reasoned that the mold was perhaps manufacturing a substance that inhibited the growth of the encroaching microorganism. Through a series of elaborate experiments he isolated this substance, penicillin, named for the mold growing on the container, *Penicillium notatum*.

Imagine how the situation would have evolved had Fleming applied the narrow view, which asserts that no relevant associations exist between the microworld of subatomic particles and the level of human behavior. He might have said, "This observation, as interesting as it is, is of no conceivable consequence to man. It involves a world apart from our own, the world of bacteria and fungi. This world is too distant from our own to be of any importance to us. Moreover, we are concerned in this small and distant world with the laws of bacteriology, which were worked out for bacteria, not for humans. To extrapolate to the level of human affairs would be reckless—sheer nonsense and bad science. These are laws of bacteriology, not psychology, and have nothing whatsoever to do with human affairs."

Such a position is absurd, and scientists obviously (and fortunately) do not follow such thinking in the disciplines of bacteriology and mycology. But this is indeed the concealed position taken by scientists in general who insist on a rigid separation between organizational levels in the universe, no matter how distant and far apart. As Fleming's discovery illustrates, scientists themselves seem to function on a practical level as if difference in size were indeed meaningless. They assume that relevances for humans *can* be found in the infrahuman levels of order in nature.

The objection that although living bacteria might impact on the human level, whereas dead and lifeless electrons, protons, or neutrons cannot, seems difficult to defend. As the molecular biologist Delbrück has pointed out,[13] as we descend the levels of organization in nature there is simply no clear dividing line between the world of the living and nonliving. We may wish to think of bacteria as alive and single molecules as dead, but what, for example, shall we do about viruses? These primitive "beings" defy any easy classification, and pose a thorny issue for those who insist on dividing nature with rigid divisions of "dead or alive." Viruses are composed of a conglomeration of DNA molecules surrounded by a jacket of protein. These simple creatures have no means of replicating on their own, but are dependent on the life processes of more complex beings such as ourselves. They suggest that the place to draw the line between life and nonlife is determined only arbitrarily, and that the very effort to sunder nature into the living and the nonliving may be a misguided task. This seems to be the position taken not only by

Delbrück, but by the physicist David Bohm, who states that the world of the nonliving is a fiction.[14]

The poet and mystic understand the unity between the world of the living and nonliving. The mystical record *is* a record of the affinity of the human spirit with the entire cosmos. This is an ancient stirring, one which is finding expression in the language of scientists such as Delbrück and Davenport. Rustrum's words embody this historical idea:

> Why . . . dissociate ourselves from a single atom beneath our feet?
> . . . What is the purpose of presuming for dignity's sake alone that human life is dearer than other forms of life in the cosmic whole? Can we not exalt all life without losing our own prestige? Are we not a constituent of the whole?[15]

THE STRUGGLE FOR CONSISTENCY

We have seen in Part III how life on earth would not exist but for the features of the distant universe. The elements which comprise our bodies were hewn in the stars. The process of evolution is dependent on being fueled by a certain frequency of mutations, which are caused in large measure by the bombardment of life forms by cosmic rays from outer space. Were it not for this invisible, silent rain, life as we know it on earth would not exist. We would not be here now, nor could we continue without the universe around us.

Not only are we materially and morphologically tied to the ecology of the universe, the physical behavior of our bodies and all about us is contingent on its large-scale features. This is the lesson of Mach's principle. The physical laws governing each step we take, even the blinking of an eye, are determined by the composition of the cosmos.

This profound lesson of modern science is strangely surprising. For the goal of science, we believe, is to analyze nature, to probe its secrets, to tease it apart. The word *analysis* is derived from the Greek word *analyein*, meaning "to break up." It is little wonder, therefore, that science is seen by most nonscientists as a menacing protagonist of fragmentation, isolation, and destruction. It is the very nature of science to divide the world into bits. That science would point in the direction of cosmic unity is a surprising event.

But not only is modern science describing man in terms of the features of the cosmos, there is the unmistakable suggestion that the universe is the way it is because we are the way we are. This implication lies at the heart of the interpretation of "quantum reality" offered by many modern physicists. According to this view, a fixed, objective universe is illusory. As d'Espagnat has said, the belief in an immutable objective reality is in conflict not only with the quantum theory, but with facts drawn from actual experiments.[16]

Is our "shaping" of the universe directed toward the large-scale aspects of the cosmos, or toward the microscopic realms which we cannot directly perceive? It is likely that our influence extends in both directions. Bell's theorem, which we have examined, suggests that conscious human activity influences the behavior of subatomic particles in actual laboratory experiments. But we may shape the mighty events in the universe as well.

The implication that human consciousness is a factor in determining the features of the "real" world is affirmed by physicist H.S. Stapp, one of the foremost spokesmen on the issues raised by Bell's theorem. Stapp contends that Bell's theorem is the most important result in the history of science, and that it demonstrates the effect of human consciousness *at the level of the macroscopic*, as we have seen.

The impact of our consciousness lies both in the direction of the very small and the very large. The sword of consciousness cuts both toward the galaxy and the atom. In the flowing connectedness that exists across all levels of organization in the cosmos, in which consciousness affects and is affected by events in the universe, it appears as might a mysterious sword in a Zen koan—in the act of cutting, it cuts and is cut at the same time.

In view of the apparent omnidirectional flow of information in the universe, a flow in which conscious human beings are seemingly enveloped, it would be astonishing if the behavior of subatomic particles were *not* tied to the behavior of man. We are involved here with a struggle for consistency. We are willing to entertain bidirectional interactions between man and the large-scale features of the cosmos; we are willing to examine how man's consciousness may even shape events in the subatomic world. Are we to refuse to speculate that our day-to-day experience might also bear correlations with what occurs in the subatomic realm?

I feel there are compelling reasons to entertain this idea, not the least of which is logical consistency. We ought to *expect* these associations to exist because of the patterns of connectedness that science has already demonstrated. I realize, however, that neither logical consistency nor endless examples of photons and penicillin will ever convince the skeptic who is unmovably entrenched in his position that to analogize between atoms and humans is to recklessly join dispassionate science and human values. Like oil and water, they are immiscible.

On balance, I find it hard to conclude that we live in an immiscible universe. Miscibility and organicity seem the rule. With Wigner, I believe that physical objects and spiritual values share a similar kind of reality. For me the fusion of physical objects and human values is further evidence of this universal quality of miscibility.

In Part IV we shall attempt to build a new model of health, disease, birth, and death in an effort to translate descriptions of subatomic reality into human terms. The relativistic view of space-time will be put to the same purpose. I believe the model that will emerge is not only consistent with our theoretical descriptions of how the world behaves, it is consistent with human experience as well.

ONENESS AND MODELS OF HEALTH

Our current models of health suggest that we find ourselves in a universe in which we do not belong, into which we have been thrust by accident. Our very existence is the result of chance mutations in a hostile environment. What initiated the chain of life is unknown, perhaps some chemical accident which we may never decipher.

In a stance of desperation we battle disease and illness. Birth, of which we had no choice, will end inexorably in an equally choiceless death, all in a universe that one day will itself die.

Against this view of man's place in the universe stand the new observations we have examined above. The theory of dissipative structures, as we have seen, also emphasizes an organizing principle operating at all levels in the universe. This principle, or something like it, eventuated in the formation of life—an "uphill event" that has become increasingly more complex in defiance of the entropic downhill drift of the universe as a whole. Disease can occur in this universe, but offers to human beings what any natural perturbation offers: the chance to evolve to a new and higher level of psychophysical complexity. Disease is no longer a categorical tragedy. Without it, as we have seen, our own species' survival mechanisms, such as our immune capacity, would have never developed; for without challenge, without perturbations, escape to new levels of internal richness does not occur.

Disease in this context is tied to life and progress. Life as we know it *demands* disease; it is unthinkable without it. Disease becomes more than a blackish prelude to death. It becomes the harbinger of life.

The principle of oneness that is revealed through Bell's theorem and through the connectivity we observed in the biodance takes us away from the edge of Monod's menacing universe. In essence it says that through the unbelievable richness of contact that every human has with the universe at large *and* with every other human being, our concept of death is wrong. In a universe of oneness, death is impossible. The richness of connectivity renders personal extinction impossible, because *personal extinction is possible only in a universe of personal isolation.* We do not live in such a universe.

The failure to feel the universal oneness that envelopes us all perpetuates the greatest illusion of modern man: the inevitability of personal extinction. This illusion can be countered by an appreciation of the quality of oneness in the universe so well described by modern science.

The modern tradition of equating death with an ensuing nothingness can be abandoned. For there is no reason to believe that human death severs the quality of oneness in the universe. If we participate in this universal quality before our death, our survival after death is *demanded.* The oneness principle endures, and we with it.

> One Nature, perfect and pervading, circulates in all natures,
> One reality, all-comprehensive, contains within itself all realities.
> —Yung-chia Ta-shih[17]

SACRED GEOMETRY

IV

Synthesis

CHAPTER ONE

SPACETIME AND HEALTH

. . . We must not speak of any mind or intelligence in nature—because it is taboo. Might it not make things less complicated if we were now to infringe the taboo and concede that what we call unconscious, or unself-conscious, mind is in fact the inwardness of nature as well as ourselves?

—OWEN BARFIELD[1]

HEALTH: THE TRADITIONAL VIEW

If we were to describe the everyday assumptions that guide our thinking in matters of health, what kind of picture would emerge? First, perhaps, we would assume that our body is an object. Quite obvious to most persons it occupies a specific space that is not shared by other bodies. In this sense it is an isolated, self-contained unit, demarcated from all other existing bodies.

Moreover, the body is material. It, like all else, is comprised of individual building blocks, the atoms. These atoms come together, forming specific patterns, and through ways that are mysterious to us take on the quality we call life. This quality, we believe, is not shared by most other objects in the universe, which we regard handily as being separated into halves: the living and nonliving.

One of the most obvious features of bodies is that they not only exist in a specific space, they persist but for a finite time. Bodies eventually die. Life, that undefinable quality, ceases with the death of the material body. It cannot be otherwise, for bodies are isolated from each other in time and space; thus, the life quality each possesses is extinguished when the individual body dies.

Although the pattern of the body is destroyed when it dies, the matter that makes up the body persists. It, like all other matter, is absolute. It cannot be created nor destroyed.

Bodies exist, quite obviously, in a time that is composed of a past, present, and future. An indisputable fact is that birth and death occur in this flow. These events, standing in a flowing time, never recur after happening once. Birth and death are the poles of life, demarcating our existence.

Events in life quite apparently happen in this flow of time. One such event is disease, which, we are told by modern bioscientists, occurs because of a cause rooted in some malfunction at the level of the molecules that make up the physical body. Disease originates in individual molecules that make up individual bodies, and is thus an individual process and experience. Disease, like bodies, is therefore confined in space and time.

Health, like disease, we suppose, is similarly located in the body and in the experience of specific, isolated persons. It is an individual process that is unshared. It belongs to each of us alone. And although health and disease certainly generate psychological experiences, they are at heart body phenomena since they express happenings deep within our physical structure at the level of our constituent molecules.

We enjoy health and loathe sickness and disease. We thus accept without questioning that health is a positive, and disease a negative, human event.

Since disease affects individual bodies, therapy is also aimed at individual persons. To treat one person for disease occurring in another would be patently absurd. Therapy, like disease, must be localized; it must be directed at specific problems that are confined to specific patients.

Since illness is the result of objective disturbances in our physical structure, therapy itself must be objective. Physical malfunctions require physical interventions, since the entire disease process is a physical phenomenon.

Disease is a body affair, standing quite apart from psychological events. Although there are obvious examples that mind and body interact, the overwhelming cause of human suffering and disease is physical in nature. When human psychological events do figure into the equation of health, they do usually by interfering, by causing trouble. Psychosomatic disease is a reality that we accept, illustrating our belief that when the mind intrudes in matters of health and disease, it functions mostly as a troublemaker.

Since health, like disease, is confined to individual bodies the maintenance of health is an individual affair. What we do to either enhance or destroy our health is a matter of personal concern, since such effects are confined to isolated bodies.

Occupying a specific demarcation in a flowing time, life is a one-time event. Since it never happens more than once, its duration is of ultimate importance: to live long is desirable and is the primary goal of our efforts to remain healthy. Analogously, a short life is tragic. Death is a final, absolute event—the enemy of life. It is to be resisted at all costs. Its defeat is a primary mission of the healing professions, along with the extermination of pain and suffering, which are themselves seen as menacing, malevolent, negative events.

While this general description of birth, death, health, and disease would not find complete acceptance by everyone, it nonetheless is a typical expression for most persons. It should be obvious by now that it is based on a particular view of the world, which conforms largely to common sense. Its primary features are those of a flowing time; the idea that all matter is composed of discrete particles; that the behavior of these particles is controlled by iron-clad laws of cause and effect; that matter exists independent from space; and that space can be regarded as being uninfluenced by time. An interpenetrating feature of this view is that of fragmentation and isolation. Bodies, as in the classical view of atoms, stand alone, both in space and in time. Although they form patterns, at heart they are single units in a deep, fundamental sense. Connectedness is seen only in terms of interaction of quintessentially separate bits and pieces.

THE LIMITATIONS OF THE TRADITIONAL VIEW OF HEALTH

It is becoming apparent that this view of the world is a limited one. The great revolution in physics which has occurred in our own century came about because of the glaring deficiencies in this description of the world. No matter that the traditional picture of the world conformed to the dictates of common sense. When put to the test by critical scientists, this view of the behavior of the universe was shown to be incomplete. As we have seen, this Newtonian description was radically revised, resulting in wrenching redefinitions of previous assumptions. All the accepted features of Newton's vision—the nature of space, time, matter, and causation—were cast in new forms. And even though they proved incomprehensible to the senses, the new descriptions proved exceedingly accurate: no experiment has ever been conducted that has disproved the quantum and relativistic theories of the way the world works.

If our ordinary view of life, death, health, and disease rests solidly on seventeenth-century physics, and if this physics has been scuttled in favor of a more accurate description of nature, an inescapable question occurs: must not our definitions of life, death, health, and disease themselves change? To refuse to face the consequences to these areas is to favor dogma over an evolving knowledge. Moreover, the modern view of the world leads, as we shall see, to a model of health that is as humane as the present views are grotesque. We have nothing to lose by a reexamination of fundamental assumptions of our models of health; on the contrary, we face the extraordinary possibility of fashioning a system that emphasizes life instead of death, and unity and oneness instead of fragmentation, darkness, and isolation.

Because I believe that a new model of health must rest solidly on the new notions of space and time that are provided by modern physics, I have called this new description a "spacetime model." What might it look like?

THE SPACETIME MODEL OF HEALTH

To begin with, the body ceases to appear as a mere object, surrounded by empty space. We know that the characteristics of both massive bodies—such as human bodies—and the space surrounding them are interdependent. Neither space nor matter is absolute. Matter is not separate from the space that surrounds it, nor is space separate from the matter that it encloses.

Not only is this relationship true when the body is viewed as a 150 pound object, it is true when the body is viewed at the level of its atoms. The modern view tells us that atoms do not stand alone, but are in a fundamental dynamical relationship with all other atoms. These relationships between "particles" are such that it is problematic to define what, even, a particle is. Physicists tell us that all atoms are in essence connected to all other atoms in the universe. Not only are the behavioral patterns of each atom affected in theory and in principle by the behavior of all other atoms in the universe, the converse is true: each atom, by its own behavior, exerts change on the behavior of all other atoms, however distant. As Eddington put it, "When the electron vibrates, the universe shakes." The compositional "parts" of the body, then, appear more as patterns and processes than as discrete units and objects. If an objective character can no longer be assigned to the body's atoms, it seems a most difficult task to continue regarding the body itself as an object, separate in space and time from all other physical bodies.

The virtual flood of chemicals entering and exiting the body account for its total renewal, down to the very last atom, every few years. This process, the biodance, is a nonending stream between bodies that live not only now, but which lived in the past. Even from the point of view, then, of elemental biology and physiology the body behaves more as pattern and process than as an isolated and noninteracting object. Bodies do not stay put; they are alive in space and time. The boundary of our physical self, our skin, is an illusion. It is no boundary at all, being constantly regenerated in only a matter of days. This "boundary," which feels solid to touch, is constantly fading, reforming, and fading again in the endless round of biodance. Thus, when scrutinized at the level of the whole or at the level of its constituent parts, the vision of the body as an object fails.

Because all bodies interact with all other bodies in this process, health can be seen as a shared phenomenon. It extends to all other bodies. Health is not just an individual affair. Like disease, it can be spread. Efforts toward health care, therefore, transcend the actions of single individuals. What *one* person does to improve—or to diminish—his health has vital consequences to *all* other persons.

Therapy, analogously, can never be directed only at single individuals. The efforts of physicians only *seem* to apply to individual patients, since all bodies are interrelated in a dynamic sharing. Individual therapy is a masquerade, a tongue in cheek event, an "as if" effort on the doctor's part. Therapy is consequential for all persons at once since there is, in a sense, only one physical body which, through an endless streaming of interconnected events, is expressed illusorily as individual life forms.

Since no demarcations in time exist in a nonflowing, nonlinear time, past, present, and future become arbitrary divisions. The ordinary way of marking life at its poles by birth and death becomes suspect. We can begin to see birth and death as events occurring at either end of the asymmetric unfolding of happenings that we call life, but that carry no absolute status as an ultimate beginning or an ultimate end. Death, in the new view of health, becomes effete. The ordinary goal of health care, that of forestalling the moment of death, fails as a rational effort on the part of both physicians and patients, for there is no ultimate end to be saved *from*. Because the flow of time is seen as a psychological event not representing a true feature of the physical world, the ordinary sense of urgency that we feel is reduced. Along with this lack of respect for a pernicious flowing time, the epidemic of various forms of "hurry sickness" begins to abate. We cease to destroy ourselves out of a sense that time is running out, that there isn't enough of it, that we are approaching our final end.

And, since all bodies are coextensive through actual dynamical physical processes, the notion of individual death is absurd. Because bodies are *not* individual, but living, sharing processes, only a collective death of all bodies can extinguish any one of them. For *one* to die, *all* must die. The *entire pattern* of interdigitation must be interrupted, not just individual processes. However, when seen against the backdrop of a nonflowing time, not even the entire disruption of all life processes would result in an ultimate end, since such finality only makes sense in a flowing, linear time composed of a past, present, and future. In spacetime, the notion of finality is transcended. We thus abandon death and its spectre of fear, suffering, and inexorable decline of life.

Life is not the property of single bodies in the new view. Life becomes a property of the universe at large, connected, as are all living bodies, to all other things. We see ourselves not as an anomaly, as life stranded in a minor galaxy in a hostile universe, but as an effulgent expression of a universal quality: that of life itself.

Molecular theories of disease causation are now seen in a different way than in the traditional biomedical model. For we recognize in the new view that isolated derangements at the level of the atoms simply do not occur. The modern rule is that all information is everywhere transmitted. Crisp, causal events that were once thought to characterize each and every human disease fade into endless reverberating chains of happenings. In the new view we see the molecular theory of disease causation as an outmoded, picturesque description. Discrete causes never occur in individual bodies because of the simple reason that discrete, individual bodies do not themselves exist.

The goal of traditional medicine, that of an utterly objective therapy that could be aimed with accuracy at the causal event of every disease, is transcended. For we know in the modern view that we cannot stand apart from nature and intervene dispassionately and objectively. We know through Heisenberg's uncertainty relations that this was so for the tiniest parts of matter, such as electrons. Interaction causes change—whether between the scientist and the object of his scrutiny, or between the physician and his patient. The interaction of humans generates genuine perturbations in the psychophysical state of both. Because of these interactions, complete neutrality in therapy is a pipe dream. That we ever thought it possible reflected our blindness toward our connectivity.

In the modern view, because of these profound interrelations between consciousness and the physical world, rather than attempting to *extinguish* the subjective element in the healing process, we tend to *maximize* it; for we see it as a potent force in exerting purposeful change. Furthermore, we reason that this change can be initiated by patients as well as professional healers. In our new view of health, therefore, each patient has the potential of being his own healer. Healing becomes democratized in the new view.

Since the body-as-object is an idea we reject in the modern view of health, our notion of the patient changes. Patients are no longer seen as objects "to whom" or "for whom" something is done. In the new view patient and therapist form a unit through the processes that connect all beings. Patient-oriented therapy is a boomerang, affecting the therapist at the same time. From the modern therapist's perspective, thus, patient therapy is self-therapy. To heal another is to heal oneself.

In the new view of health we cease to see disease as entirely negative. Health, too, is not altogether positive for us. The fact is, the distinctions between health and disease at a point begin to blur. Why? For one reason, we have come to see the impossibility of events such as health and disease as being "local"—i.e., they are connected and dependent on all distant happenings in the universe. This degree of connectedness suggests that "good" or "bad," "health" or "disease" are capricious and arbitrary judgments. In the new view we attach little value to health and disease. Rather than seeing them as either good or bad, to us they seem to be simply a statement of the way things are. For us this is not a statement of passivity and blind acceptance, for we can still act to change the physical state of the body. It is merely a feeling born of the recognition of the interpenetrating oneness of all things.

We no longer insist in the new view that length of life is of critical importance. Long-lived existences have no intrinsic value over short-lived ones. A short life is not tragic—although we continue to act to preserve life. It is simply that length of life is meaningless for the reason that passage of linear time does not occur. Our acts of health, therefore, no longer carry the old traditional quality of desperation. For us, there is no final end. We have escaped from the River of

Time. For us, time is no longer the devouring tyrant it was once presumed to be.

For what is there to die? In the new view, the body is "dematerialized." Matter is no longer absolute. It is transmutable to, and from, energy. The grotesqueness of death demanded a type of matter that was absolute, separated from all other, independent from all other. The new model of health includes matter as originating from, and disappearing into, the energy-containing void. We know through actual physical experiments that these transfigurations occur at all times and in all matter. This relentless shuttle between the worlds of form and nonform are not confined to the arbitrarily defined world of living matter, and do not cease when "death" occurs.

No longer in the new view do we hold even to the idea that we have a determinable location in space and time. Connected as we are to all other bodies, comprised as we are of an unending flux of events themselves occurring in spacetime, we regard ourselves not as bodies fixed in time at particular points, but as eternally changing patterns for which precise descriptive terms seem utterly inappropriate.

THE NECESSITY FOR A NEW MODEL OF HEALTH

Why should we want to attempt to view the human processes of health and disease in terms of the new physical views offered by quantum physics and relativity? In the first place, as the physicist Wheeler has observed, *everything* is quantized at some level: "The world at bottom is a quantum world; and any system is ineradicably a quantum system."[2] This suggests that eventually our concepts of how our own bodies work will have to give due regard to quantum physical events and the probabilistic, statistical subatomic world. At present, most bioscientists believe that the subatomic events are too small to be of practical importance.

Some scientists go so far as to adamantly reject any attempt to mix quantum physics with biological investigations, exhibiting a point of view that is so emphatic as to resemble prejudice. ("Electrons and human beings aren't the same.") This attitude is hardly becoming to a scientist, and is certainly not a scientific position. Such scientists might as well argue that the principle of flight is a natural phenomenon that applies only to smallish things like hummingbirds and bees, but is irrelevant to man, who could never be supported by invisible molecules of air.

There are suggestions that when we delve into our bodies at the deepest levels we shall have to deal with quantum events. Niels Bohr proposed that conscious thought might involve such minute exchanges of energy that only a quantum physical explanation would be adequate to describe consciousness. More recently, Walker[3] has offered the first attempt to render a quantum physical description of consciousness. His work stands as an early venture into murky waters, its significance lying in the direction toward which it points: that in man's attempts to explore his body-mind, he cannot forever avoid the quantum realm.

Our basic understanding of neurophysiologic events in the brain also points in these directions. We have viewed the brain for decades as an architectural assembly of hard wiring. Neurons function as conduits for electrochemical information, much as a wire conducts electricity. The synapses, the junctions between neurons, are the clefts over which this information is passed from one neuron to another. The whole contraption is conceived as functioning in binary on-off terms—either the neuron "fired" or it didn't. The situation now seems far more complex. Far from being silent in the interval between firing, the synapse is the site for so-called slow wave potentials. A kind of electrochemical conversation is always going on in the synaptic cleft—sometimes in loud tones, but *always*, at least, in hushed whispers. The traditional on-off concepts of neuron functioning are inadequate to explain these events, for there apparently is not an "off." These events, it is suggested, involve levels of energy where quantum events become decisive, so that an adequate understanding of elemental energetic mechanisms in the brain may therefore demand the application of quantum concepts.[4]

Far from being invisible, quantum events may intrude into our lives in excessively obvious ways. Earlier we examined Bell's theorem, noting that conscious decision making determined the actual outcome of experiments. It would be wrong to view this discovery as a mere laboratory triviality. The significance of Bell's theorem is stated by Henry S. Stapp:

> The most important thing about Bell's theorem is that it puts the dilemma posed by quantum phenomena clearly into the realm of macroscopic phenomena. . . . it shows that our ordinary ideas about the world are somehow profoundly deficient even on the macroscopic level.[5]

TABLE I

A SPACETIME MODEL OF
BIRTH, LIFE, HEALTH, AND DEATH

Traditional View	*Modern Physical View*
1. The body is an object, localized to a specific space.	1. The body is not an object, and cannot be localized in space
2. The body is an isolated, self-contained unit.	2. The body is in dynamic relationship with the universe and with all other bodies through actual physical exchange—the "biodance."
3. The body is comprised of individual building blocks, the atoms.	3. "Building blocks" and "atoms" are inaccurate descriptions, since all particles can only be understood in relation to all other particles.
4. Health is an individual affair, affecting a single body.	4. Health extends to all other bodies, since all bodies are in a dynamical relationship. Individual health is an illusion.
5. Illness is a process experienced by individual bodies.	5. Illness is a collective event, since all bodies are related. Individual illness is an illusion.
6. Therapy affects individual bodies.	6. Therapy affects all bodies.
7. Health maintenance is a personal affair.	7. Individual efforts to maintain health extend to all persons.
8. Neglect of health damages single bodies and is an individual affair.	8. Neglect of health negatively affects all persons and is a collective affair.
9. Birth and death are demarcations at the poles of life.	9. No demarcations in time exist.
10. Time flows.	10. The flow of time is a psychological, not a natural, event. No physical experiment has ever detected the flow of time.
11. Events in life happen.	11. Events in life do not happen, they simply "are." It is the "asymmetry" of the occurrence of natural events that generates the impression that they occur in a one-way flow of time.
12. The matter that comprises the body is an absolute.	12. Nothing of the body's matter is absolute. All matter, as well as space and time, are relative in the modern view.
13. Death is a final, absolute event.	13. Death is not a final, absolute event, since it refers to a body that is coextensive with all other bodies, and whose matter is not absolute.

TABLE I (*continued*)

A SPACETIME MODEL OF
BIRTH, LIFE, HEALTH, AND DEATH

Traditional View	*Modern Physical View*
14. Life is a property of individual bodies.	14. Although individual bodies are indeed alive, the interrelatedness of one body with all others, and with the universe at large, makes life a universal and not an individual process.
15. Therapy is directed at individuals, since it is individuals who become ill.	15. Individuals do become ill; but because of the interrelation of all bodies, therapy can be directed to *any* body. Therapy is all-pervasive because all bodies are related.
16. Disease occurs because of derangements at the level of molecules [the molecular theory of disease causation].	16. Atoms and all subatomic particles that constitute the body are in dynamical relationship to all other such particles in the universe. Where does the breakdown originate—in the body, or elsewhere in the universe? Localization of disease causation to specific bodies, or to specific levels within bodies, is inaccurate.
17. Disease is molecular misbehavior and is thus an objective affair. Therapy, therefore, must also be objective.	17. Objective therapy is an illusion. Intervention in nature, as well as scrutiny of all types, changes what is observed. The observer cannot separate himself from the outcome of the observation, so that objectivity in its pure sense is an impossibility.
18. Disease is a body affair.	18. The influence of consciousness on the physical processes occurring in the body obliterates this distinction.
19. Disease is a negative, and health a positive, affair.	19. Connected and dependent as they are on all distant happenings in the universe, the characterization of local events as either good or bad seems a capricious and arbitrary human judgment.
20. To live long is desirable; a short life is tragic.	20. Length of life is meaningless for the reason that passage of linear time does not occur in nature.
21. The body is material.	21. Matter has become "dematerialized"; therefore, the body is not strictly material.
22. Bodies have a determinable location in space and time.	22. Connected as they are to all other bodies, the location of any single body in space and time is at best an approximation.

The implication of Bell's theorem is that it is important in our ordinary everyday affairs. Why is it not obvious that this is so? Are the effects too small to be noticed? If they exist, are they too trivial to matter? It is premature to conclude that these events are meaningless in our lives simply because we do not notice them. No one, after all, has ever "noticed" gravity—only its effects. Our lives are full of phenomena whose cause we can only guess at. To dismiss Bell's theorem as meaningless at the level of human experience would be to commit the logical error of the icthyologist who, after seining the entire ocean with a net of one-inch mesh, concluded that the ocean contained no living creatures smaller than one inch in diameter. In looking for day-to-day effects of quantum phenomena such as those implied by Bell's theorem, we simply may need to tighten the mesh in our perceptual net.

Curious examples of this sort keep turning up. In the 1960s a new clinical syndrome in medicine was first described, called hyperosmolar coma. This disease was recognized to be due to a variety of causes. It was a serious problem, fatal in a high percentage of cases. Following the first description of it an avalanche of reports of the illness followed, and it was quickly recognized to be a very common clinical entity.

The baffling question was, where was it hiding before it was first reported? How could hyperosmolar coma go undetected? How could such a devastating clinical illness, which presented itself in such spectacular ways, have been missed for so long? It is now generally agreed that the disease was present before its initial recognition with probably the same frequency as afterwards. But following its discovery the mesh in the perceptual net of physicians tightened, allowing it to be captured with great regularity. It was the perceptions of physicians and not the disease itself which were in hiding.

THE SPACETIME MODEL AND DEATH

One of the most apparently preposterous aspects of the spacetime model of health is the redefinition of death. Let's take a closer look.

Death and Time

Fashioned as it is on a classical, traditional view of linear time, our concept of death is that it rushes to meet us in a one-way flow of events. Santayana epitomized our frailties in dealing with this inexorable onrush:

There is no cure for birth and death, save to enjoy the interval.

And Bertrand Russell described the finality with which we view death in his usual piquant way by allowing that when he died he would rot, nothing of his ego remaining.

Visions of an afterlife have always been viewed by hardnosed skeptics such as Russell as a cowardly hedge against the obvious final end that death brings to all men. Russell's view of death, together with the views of those who believe in an afterlife—be it heaven, hell, or some variation—is based on the old idea of time as a one-way street.

But we must some day come to terms with this most important and painful fact: our "modern" view of death is utterly dissonant with the modern view of time. The modern notion of time is that it does *not* flow. This new definition cannot be bent to accommodate our ordinary concept of death as the culminating event of a lifetime spent in a flowing time. As the physicist-mathematician P.C.W. Davies states, no physical experiment has ever been performed that detects the passage of time. This statement may at first glance seem preposterous. But Davies is describing the view of time inherent in modern physics—relativity and quantum mechanics—and not the traditional, Newtonian concept of time, which belongs to classical physics and which we ordinarily associate with all science. Although physical experiments attempt to look at the world objectively, as soon as the objective attempt is made the passage of time disappears like a ghost into the night. As Davies states,

Far better to regard the world as a *total phenomenon*: in the words of the German mathematician Hermann Weyl (1885-1955), "the world doesn't happen, it simply is."[6]

Our view of death is inconsistent with this definition of time. We are out of step with current scientific concepts, and our error is as monumental as if we still believed the world to be flat.

The notion that time flows in a one-way fashion is a property of our consciousness. It is a subjective phenomenon and is a property that simply cannot be demonstrated in the natural world. This is an incontrovertible lesson from modern science, a lesson that has been enormously difficult for modern man to comprehend. A flowing time belongs to our mind, not to nature. We serially perceive events that simply "are"; and the serial perception of many such events eventuates in what we interpret to be an indisputable fact of nature, the flow of time.

The physicists who at the turn of this century revolutionized the older views of time did so by calling into question these "indisputable" aspects of nature. They did so, however, not by intuitive leaps of their own consciousness so much as through an attempt to answer a persistent question that would not go away: what view of time must be constructed to explain certain observations that keep appearing in atomic experiments? A new view of time was demanded by the actual data that flowed from the laboratory.

What was the new view of time that arose? We have examined it earlier, but a succinct review of the modern concept can be found in a fuller remark of the mathematician Weyl:

> The objective world simply is, it does not happen. Only to the gaze of my consciousness, crawling upward along the life line of my body, does a section of this world come to life as a fleeting image in space which continually changes in time.[7]

This view is an affront to common sense. It is entirely incongruous with how we "know" time behaves. It was no less an affront, however, to the scientists who fashioned this new view than to us nonscientists who must assimilate it.

Death and Common Sense

Our concepts of death are founded on common sense, which we look to as a benchmark any time we try to fathom ideas we cannot objectively pin down. But it may be ludricrous as well as useless to attempt to use common sense to fashion concepts of death. *None* of us has any firsthand personal experience in the matter. Moreover, there are no sources to which we can look with absolute confidence. Serious objections can be raised against all known accounts of persons who have "died" briefly, only later to regain consciousness and relate their experience.

In spite of the limitations, however, a common sense approach to the formation of concepts about death seems to most persons the only available means to get at the problem. But for those who are disposed to follow this approach, Einstein's caveat should not go unnoticed: common sense is merely the deposit of prejudices laid down in the human mind before the age of eighteen.[8]

The most serious objection to incorporating common sensical and "obvious" notions of how nature behaves into our death concepts (besides their tendency to reflect hidden prejudices) is that these approaches diverge from the physical descriptions of nature that are given to us by modern physics. We ought to be consistent with science, if possible, in describing the world, *if* we wish our descriptions to be considered objective. Death is a part of the natural world as much as is life; and when science speaks about the natural world, which includes the phenomenon of time (and, therefore, death), we ought to listen to what is said. We cannot pick and choose, extracting only those modern scientific views we find palatable. We must look at the complete picture science gives us, and, therefore, we cannot ignore what modern physical science has revealed to us about the nature of time.

There is now a deep stirring in our consciousness as a culture about death. Thanatology is a respected area of study. "Death and dying" are popular subjects not only among the laiety but among medical professionals as well. In medical schools students are given lecture series on how to deal with dying patients by clergy and psychiatrists alike. "Personal growth centers" have resident professionals who share their wisdom about death. Death education is a central theme of several journals that have only recently appeared. It has become culturally acceptable to scrutinize death as never before. Once considered only a priestly function, we now recognize that persons with diverse points of view can contribute to our collective knowledge about death.

But almost without exception these approaches merely pour new wine into old bottles, for they are stuck in a world view whose attitude toward time is archaic. *No* current thanatologic endeavor can yield fruitful results without accepting what is at the same time the most marvelous and astonishing discovery of our era: time is not a river.

Death and the Asymmetry of Time

We have a habitual tendency to link birth, health, and illness to form a continuum eventuating ultimately in death for each of us. This process is laid onto a background of linear time, and generates the general notion that death inevitably follows birth, and that disease and decline invariably cause death.

Other points of view are possible, however, one of which is expressed by Alan Watts:

> . . . lack of rain, famine, and death are simply . . . ways of looking at, and describing, the same event. Given living organisms, lack of rain = death. The notion of causality is simply a lame way of connecting the various stages of an event which we have distinguished and

separated for purposes of description; so that, beguiled by our own words, we come to think of these stages as different events which must be stuck together again by the glue of causality. In fact, the only single event is the universe itself.[9]

Watts' view is strikingly similar to that of the modern physicist, for he is essentially invoking the modern concept of time as being either symmetric or asymmetric as described by Davies (see page 165). Like Watts, the physicist has removed the "glue of causality" from the collection of asymmetric events we continually confront in time.

"The only single event is the universe itself." It is an event that at once enfolds all of us, including our birth, health, illness, and death—and the time we perceive. With the causal glue removed, each of our seemingly successive life events simply stands on its own. If we can say with Watts that, given living organisms, lack of rain *is* death, then so, too, birth is death—as are health and disease.

The modern view of time, thus, validates another view of the stages of our life and the events that comprise them.

Death and Time: A New Model

How might a concept of death be structured which would incorporate a view of nonlinear time that is consistent with the postulates of modern physics? One of the most creative approaches has been put forward by the psychologist LeShan.[10] Commenting on the possibility of surviving biological death, LeShan formulates a view of birth, life, and death which entails a nonlinear time concept, a view that is consistent with modern physics. He observes that birth and death demarcate life at both ends, forming boundaries to life. Noting that time in the modern sense cannot be bounded, he arrives at the conclusion that death as a finality is inconsistent with a modern world view. He utilizes other modern physical concepts such as field theory to build a logical case for survival of death. His treatise is one of the clearest to date in the attempt to apply the new concepts of time, space, and matter in building a fresh idea of death.

But however consistent LeShan's logic is with the new view of the physical world, it is equally *in*consistent with ordinary human experience. Survival of biological death seems patently absurd. Death is an obvious and grotesque fact of life, and the cleverest logical machinations will not make it otherwise. One cannot *reason* death away. And, after all, one can *reason* the wildest schemes into believability, such as the ancient notion that the earth was supported by a human of unimaginable strength who in turn stood on a supporting tortoise. Logic is deceptive—as changeable as fashion—and in the end it is to one's own experience one must look. Again we are back to common sense as a guide to building concepts of death.

But do not these objections against the use of reason in approaching the idea of death follow a *reason* and logic all their own? We find ourselves *reasoning* in unconscious and convoluted ways that it is hopeless to rely on *reason* in attempting to understand an event so *un*reasonable and unfathomable as death. We cannot escape the use of reason any more than we can escape our own shadow. We must employ logic to some degree in *any* attempt to understand events in our lives, even if we conclude that such events can only be understood in intuitive and nonlogical ways. Whether we are attempting to decipher complex events, such as how the process of photosynthesis occurs, or whether we are pondering the meaning of death, we cannot hide from our faculty of reason.

What can we reasonably say, thus, about an approach to death which invokes a concept of time that goes beyond the ordinary linear view? Is it reasonable to attempt to fuse ideas from modern physical science to concepts of death? Or do these counterintuitive new views of nonlinear time deserve to stay where they originated, in the laboratory? Is there any realistic hope of incorporating them into a concept of death that has personal meaning when they seem so bizarre, so foreign to the human sense of how the world actually behaves?

These are cogent questions, and no doubt have been asked in kind in all periods in history when objective findings seem to trammel the reason of reasonable men. It is helpful to recall that history records the stunning irreverence of science for what passes for common sense. The history of science *is* the history of the wrenching process of common sense accommodating itself to scientific fact. The assertion in our day of a new view of time that is foreign to the senses surely engenders no more amazement and discomfiture in the average man than did the claims of Copernicus and Galileo in their own day. Thematically the assertions change; the reactions they evoke do not.

The resiliency of the human mind to accommodate ideas that were once incomprehensible is an amazing feature of our consciousness. If we are tempted to think we can never adapt to a new view of time which would mandate a new concept of death, we have only to review equally radical transformations in human thought: the evolu-

tion from the Ptolemaic to the Copernican model of the solar system;
the emergence and acceptance of Darwinian evolution; and the
transition in our own century from a classical, Newtonian view of
the world to the counterintuitive picture of quantum mechanics and
relativity.

In view of such remarkable transitions in human thought it would
be a naive mistake to suppose that radical new views of time, life,
and death were impossible for us to accept. It seems inevitable that
such restructuring occur. Just as Bishop Wilberforce's clerical logic
could not prevail against the evidence for the evolution of species,
our own views of time, life, and death—couched as they are in
myth, tradition, and common sense—must themselves be scuttled
and revised to be consistent with the evidence for a nonlinear time.

The historical panorama of the evolution of great ideas serves us
notice in our time: concepts of what is real are not written in stone.
Heraclitus was correct: the only constant thing is change. We have
never had, nor shall we ever have, a sure, immutable fix on reality.

The Perception of Linear Time: Possibility for Change

Dependent as they are on concepts of time, our definitions of life
and death are overripe for change. There are sure and certain rum-
blings that the change is upon us. The poet William Carlos Williams
said, "A new world is only a new mind!" Modern physical concepts
have given us a new world—and have dragged us, reluctantly,
toward a new mind. The new mind is everywhere flowering, and
part of the new fruit is another variety of Coleridge's rose, plucked
in heaven during a dream and present in our hand on waking. It is
an unbelievably beautiful flower, a new and emancipating vision of
death.

Why does a traditional linear view of time exert such a compelling
psychological force? For most persons any other view of time is
unthinkable. The parcels of time—past, present, and future—impart
a meaning and pattern to our lives without which we envision
chaos. We even use the capacity to differentiate past, present, and
future as a criterion for sanity, judging those who are disoriented in
time psychologically sick. And we tend to view those cultures whose
view of time is different than ours as primitive and uncivilized.

Even those among us who have slain the notion of an absolute,
linear, flowing time—the physicists—as a group demonstrate a peculiar stance with regard to the modern physical definition of time. It
is as if the new views of time are fit only for their laboratory; and

since their lives must be in large measure conducted outside the laboratory, another view of time must be employed—the everyday past, present, and future of the average man. There is little evidence that the new views of time exert any significant force in the way physicists order their own lives.[11]

The most notable exception is that of Einstein. There is clear biographical data that his personal vision of life and death were deeply influenced by the new concepts of space and time. For Einstein these ideas filtered from the laboratory into the world of the everyday, where they had relevance to the most poignant affairs of men, affecting, even, the meaning of death itself.

In 1905 Einstein published his treatise on special relativity. At the end of this paper, which was to change forever our concepts of space and time, he thanked his dear friend Michele Besso. It was Besso, when they were workers together in the patent office in Bern, with whom he had agonized over these ideas when they were seminal. Their deep friendship endured for a lifetime, and in 1955 when Besso died (shortly before Einstein), he wrote a letter to Besso's surviving son and sister:

> The foundation of our friendship was laid in our student years in Zurich, where we met regularly at musical evenings . . . later the Patent Office brought us together. The conversations during our mutual way home were of unforgettable charm. . . . And now he has preceded me briefly in bidding farewell to this strange world. This signifies nothing. For us believing physicists the distinction between past, present, and future is only an illusion, even if a stubborn one.[12]

What is the difference? Why did the new ideas of the universe penetrate the thinking of Einstein to the extent of modifying his attitude about death, whereas they have little apparent impact on the deeply personal philosophies of most physicists who work with them? We can only speculate. But surely his unparalleled personal involvement with these concepts was influential in his life as in no other. For him there was no casual acceptance of the new description of reality. Indeed, the process of shaping the new concepts very nearly devastated him:

> I must confess that at the very beginning when the Special Theory of Relativity began to germinate in me, I was visited by all sorts of nervous conflicts. When young I used to go away for weeks in a state of confusion, as one who at that time had yet to overcome the state of stupefaction in his first encounter with such questions.[13]

What does Einstein's experience tell us? Simply that as a potentially transformative power in our everyday life, these new concepts of space and time are not effete. Their effect is not trivial, but is of powerful and beautiful proportions. As Castaneda's Don Juan might say, they are a path with a heart. The modern views of spacetime offer the potential of altering the spectre of the finality of death for every man. Einstein's personal spiritual and philosophical transformations that flowed from his remarkable insights are possibilities for all of us. As great as it was, his gift to us of the power over the atom is insignificant in comparison to showing us a power over death. Einstein's most important legacy may turn out to be the understanding that in the matter of death, as with space, time, and matter, we had it all wrong.

There are a few current physical scientists, however, who anticipate the unsettling effects of their ideas, realizing that their radical new descriptions of the universe are far more than laboratory curiosities. As an example, Davies, the British physicist-mathematician, observes,

> . . . experimental and theoretical advances in the scientific understanding of space-time physics and cosmology have an impact on society, as do all forms of human intellectual activity. These advances have not always been assimilated into the mainstream of knowledge with equanimity. Sometimes, the implications of new models of the universe have appeared so unpalatable that they have been fiercely resisted by the establishment, such as greeted the Copernican revolution.[14]

We can expect no less resistance to redefinitions of the religiously charged matters of life and death. The ghost of Bishop Wilberforce still walks, appearing whenever entrenched hallowed notions are threatened. But in their great debate over Darwinian evolution, Huxley survived the Bishop's vituperative attack, and the disconcerting new ideas of life and death will survive for the same reason—because they are consistent with the most precise definition of the world we have yet made.

The ordinary view of death must fail because it is based on two erroneous assumptions—that the body occupies a particular space, and that it endures through a span of linear time. The first assumption, that the body can be localized in space as one might localize a stone or a tree, is inconsistent with what we know of the dynamical relationship of living things with the universe of which they are a part. Earlier we examined this relationship, the biodance, the endless streaming of matter which irreverently disregards our idea of a bounded body.

Moreover, the modern descriptions of the interrelatedness of the particles that make up the body are at variance with the notion of any self-contained object, be it body or otherwise. All particles, we saw, can only be described in terms of their relationships with all other particles. None stands alone. Although these descriptions of connectivity were worked out for subatomic particles, it is exceedingly unclear how human bodies can exist in isolation, composed as they are of particles which themselves are never isolated and bounded.

We saw that the view of life as an enclosure in time, bounded by birth at one end and by death at the other, is as spurious in light of modern concepts of spacetime as is the notion of a spatially bounded body. For time is no mere backdrop against which events are played out. It can only be said to "pass" in our minds. We *introduce* the concept of a flowing linear time into the universe, but we have never been able to experimentally point to this property in the world.[15]

Where, then, are we—without bounded bodies, occupying no discrete interval of time? These assertions seem audacious, preposterous, leaving us with the temptation to dismiss them out of hand as some irrelevant jetsam of science, about as useful as the concept of the body humors of an earlier time. The confusion and psychological disarray we feel on first encountering these new concepts engenders an impulse to "hang it all" and retreat to where we *know* how things behave.

Knowledge of Death through Knowledge of Life

Perhaps there exist fresh approaches to these difficult new concepts that can clear our confusion. One such approach is to ask just what is it that makes human bodies special, what is it that sets them apart in the world. In other words, what is *life*? What is the quality whereby we separate ourselves from the nonliving part of the universe? What is it that is extinguished when we die, converting our bodies to the nonliving realm from which we presume they originated? An understanding of the quality of life must surely help us in our task of understanding the meaning of time and death.

What is life? Our musings over what constitutes death are bound to be premature and preliminary unless we can know what it is that death annuls, what it is that ceases to be when death occurs.

Death, we say, is the end of *something*; and this something has been the grail of both philosopher and scientist through the ages. No attempts to analyze the life quality have ever proved completely satisfactory to either scientists *or* philosophers. Earlier we saw how the mind-body problem is the crux of the question, the conundrum of how apparently lifeless matter combines in astonishing complexity to produce conscious life.

Because we have failed historically to understand what life is, it is tempting to think that perhaps we have erred in ways that are not subtle, but in massive and flagrant ways, ways which involve misperceptions of the behavior of the universe itself. We perhaps are simply out of touch, groping in nature with crude tools that are inadequate for the task. Just as we learned that our Newtonian common sense approach to understanding nature was discrepant with the revelations of quantum theory and relativity, we may too learn that revolutionary approaches to the question of life will be necessary before we can approach a proper understanding.

During the early period of this century when the foundations of quantum theory and relativity were being fashioned, a student was delivering a paper in which he was attempting to elaborate a novel and difficult idea. His listeners seemed perplexed with his explanation, and in frustration he turned to Professor Niels Bohr who was in the audience and asked, "Do you think this idea is crazy?" Professor Bohr replied, "Yes, but I do not think it is crazy enough."

Perhaps our attempts to understand the relation of the quality of lifeless matter to life itself have failed for the reason that they, too, are not crazy enough. It is not that embarking on a course of insanity will bring us nearer to solutions, but simply that a departure from common sense assumptions about the nature of life may be required.

Novel attempts are being made. The physicist Evan Harris Walker has suggested that the basic "unit" of consciousness is the quantum itself. The molecular biologist Delbrück has also put forward, as we noticed, the proposal that the life quality is possessed by fundamental organizational units of living creatures, such as atoms and molecules themselves.

Are these proposals an emergence of vitalism in a pseudoscientific dress? Are they desperate attempts to find meaning where none exists? We should be cautious in our criticisms, recalling Bohr's defense of craziness as a fruitful quality of scientific conjecture.

Creative attempts to understand the life quality are necessary steps we must take before we can understand the process of death, for the meaning of death demands an understanding of what life is. We must be adventuresome; and we can be certain that adherence only to common sense in these attempts will lead us in circles. The physicist Freeman Dyson's words will serve us well: "For the idea which at first glance does not seem crazy, there is no hope."

The strategy of attempting an understanding of death through a proper comprehension of the life quality is logically attractive, but it is a goal not easily met. For most of us, the tasks of deciphering life *and* death seem equally hopeless. How can we improve on the record of failure of all the brilliant scientists and philosophers who have ever lived? The questions remain unanswered. Why?

The answers to questions of life have always eluded us because we always deface the picture of the world before we begin to probe it. We unknowingly smudge the canvas, then wonder why we cannot bring it into focus. We seek clear visions in clouded places. How do we commit these errors? By judging the world to be other than it is. Birth, life, and death are events occurring in nature, whose spatio-temporal characteristics we are only dimly beginning to see. We shall never clearly understand these great questions until we comprehend the quintessential spacetime nature of the world in which they occur, and from which they cannot be extracted. In ignoring the new physical picture of the world, we are dooming ourselves to the same frustrations and failures of the questioners who have come before us. A distorted reality reveals distorted answers.

HEALTH AND THE EXPERIENCE OF SPACETIME

It is the contention of this book that a truer image of the world will give a truer description of events occurring in it, such as birth, life, and death. Furthermore, the meaning of certain life qualities that are our concern—such as health and disease—can only be comprehended through a view in which modern physical definitions of time, space, and matter are properly regarded.

What happens to our health when we actually begin to conceptualize the world in a new way? When we step beyond a linear time, when we cease to partition the world into past, present, and future events, it is *not* axiomatic that we begin automatically to experience heightened health. I shall relate a clinical example that I hope will illustrate the problems which sometimes occur.

Janet was a twenty-eight year old patient who came for a diagnostic evaluation because of complaints of anxiety, depression, and "spells." She had for four years experienced episodic weakness, sensations of flushing and heat, and palpitations. These were not trivial symptoms: twice she had automobile accidents associated with the spells.

Quite appropriately, she had been investigated by neurological specialists. No evidence could be adduced for any specific neurological disorder. Thereafter she saw various other specialists, including an internist and a cardiologist, with similar negative findings. Eventually she came under the care of a family physician who felt that the entire syndrome was the result of "nerves." This conclusion seemed reasonable enough, especially in view of the extensive evaluations that had preceded his diagnosis. By this time she was extraordinarily depressed, not sleeping, and desperate. She was given an antidepressant medication for this problem, which in her had a paradoxical effect: it made her even more anxious and depressed.

She came to me for yet another diagnostic endeavor, tearful and upset. It was clear why her previous physician had concluded that she had a bad case of "nerves." However, on probing her history with her, a curious story emerged. She decided, she said, to reveal these events finally out of frustration, thinking they might have some relevance to her illness. Never before had she told a physician these things, fearful that they might think she was "crazy."

She described how she, since the age of five, had experienced abilities that are commonly termed psychic. She could predict events before they occurred—events that usually related to significant illness in loved ones, or to tragic happenings. She developed by the age of twelve the capacity to abolish the sensation of pain in her body. Cuts, scrapes, and visits to the dentist were dealt with in this fashion. She shared this special knowledge only with her mother, who was forever urging her to "give up" these things, fearful that no good would come of them.

She was fairly comfortable with these unusual talents until her early twenties, when she began to see them as a burden, even as a menace. She could not turn them off. Events could be seen into the future, and distant happenings could be visualized periodically. She began to be very disturbed by these phenomena, and her symptom complex gradually began to develop.

Trying to channel her abilities in some useful direction, she became employed by a local police force, where she was informally relied upon to apprehend critical information. She was particularly disturbed when she had the vivid experience of "seeing" the drowning of an infant in an apartment complex—one hour before it occurred. She informed the police officers that the event would occur (by this time they had begun to take her predictions seriously), but that her vision was incomplete: she was unable to specify which apartment was involved. The discovery by the police one hour later of the actual event left her shaken. Shortly thereafter her physical symptoms became pronounced.

Janet's experience of space and time were extraordinary. For her, neither space nor time were bounded. They did not stay put. She had an unexplainable sense of distant happenings—of happenings distant both spatially and temporally. She could violate the presumed unidirectional flow of a linear time at will. Time for her was no river, unless we are to say that it was a most peculiar river, simultaneously flowing both forward into the future and backward into the past.

Persons like Janet are by no means rare. Like her, many of them tend to resist revealing their unusual abilities. Janet's attitude was characteristic of many such persons: they fear being thought mad. And frequently the internal tension resulting from living in a sociocultural setting that roundly judges visions as hallucinations creates ill health. Psyche and soma cease to function harmoniously and the psychic pays the price for his/her unusual abilities with physical malfunction. Janet was cautious, perhaps wise. She knew the potential danger in being frank and open with her physicians, in spite of asking for their help. She concealed vital clinical information for fear of being thought insane.

Janet's physical examination was entirely normal. No other diagnostic studies seemed necessary. Instead of using more medication, she was invited to learn some techniques through biofeedback therapy to control her sensations of palpitations, anxiety, and panic. As she quickly learned these skills, she began to feel once again at one with her body. She was a "natural" at learning biofeedback techniques, having no trouble whatsoever in entering the states of deep relaxation where rapid mastery of these skills occurs. She found that the experiential spacetime dimensions she entered in biofeedback therapy were common to those she had experienced during meditation years earlier. She saw similarities between these dimensions and her precognitive skills. She eliminated her symptoms, and remains asymptomatic as of this writing. Her psychic experiences continue to occur as frequently as before, but they no longer frighten her. She has come to view them as a natural expression of her particular resonance with the world. She is well, in spacetime.

If continual participation in traditional linear time can result in a chronic sense of anxiety and urgency, leading to various types of "hurry sickness," it should also be obvious from Janet's case that an unenlightened entry into spacetime—the experience of a nonlinear time experience and an unbounded space—are no guarantors of health. It was not until Janet encountered validation of her own construction of reality that her health improved. Eventually she was able to use her experiential mode of spacetime to the advantage of her own health. It was not until she stepped outside the traditional mode of effecting positive health change, that of using drugs and relying on professional healers to *make* her healthy, that she was able to effect a cure. She had been attempting to do the impossible: to function as a patient in someone else's world construct, while maintaining a spatial and temporal perspective that was entirely different from the doctors'. Sensing the rightness and validity of her own sense of reality, she was able to become her own physician. She healed herself.

How can we comprehend the spacetime model of health? Are special qualities of intellect and perception required? Almost certainly this is not the case. I am certain that the prevailing belief that an understanding of the modern idea of spacetime is possible only for the scientific specialist with mathematical expertise is wrong. Without thinking about it, all of us use this mode of perception frequently.

Consider what goes on in our consciousness when we use our faculty of imagination. We visualize—we make pictures in the mind of something occurring. Although we stand apart from what we are visualizing as we see it happening in our consciousness, we may be completely drawn into it if the visualization is particularly vivid. However, sometimes (and perhaps most times) we sense a distance from the image we are making. We *know* we are imagining, and thus feel as if we are looking on.

There is a curious quality of this process which has to do with our time sense. The sense of time that we ordinarily have, that of a flowing, linear process comprised of a past, present, and future, seems suspended in moments of imagination. These pictures in the mind change as events unfold, yet they do not convey to us the sense of time flow. In the imagery process there is no sense of time urgency. Time seems suspended, although events clearly "happen" in the image itself.

We ordinarily think this is impossible. Anything that "happens" must involve a linear experience of time. How can things happen outside of time?

This quality of time that we experience in the imaging process is strongly similar to the modern description of time given by the British mathematician-physicist P.C.W. Davies, which we have already examined. Davies contends that a flowing time is not a quality of the world itself, but is a psychological illusion, albeit a mysterious and persistent one. Nowhere in modern physics, Davies contends, must one postulate a flowing time of past, present, and future to account for the findings of modern physical science.

Time Symmetry and Asymmetry

As Davies explains, the understanding of *symmetric* versus *asymmetric* physical processes is a key to understanding the modern view of time.[17] A symmetric process is one which, if viewed forward or backward, could not be distinguished. An example is the movement of a uniform process such as a swinging pendulum. Although minute variations in the uniformity of the pendulum's motion occur, they are not apparent to the naked eye. If a movie of such a phenomenon were run forward or backward, we could not tell one direction from the other.

Most occurrences in nature are not of this sort, however. We *can* tell if most happenings are moving forward or backward. The growth of plants and animals clearly can be distinguished from youth to old age. We never see flowering plants going backwards to form sprouting seeds, nor do we ever see human beings growing younger. Things in nature, for the most part, proceed one-way. These processes are called asymmetric. They have a backwardness and a forwardness to them which we have little trouble distinguishing.

Suppose we were to make a movie of a person growing older. We now cut up the movie into its individual segments and lay them in a stack. Even though we have dismantled the movie in this way, the stack itself still possesses "time asymmetry." We still have a collection of events that have a one-wayness to them. Yet there is *nothing* intrinsic to the stack of still frames, Davies tells us, nor in the assembled movie itself, which is the equivalent of flowing time. The sensation of a flowing time occurs when we witness the unfolding of asymmetric processes in nature, as in the movie of the aging person.

It is the process of time *asymmetry* and not time *flow* which is intrinsic to nature. The sensation of time flow belongs to the mind, and not to nature itself.

Time and Imagery

In the process of imagery we step outside the sensation of a flowing time, and we view asymmetric occurrences in the mental pictures that we make. The sense of time involved reminds us of the physicist's statement: events in nature do not happen, they simply are.

Who has never imagined? Who has never daydreamed or let the mind wander? This kind of mental exercise is surely found in all thinking humans. For this reason the ability to comprehend the modern view of time is, I feel, a faculty common to all persons. It is no less a part of our sensory capacities than touch, hearing, and sight.

Time and Illness

We are coming to the understanding in medicine that some diseases are the result of a disorder of time perception. As we have observed several times in this book, the sense of time urgency is associated with a sobering variety of physical problems. For example, anxiety, stress, and tension figure into the development of atherosclerotic heart disease and hypertension, the two most common causes of death in our society.

The chronic misjudgment of the nature of time should be seen for what it really is: chronic disease itself. It is a silent process, but for many of us an inexorable one leading to disease which can be fatal. We do not ordinarily judge it in these terms, of course, and too frequently ascribe our sense of time urgency to "nerves." Having misjudged the cause of our distress, we misjudge the solutions—tranquilizers and alcohol are too often the most commonly trusted antidotes.

Time and Therapy

Time urgency has been recognized by an increasing number of persons in medicine, however, for the disease it is. Promising treatments are evolving. It is interesting to observe that most of these newer methods of treating "hurry sickness" and time urgency—biofeedback, relaxation, and meditative techniques—lure the subject in very subtle ways into a new way of perceiving time. They ask the patient to step out of a chronic, habitual way of sensing time as an inexorable flowing process into an alternative mode of time perception. They ask the patient to "stop" time. They invite him into the realm of spacetime, although this invitation is never explicit.

Every single method in current use to teach patients these skills relies on some form of mental imagery. Visualization techniques abound. Patients learn to relax by making pictures in the mind. The skillful therapist learns to employ images in individual ways, ways that are most effective for a particular subject. But regardless of what particular image is used on any given subject, the process involved in making the mental image is the same: the subject is stepping outside a flowing time into a static time wherein he sees time-asymmetric events (the image) occurring. If practiced regularly these techniques are extremely effective in helping patients adapt to a way of being in which time is judged in ordinary waking consciousness as less urgent, less hectic, and less anxiety-provoking.

Most persons learn these skills easily and they come to enjoy the imagery process. Why? The new mode of time perception feels good. To be forever bogged down in a sense of time urgency is defeating. Stress and anxiety for most of us are unbearable without periodic alleviation. Thus, to involve oneself in a new mode of time perception is to experience good feelings.

We have seen earlier that participation in the states of consciousness that we typify as being serene, calm, and relaxed generate physiological changes that can be measured. The changes that occur are as real as those produced by any drug. Changes in hormonal levels in the blood, variations in heart rate and blood pressure, and changes in levels of muscle tension and blood flow to certain regions of the body accompany a subject's imagery efforts. Thus, since the processes of imagery and visualization are involved in these states, we can begin to see these processes as potent therapeutic agents. They are "medicine" in the truest sense, as real as drugs and surgical procedures.

How do these techniques work? Some observers believe that the actual content of the image is crucial to what changes follow in the body. For example, if one wishes to make one's hands warm (a valuable strategy for persons with migraine headache or Raynaud's disease), one thinks of a wonderfully warm wool blanket wrapped around the hand, or of warming the hands in front of a roaring fire. Yet the actual picture that one forms in the mind is probably not as important as we might think. Many persons can develop the ability to increase the temperature of their hands quite skillfully no matter what image they make—even using visualizations of white, frozen hands held in ice water.

How is this possible? Regardless of the image that is made, the subjects do at least one thing similarly: they are exchanging their usual sense of time perception for one in which time ceases to flow. They are witnessing time-asymmetric events, whether the image is that of holding the hands before a fire or immersing them in ice water. They are seeing events unfold in their imagination, but they have ceased to place them in a flowing time. Even though the events are sequentially changing, they are not happening in the usual linear sense; they simply are.

This perspective annuls the psychological experience of linear time. The subject is physiologically calm as well as psychologically serene. And in most cases the physiological response that accompanies this experience of time is that the hands warm, regardless of the image.

Viewed from this persepective all the current relaxation techniques—biofeedback, autogenic therapy, transcendental meditation, progressive relaxation, etc.—are time therapies. They invoke a specific psychological mode with regard to time perception.

A close examination of meditation techniques used through the ages reveals that they resonate with a modern view of time and space. There are endless examples of how time can be annulled as one meditates. One Buddhist technique is to imagine that one is meditating sitting by a river. As distracting thoughts enter, disturbing the clarity of mind, the meditator is asked to visualize the cluttering thought as a log far upstream, just coming into view. The attention remains focused on the log as it floats slowly downstream, finally disappearing out of sight. In this imagery process, distracting thoughts are transformed into a process that is witnessed as a time-asymmetric event which gently unfolds in the mind. One becomes unaware of a linear time flow while observing this phenomenon, for the observer has stepped outside of time. He has stopped time. He has calmed the mind.

Another technique offered to novices to still the mind and neutralize interfering thoughts is to imagine that with each outflow of the breath a number descends into the body, coming to rest at the bottom of the stomach. "One," "two," "three," etc., are seen lying in a pile, gently resting. At the end of some arbitrary sequence—perhaps eight to ten breaths—the process begins again. This simple technique has a surprising and subtle effect. If one were merely to count one's breaths he would likely be drawn into a sense of a linear time as a result of counting a linear sequence of numbers. But the imagery process destroys this. The numbers, although counted linearly, are lying in a heap, one on top of others. They seem to go nowhere. They are just numbers and numbers alone, not part of the temporal sequence that we sense when counting sequentially. They are like a movie strip which is cut into individual clips and stacked one on top of the other. The stack possesses time asymmetry, but gone is any property of time flow. The stack of numbers, thus, aids the meditator in escaping the linear time of ordinary awareness. By helping the meditator step into spacetime, the sensations of urgency that result from the comprehension of linear time are defused. The mind is centered and the meditation becomes more powerful.

Many pastimes, hobbies, and diversions share this capacity to "kill time," and frequently those who engage in them are said to be "killing time." This is an accurate description of the felt changes in time flow. In doing something repetitive—for example, needlepoint, where repetitive stitches follow one on the other—one can step out of time into a complete absorption in the project. Although the stitches form a sequence, each stitch can have its own "is-ness." It can escape its position in sequence, and experientially seems to bear no strong temporal association to the stitch that came before it or that comes after it. Each stitch stands on its own. The preoccupied needlepointer indeed "kills time," having stepped into the nonflowing realm of spacetime through total absorption in his/her work.

Time and Athletic Achievement

Many athletes have described experiences of time that resemble nonlinear, nonflowing spacetime. In his remarkable book, *The Ultimate Athlete*, George Leonard chronicles many nonordinary experiences of time. He says,

> Thousands of such events occur every day, in sandlots and city streets and giant stadiums. For the most part, they are unreported and thus only faintly experienced. The culture goes on distracting itself with extravagant spectator events and consumer products and restless travel, all the while ignoring the vast riches that lie as close to us as our own experience. These riches are by no means limited to the field of sports, but are especially abundant there. The intensity of the experience, the intricacy of the relationships, the total involvement of body and senses, all come together in sports to create the preconditions for those extraordinary events that the culture calls "paranormal" or "mystical."[18]

One of the most celebrated descriptions of an experiential immersion in spacetime is given by ex-San Francisco 49er quarterback John Brodie. In an interview with Michael Murphy, founder of Esalen Institute, Brodie described this nonordinary way of perceiving space and time.

> MURPHY: Can you give me some examples of the aspects that usually go unrecorded, some examples of the game's psychological side or what you call "energy flows?"

> BRODIE: Often, in the heat and excitement of a game, a player's perception and coordination will improve dramatically. At times, and with increasing frequency now, I experience a kind of clarity that I've never seen adequately described in a football story. *Sometimes, for example, time seems to slow way down, in an uncanny way, as if everyone were moving in slow motion. It seems as if I have all the time in the world* to watch the receivers run their patterns and yet I know the defensive line is coming at me just as fast as ever. I know perfectly well how hard and fast those guys are coming and yet *the whole thing seems like a movie or dance in slow motion.* It's beautiful.[19] [Emphasis added.]

In 1972 Duane Thomas, then a running back for the Dallas Cowboys, led his team to a Superbowl championship. Thomas later described his spectacular ability in ways that sound almost mystical. He spoke of his ability to see whole patterns develop in slow motion. He could sense the complex motion around him with a sense of time that allowed him to pick and choose one option over another.

In 1973 one of the most unheralded woman athletes of our time, Beverly Johnson, accomplished the first all-woman's ascent of one of the most formidable formations of granite in the world—El Capitan in Yosemite Valley—with Sibylle Hechtel. Five years later she completed the first (and to date, the only) solo woman's climb of El Cap. A television crew was waiting for her as she finished. In an interview, which was aired nationwide, a newsman asked her what she was thinking during the long arduous hours spent scaling the vertical rock. She replied that she kept telling herself, "How do you eat an elephant? One bite at a time."

One bite at a time. Beverly Johnson's description is a "time strategy" employed by many athletes. Long distance runners frequently describe "staying in the moment," remaining centered in the present, focusing their attention on what is happening *now*, not becoming preoccupied about the grueling distances lying ahead. "One bite at a time" and "staying in the moment" take one out of a linear struggle to climb a mountain or complete a marathon, and for the athlete diminishes the anxiety and energy expenditure which would only be increased by concentrating on "how much farther do I have to go?"

Such time strategies seem to divide time into nonflowing, nonlinear segments in which events do not happen in the usual sense, but simply are. This experience of time closely resembles the time of the mystic or the meditator. It also resembles the spacetime description of the modern physicist. This experience of time recognizes an *asymmetry* of time in which a direction of events can be distinguished as they unfold, but that denies any flowing quality of time itself.

Descriptions by athletes of such events abound. These are common, and are not purely the experiential province of the professional athlete. The time-defying total absorption of the backyard athlete or the "runner's high" of the professional marathon runner may be similar in origin. These experiences suggest that an alternative to the ordinary means of experiencing space and time lies within all of us.

One of the most provocative speculations about high achievement in athletics comes from Pat Toomay, who spent several years with the Dallas Cowboys as a defensive end. Toomay is an exceptional athlete and an eloquent one at that, having given some quite irreverent but penetrating descriptions of professional football.[20] He has a fascination in probing those rare moments in the lives of most athletes when everything functions perfectly—knowing the flow of a play before it develops, where the ball carrier will run, where the ball will be thrown before it is released. In baseball, the ball and bat become one: the batter can't miss. For the pitcher, the curve ball breaks perfectly, the fast ball is alive, and hitters are retired in effortless sequence. For the basketball player the ball and the net form an arc of oneness from the moment of the ball's release. In all these moments there is an unexplainable and ineffable sense of perfection and flow.

Toomay proposes a model for such high achievement which is based on the physicist David Bohm's idea of the implicate and explicate order (see Part III, Chapter 5). It is the implicate order that is unseen and undefinable, which enfolds and underlies all. Its qualities are oneness, unity, perfection. The explicate order, on the other hand, is the multifaceted and nonharmonious world of the senses, the world of the ordinary and everyday. Toomay suggests that moments of protracted perfection in athletic achievement occur when one transcends the explicate level and participates in the concatenated, unitary perfection of the implicate domain. In this state, perfection in perception and execution for the athlete are less a matter of *doing*, and more a matter of *being*.

It is well known that most children have a highly developed capacity for total absorption in a task. In certain situations children can use this ability therapeutically. To illustrate, I shall share the story of Mark, a six-year-old boy who was referred to my biofeedback laboratory for treatment of hyperactivity. Hyperactive children are a literal embodiment of "hurry sickness." They cannot be still for very long. Their constant activity is disconcerting for their parents and peers. Because they are constantly in motion they cannot focus their attention. Although they are usually intelligent they may be judged to be slow intellectually, for it is only with great difficulty that they can stay "on track" long enough to complete a task. Like most children, Mark learned to master biofeedback techniques very easily. (Children don't know that humans supposedly cannot control such things as heart rate, blood pressure, muscle tension, and skin temperature!) He was intrigued by his accomplishments and seemed to make the logical connection between being calm, still, and in control of his body, and being successful while working with the biofeedback instruments. Whereas he said he ordinarily felt "all nervous inside" most of the time, he ceased to feel that way when he was relaxed and performing well in biofeedback sessions. A marked change in his behavior became apparent, both at home and at school. Not only did his performance at school change, his relationships with his parents and peers improved.

After a biofeedback session the biofeedback therapist asked, "Mark, what happened to all the nervousness inside you?" He replied, "It's gone now. When I feel that way I just let it go out through my big toes!" With the magnificent imagery that seems natural for most children, he went on to describe how he would imagine the nervousness as a substance which he released through the tips of his big toes. Why the toes? "Because they're in my shoes, and nobody else can see me do it!" he replied.

Mark's image was typical of the imagery process in general. He distanced himself from the event he was seeing. His image then evolved in his imagination as a time-asymmetric event while he stood outside time, looking on. This time therapy, this imagery, was effective in neutralizing his own particular hurry sickness, hyperactivity.

Monica was a patient who came for treatment for severe pain in the left side of her neck. Her pain began with a skiing accident in which she injured her left shoulder. The shoulder injury healed, but she was left with recurrent pain due to spasm of the trapezius and paracervical muscles, key muscles that involve the shoulder and neck region. Invariably she would develop a generalized tension headache after the neck and shoulder pain had persisted for several hours. A thorough evaluation by her orthopedist and neurologist had revealed no specific abnormality. Loathing pain medication, she came seeking relief through biofeedback therapy, hoping to manage her problem by her own devices.

There are a variety of images that can be used effectively in manipulating the sensation of pain. The technique which Monica used to abort her discomfort was to visualize the location of her pain as a small glowing red ball.[21] She would focus as intensely as possible on this image, and when it was extremely vivid she would cause the ball to begin to move, ever so slowly, outside her body. She would center the ball about six feet in front of her. Then this small red ball of pain, glowing intensely, would begin to grow. It would enlarge to the size of a basketball, hovering in space. Moreover, it was suspended in time. Monica's description of this state was that time "stood still." Although events were "still going on," such as the red ball continuing to shimmer, time had ceased to flow. This was the time of spacetime.

Time-asymmetric events continued to happen—the ball continued to glow, and she would make it change colors. As it changed eventually to white, it ceased to shimmer and it began to shrink. When it became its original size she placed it back in the body at the original site of the pain. At the conclusion of this imagery sequence during which she learned to keep her muscle tension at extremely low levels as measured by the biofeedback apparatus, the pain would be markedly diminished or gone entirely. Monica's entry into the realm of spacetime was for her a therapeutic journey. In a few weeks her pain ceased to recur.

In discussing man's concept of time in Part II, we saw how the perception of pain was allied to our perception of time. For the person experiencing pain, time drags. Minutes seem like hours. But time never *stops* perceptually; it flows inexorably, and ever so slowly, when we hurt.

Clinical experience suggests that a key to manipulating pain perception—as Monica's descriptions suggest—is in *stopping* time.

The physician, nurse, or therapist who aids the patient in pain is more than a dispenser of analgesics. He can be a guide. He can be one who shows the sufferer the way through the corridors of time to the still point where time ceases to flow, and where pain abates. And the patient, the suffering patient—how can we avoid the conclusion?—becomes a time traveler.

The new physical description of time is grist for everyman's mill, as the above clinical cases illustrate. The relevance of the new definition of time goes beyond the physics laboratory to impact on the lives of anyone who suffers from a time-dependent disorder, or hurry sickness—which, unfortunately, includes almost all of us.

ILLNESS AND THE EXPERIENCE OF SPACETIME

How might a spacetime model of health appear to one who is sick? How would one begin to implement these views while actually suffering from illness?

In thinking about these questions it is wise to remember a fact that is frequently forgotten when we are healthy: there is something utterly oppressive about being sick. It is a state of being so far removed from ordinary experience that the well cannot properly speak of it.

This fact became apparent when I recently found myself suffering from a viral upper respiratory illness, which is the medical term for the common cold. I have been blessed with excellent health and did not take well to having a cold, no matter how "common" it was. The headache, malaise, sore throat, and cough completely unbalanced me. I became depressed about not being well. As aches and fever developed my mind ran to thoughts of more serious maladies— what is it I *really* am suffering from? What is this illness turning into? I could not do my work I felt so bad. Finally I went to bed, telling myself it was time to retreat, to cease struggling and let the body's wisdom prevail. I thought of advice I had given sick patients before, and *none* of it came as any comfort. For two days I was more than physically miserable; psychologically I was helpless.

My experience was enlightening. What, I asked, can persons who are actually in the throes of illness do to get better? Are we as therapists fooling ourselves to assume that, in addition to taking the medicines we give them, sick patients have the capacity to initiate mind-body events that might act in healing ways? If the common cold wreaks so deadly an effect on one's spirit, what does the patient with a chronic disease experience? At least I could assume that my illness was self-limiting and would be over in a matter of days. I wasn't faced with the knowledge that I was incurably sick, that my illness would lead to my death.

I have no sure answers as to what self-healing capacities are actually possible for sick patients, for persons who *feel* ill with mind *and* body. But I have come to believe that the actual experience of the world—the spacetime construction we call reality—is distorted through being ill. It is drastically different from the construction we make when we feel well. Concepts of time duration change remarkably: time slows; we feel we have been sick forever, that our illness shall never end. The experience of our place in the world changes. When we are ill we feel separated and isolated from those who are well. We sense a profound difference in our "space quality"—the sense of relatedness and connectedness with all else evaporates and we feel closed in, and fragmented from those around us.

When we are sick we become a Newtonian object: a bit-piece stranded in a flowing time.

Can we develop, even when ill, a modern spacetime sense? Can we maintain a clarity of vision that reveals to us our oneness in time and space with all else? Records tell us that this awareness *does* come at certain stages of illness, breaking through like the sun on a cloudy day. This vision is common, for instance, in the survivors of near-death experiences. At least the vision is *possible*.

Moreover, can we help our patients and our sick friends toward this comforting vision? This is a task for the medicine of the future. It is a task that should be viewed, in my estimation, with the utmost priority, since its successful implementation would strike at the most burdensome aspect of being sick: that of isolation, separation, and the fear of death.

A spacetime view of the healing process suggests a theoretical framework to begin this task. After all, as we have seen, the new view compels us to observe that it is not only disease that can be spread, but health as well. Health, as well as illness, is seen as *process* in the new model. It is a field phenomenon, an event spread in spacetime that goes beyond individual bodies. As such, the healing message from the well to the sick *can* get through, can penetrate to the isolation and sense of morbid aloneness that is part of the felt experience of being sick. Moreover, in the new model this information is transmitted obligatorily. We need not decide whether we *can* conceivably help sick patients and friends. The matter simply is not ours to decide.

The most hideous aspects of illness are the distortions in space-time that sick persons experience. These distortions accentuate pain, suffering, and anguish. The spacetime view of health and disease tells us that a vital part of the goal of every therapist is to help the sick person toward a reordering of his world view. We must help him realize that he is a *process* in spacetime, not an isolated entity who is fragmented from the world of the healthy and who is adrift in flowing time, moving slowly toward extermination.

To the extent that we accomplish this task we are healers.

SPACE AND TIME AS EXPERIENCE: WHY THE DISCONTINUITY?

The attempt to begin to see space and time in a new way is no easy task. It is exceedingly difficult to imagine a static time, a time that does not flow. It is not easy to get a grasp on the time of spacetime, the continuum in which events do not happen but simply are. We are frustrated in trying to experience the assertion of modern physics that space and time are coupled; that we cannot experience one without experiencing the other; that we cannot know time and space singly. It is so obvious that we *do* experience them singly.

A paradox thus arises: if time and space are indeed united experientially, why do we have the persistent sensation of flowing time without having a similar sensation of a flowing space? We have patently dissimilar sensations of the two. Time flows experientially, but we see space as localized and static. There is simply no psychological sense of a flowing space. Space stays put; time does not. If these qualities of nature are indeed united as modern physics assures us, then why are they so qualitatively dissociated in our experience?

Perhaps our sensations of space and time differ in quality for a good reason—a reason which in the language of evolutionary biology is the best reason of all: survival. It is likely that in our evolutionary history we developed ways of judging space and time which were contributory to our own survival.

Perhaps in the course of our evolution we developed *many* ways of sensing and judging space and time. Which ones would have survived to the present day? Those ways that favored the survival of the individual organism through the perpetuation, by means of procreation, of his genetic packet. These types of sense perception would have been more durable for the single reason that they had greater survival value. And if a particular way of judging space and time helped an organism survive and procreate, this method of judging space and time survived along with the organism, encoded in its internal genetic program. These were survival skills, valuable in the same way that an eye or ear, or the ability to fly or run fast were valuable. They lent an edge in the struggle for survival.

Let us consider that a psychological experience that results from the sensation of flowing time is the sense of *urgency*—time is moving, things are imminent, something is about to happen. In a flowing time we *anticipate* the occurrence of events. In this flow of events I act to insure my own survival, I behave in certain ways to stay alive. A sense of urgency promotes preparation—for killing and hunting, for gathering and planting. The chance to slay this bison for food, for survival, may pass unless I act now. Thus it seems likely that the physical survival of our ancestors was favored by a sense of passing time and urgency even though, as we have seen, the time embodied in primitive culture, myth and tradition is nondurational in nature (part II, chapter 3). It is not clear that a sensation of time as singularly static would have had as great a survival advantage.

The sensation of a static space may similarly have favored survival. A nonmoving static space provided a background on which to act. Indeed, we find it hard to imagine space in any other way. If we perceived space in a way in which it seemed flowing and nonstatic, the result would be chaotic—a fact which is immediately apparent to anyone suffering from vertigo, an irksome clinical problem in which space does move. For the vertiginous patient space refuses to stand still, but whirls round and round. A space always on the move would have surely been as dangerous for our predecessors as it is for us, for in it it is difficult to act in precise, sure ways. Survival hardly seems possible in a moving world.

Thus, if we were to have designed a type of temporal and spatial mode of perception for our ancestors to aid them in their evolutionary ascent, we would likely have chosen the ones that have come down to us: those of a flowing time and a static space.

Viewed in an evolutionary context, our struggle in apprehending what the modern physical definition of spacetime is all about may reflect our biological heritage. Our view of space and time is not a matter of intelligence, of figuring things out. Were we to actually perceive space and time any other way than we do, we would probably not be here to do any perceiving at all. We would likely not have survived as a species.

Our way of experiencing space and time, thus, has likely facilitated our evolutionary ascendency. We perhaps owe our very existence to it. But this mode of perception comes with no guarantee that we perceive the world around us *accurately*. We are not assured that we perceive space and time correctly, only *naturally*—i.e., our perceptions reflect our own nature. When we struggle with the vagaries of the new concepts of spacetime, we should consider that it is our very *nature* to not understand. Something within us resists these new ideas.

"Understanding" Spacetime

A common reaction among those who first encounter the definitions of spacetime is to feel defeated. "I'm just not smart enough to understand; these concepts are for physicists and mathematicians." This feeling, which is almost reflexive, is surely inappropriate, for there is yet *no good evidence that the ability to conceptualize the modern idea of spacetime has anything to do with intelligence*. These ideas are more firmly lodged in the nonrational and intuitive part of us than in our verbal, rational self. Indeed, intellectualization may be an impediment to understanding spacetime, so removed are these ideas from common sense and logic.

This is a crucial point. There are those who reject any mention of the modern physical ideas of spacetime out of an assumption that they can only be understood by gifted scientists. Nothing could be farther from the truth. The quintessence of these ideas is ancient. The central expressions of special relativity had been worked out descriptively in oriental cultures thousands of years before Einstein's discoveries.[22] Entire cultures, as we have seen in our discussion of attitudes toward time in Part II, live comfortably and efficiently with the idea of a nonflowing time. Perhaps without exception the cultures that have most easily embraced these ideas have done so without any reliance on mathematics, but on intuition and nonrational modes of thought.

The modern notion of spacetime is not necessarily shrouded in undecipherable mathematics and physicalistic jargon. The language of science is not necessary for an appreciation of the essential meaning of the new definitions of space and time. Not only is this evident from the cultural record as we have observed, it is obvious from the statements of Einstein himself; he claimed to have been led initially to his descriptions not by breakthroughs of logical reasoning but by an inner certainty of the beauty and harmony lying at the heart of his theories. Einstein was describing intuition, not linear reasoning. It is this quality of the mind that has allowed whole cultures to apprehend spacetime prior to the modern era.

THE BIMODAL SENSE OF TIME AND SPACE

In spite of the fact that the sense of linear, flowing time may have survived as part of our biological nature because of its survival value, this is surely not the whole story. I believe there is survival value also in perceiving time in a static, nonflowing, nonlinear way. We have observed that a sense of urgency is associated with the perception of time as a linear process of past, present, and future. Our modern sense of this urgency is expressed by our feeling that there is not enough time. We are running out of it. For each of us the flowing river of time will run dry. This moving river translates for most of us into a moving treadmill on which we attempt to do more and more in less and less time. The price we pay is stress, tension, and anxiety.

There is considerable evidence, as we have seen in Part II, that the psychological effects of urgency—stress, anxiety, tension—do not stay in the psyche. They are translated into the body where they eventuate in physical ailments. The sense of urgency generates infirmity, disease, and death. So although this sense may have enabled us to behave in ways which facilitated survival at earlier stages in our evolutionary history, it surely is a two-edged sword which haunts us in modern times.

In contrast, the psychological sense that accompanies the perception of time as static and nonflowing is one of tranquility, serenity and peace. This is the time perception so well described in mystical and poetic literature. It is the sense of oneness of unity with all there is, the feeling of calm and release. It is the opposite of urgency.

Perhaps our evolutionary struggles left us with these two complementary modes of time perception for good reason. Both modes, functioning at different times in different circumstances, seem more contributory to survival than the presence of either alone. The urgent sense of time could be used to advantage in the hunt or in the fight. The sense of nonflowing time, of oneness and calm, could be called on for physiological restoration when the time for action has passed.

These two modes of time perception, working alternatively, make sense. They strike a balance not conferred by either alone. Perhaps we find within us these two capacities for sensing time because we needed one as much as the other.

CHAPTER TWO

HEALTH AND THE IMPLICATE ORDER

Everything is alive; what we call dead is an abstraction.

—DAVID BOHM[1]

WHAT IS HEALTH? There is no generally accepted answer, and one of the embarrassments of modern medicine is its inability to define exactly what it is that it promotes. Most persons tend to visualize health in negative terms—I *don't* have high blood pressure; I *don't* have an elevated blood cholesterol level; I *don't* have any obvious abnormalities on my physical examination. If my doctor can't find anything wrong, I *must* be healthy. This prevalent way of defining health does not, however, tell us what health is. And even the attempts to couch a definition of health in positive terms are flawed. The World Health Organization has defined health as the total physical, psychological, and spiritual well-being of an individual— yet these concepts are too vague to be very useful. They are not clear about what this well-being actually is, or what is meant by the proper function of the spiritual, physical, and psychological parts of ourselves.

We are helpless, even, to know clearly what is meant by disease. There seem to be no absolutes. Consider, for example, the disease called G-6-PD (glucose 6-phosphate dehydrogenase) deficiency. This disorder is caused by a genetic defect, resulting in an inadequate level of an enzyme that is necessary for the proper function of red blood cells. Under certain physiologically stressful situations, the deficiency of G-6-PD can lead to hemolysis, or actual dissolution of red blood cells. In certain areas of Africa this disease exists alongside sickle cell disease. It was discovered that natives having sickle cell disease were more resistant to its effects if they concomitantly had a *second* disease—G-6-PD deficiency.[2] In this instance, having one "disease" made one healthier—at least in the sense of conferring a relative resistence against another. But how can a true disease confer health? Disease, therefore, as well as health, defies easy definition.

Health, we ordinarily presume, somehow emanates from within us. This supposition reflects our reflexive way of attributing all characteristics such as health—and even life itself—to the behavior of our constituent molecules. Yet it is not entirely clear that this is so. David Bohm, in speaking of the living world, uses the example of a seed. Almost all of the matter and energy that emerge as the seed grows comes from the environment. "Who is to say," says Bohm, "that life was not immanent, even before the seed was planted?" And if life was immanent prior to the unfolding of the seed in its growing form, then the growing seed becomes more than the mere matter from which it began, as it takes on life itself. The growing seed has become more than the behavior of constituent molecules.

This life-energy, a term Bohm uses, belongs to the implicate order—that unseen totality that, says Bohm, underlies the external world of things and events (which belong to the explicate order; see page 104), and in which all things are grounded. Bohm has also proposed that health is the result of the harmonious interaction of all the analyzable parts which comprise the explicate order—the cells, tissues, organ systems, and the entire physical body—with the external environment. For Bohm, health is harmony, a quality ultimately grounded, as are all things, in the totality of the implicate order, and not in the particulate things themselves.

Implicit in Bohm's idea of the implicate order is the concept of flowing movement. All is flux and motion, says Bohm. This movement, this dynamism, is primary, and it is only in the explicate order of our ordinary sensory experience that we divide it, sundering the purity of motion into what eventually appear to be separate parts. These apparent divisions are, however, illusory, since the implicate flowing wholeness is unanalyzable and indivisible. The entire function of the explicate order, says Bohm, is to divide this world of oneness into parts. It is our common sense way of imposing order onto the world.

The essence of the nonobstructed, indivisible, flowing movement of the implicate order is harmony—which for Bohm is the meaning of health when this harmony is transcribed into the explicate world. But since pure flow and movement are imperfect in living organisms (breakdowns do occur), harmony—and thus health—is imperfect.

Things go wrong. The result is disease, a break in harmony. All living organisms change and die.

Seen in this way, health has a *kinetic* quality. There is an essential dynamism to it, grounded as it is in Bohm's proposed underlying implicate order, whose qualities of totality and movement have given rise to the term *holomovement*. Health is not static.

Yet how differently we ordinarily conceive health! For many of us our image of health is to be frozen at some stage of youth, whereafter things never change. We wish to capture this state in some crystallized, static form, and so remain healthy thereafter. But it cannot be so; for health is harmony, and harmony has no meaning without the fluid movement of interdependent parts. Like a stream that becomes stagnant when it ceases to flow, harmony and health turn into disease and death when stasis occurs. We return to the concept of the biodance, the endless streaming of the body-in-flux.

It is pathetic that we have lost touch with this kinetic quality of health. We view health as a frozen painting, a still collection of bits of information: electrocardiograms, blood pressure readings, laboratory values for liver enzymes, blood sugar, and kidney function. Even health facilities that overtly emphasize kinetic aspects of health care—the movement sports such as jogging—frequently convert the distance a client has run into a computerized number that indicates how many "points" he has achieved, so that the kinetic experience becomes translated into the stillness of numbers. The experience of health, its moving principle, is diminished. It is translated into dead data that, ironically, seems to reassure us more than the experience of health itself.

The harmony of moving parts implies more than the fluid interaction of the constituent parts of only the body itself. We saw in the chapter "The Biodance" that there are no bounded bodies. The concept of the body-as-parts is a contradiction in terms, since the "parts" themselves originated in the far-flung reaches of the universe and do not remain localized in any particulate way in the body once they find their way there. Furthermore they are related to all other parts in the universe, begging the meaning of "part." In its essential dynamism, the body reflects Bohm's holomovement. The harmony of body parts is the harmony of the parts of the universe, which are only momentarily localized in the form of a physical body.

Seen from this perspective, new views of body, harmony, and health emerge. Alan Watts once said that, just as an apple tree "apples," the universe "peoples." Perhaps Watts was poetically correct. We are a coalescence of the universe, however temporary—a fruit as Watts said, an explicate expression of an implicate harmony.

The idea of health as harmony, of harmony as a quality of perfectly moving parts, suggests, as we have seen, a kinetic quality of health. Is this merely an intellectual construct? Perhaps not. There seems to be plentiful evidence of this principle on the actual clinical level. For instance, our folk wisdom has it that inactivity begets illness. Elderly persons do poorly when they resign themselves to the rocking chair. To stay active is to promote health at all age levels. Although there is no clearcut evidence that physical activity actually prolongs life, few physicians (except those who are themselves sedentary) argue that it adds to the quality of life. These observations are epitomized in the maxim, "Use it or lose it!" Movement, then, may be a key in a coherent practical construct of health-as-harmony, since it seems to resonate through the level of actual day-to-day experience.

Perhaps part of our confusion as to what health actually is has been due to our dogged insistence that it must be seen in absolute terms. It, like disease, we say, has some primary status all its own. Again Bohm has implied that this may not be the case. As he observes,

> When you trace a particular absolute notion to what appears to be its logical conclusion, you find it to be identical to its opposite, and therefore the whole dualism collapses, as Hegel found. Reason first shows you that opposites pass into each other, then you discover that one opposite reflects the other, and finally you find that they are identical to each other—not really different at all. The two opposites may be first treated as independent, but you will find that each is the principle of movement of the other.[3]

At first this whole idea seems nonsensical. How can apparent absolutes blend into each other? However, science has shown us that this is possible. A century ago both space and time were considered absolutes; but the revelations of relativity have disclosed these "absolutes" to be otherwise. We have seen them melt into spacetime, such that one has become the "moving principle" of the other. Space cannot be perceived without a concomitant perception of time, and vice versa. The previous absolutes have merged.

The concept of opposites—the concept of *anything*—is allied to thought. For Bohm, pure thought is grounded in the implicate order, the domain of totality that encloses and enfolds all else. There is only *one* totality; thus, all in it are one. This includes thoughts, yes, of opposites. Bohm's proposal—and he is careful to qualify it as such—is that in the implicate domain all thoughts are ultimately one. In this territory, which is beyond analyzability, all opposites fuse.

Bohm further notes,

> . . . in music, and in visual and other sensory experience, the implicate order is primary in that the sense of flowing movement is experienced *before* we analyze it into the elements which express that movement or display it. You may listen to music and later break it down into notes which you can display either in imagination or on a piece of paper. Ultimately the same thing is true in vision, but we have become so used to fixing our attention on objects that we don't perceive this. We tend to see each object as fixed and separate, because we return to the same object (this tree, this rock) again and again. Therefore the flowing movement regenerates the same thing over and over, causing us to lose sight of the movement itself, except perhaps in the instances when we look at a stream or the sky, where there are no fixed objects to be focused on. But all our experience, including thought, begins in immediate awareness of this flowing movement.[4]

There are moments in which all of us experience the harmony of the movement we call life. These are transcendent or "peak" experiences in which we may forget not only our self-as-object, but the world-as-object, becoming one with the experience itself. Space and time are perceived at such moments in nonordinary ways. Spatially, we cease to distinguish ourselves as floating in a sea of space adrift with other objects; and temporally, time ceases to flow in a linear way. These are moments of implicate awareness.

These are also times of health, in the sense that they are experiences of perfect harmony. Yet these moments invariably change, and as they do our attention is drawn to the nonharmonious events that follow. To some of these ensuing events in life, if they are sufficiently disruptive, we attach the term "disease." We make these distinctions just as naturally as we analyze a flowing Bach fugue into its separate notes after losing ourselves in the initial hearing of it. And our repetitious fixation on such nonharmonious events creates our belief that they have some primary status, forgetting that we have abstracted them from the wholeness of the experience. The flowing harmony of experience becomes rarer as we carve those genuine moments into bit-events.

Yet health *is* a flowing movement. There is *no* benchmark to which we can refer to tell us when health leaves off and disease begins. Health and disease are the "moving principles" of each

TABLE II

HEALTH AND THE IMPLICATE ORDER

Traditional View	*Implicate View*
1. The sensory world of objects and events is primary.	1. The sensory world of objects and events is not primary. They belong to the explicate order which is grounded, or enfolded, in an underlying indivisible totality, the implicate order.
2. Health is the absence of disease.	2. Health is not the mere absence of disease, but is the manifestation of the harmonious interaction of all apparent parts that inhabit the explicate domain.
3. Health and disease are absolutes, and are irreconcilable opposites.	3. Health and disease are not irreconcilable opposites. They are the "moving principles" of each other.
4. All living matter is potentially dead. Everything awaits decay.	4. All matter belongs to the implicate order, where everything is alive. "What we call dead is an abstraction" (Bohm).
5. Life is characterized by movement, and death by stasis.	5. The implicate order enfolds all, and is flux; thus, *both* life and death are movement. Nothing is static.
6. Health can be conceptualized as proper function of body parts.	6. "Parts" exist only in the explicate domain. Therefore, health transcends the function of parts, since all parts, which consist of matter, are ultimately enfolded in the implicate order, and thus consist of an indivisible whole.
7. The ultimate goal of health care is to forestall disease and, thus, death.	7. Since death is an abstraction ("everything is alive") this is an inappropriate goal of health care.
8. Health can be expressed in terms of objective measurements—laboratory tests, physical examinations, x-rays, etc.	8. All measurements refer to objects belonging to the explicate order, and are thus not primary. They defy the unanalyzable wholeness of the underlying totality in which all material bodies are grounded. As such, all measurements are arbitrary and are poor indicators of health.

TABLE II (*continued*)

HEALTH AND THE IMPLICATE ORDER

Traditional View	*Implicate View*
9. The focus of health care is on the physical body. Consciousness is a secondary and irrelevant factor.	9. Both matter and consciousness are enfolded in the implicate order, where all things are one. Thus, all matter is to some degree conscious. Health care cannot, therefore, ignore consciousness. To focus on matter *is* to focus on consciousness.
10. Health care focuses on individuals.	10. This is an arbitrary and illusory concern of the explicate domain. All matter is enfolded in the implicate order; thus, so too are all bodies. To focus health care on one person is to focus on all, since all bodies (all matter) comprise a totality in the implicate order.
11. Therapy primarily is executed by mechanical means, by matter acting on matter—e.g., by medications and surgery.	11. Everything is alive. There is nothing in principle, therefore, preventing the use of consciousness as a primary form of therapeutic intervention at all levels of matter—from subatomic particles through molecules, cells, tissues, organ systems, etc.
12. Health care is of unquestioned value.	12. Insofar as traditional health care distorts the wholeness of the body by inappropriate concentration on function of mere body parts, it can be destructive. Health care, thus, is of *qualified* benefit, since it may create distortions in body awareness which may prove harmful and actually generate illness.
13. Transcendence of the concern about health is a mystical aberration usually leading to neglect and rejection of the body.	13. Transcendence of the concern about health may indeed lead to the view of health as irrelevant, but may also lead to an awareness of the body as being materially alive at all levels. This awareness can generate a spiritual regard for the body, a self-identity with the matter comprising it, leading to an enhanced pattern of health care.

other. As Bohm implies: perceived as they are by conscious thought, and grounded as thought is in the totality of the implicate order that enfolds all, health and illness—how can we avoid the conclusion? —are one.

The *experience* of health and illness are, of course, not one and the same. The experience of them occurs in Bohm's explicate order, the world of the everyday that we habitually dissect into discrete objects and events. And as a consequence of partitioning this world into separate objects, we find that we partition it into immiscible experiences such as health and illness.

Is there a way to experientially touch the implicate order such that our own morbid preoccupations with health and disease are transcended? Can health and illness be experienced as irrelevancies? Almost certainly this is the case. The mystical literature is alive with instances of this sort. The mystics are consistent in asserting that ordinary considerations of health and illness, even of death, can be transcended. Frequently these statements are misinterpreted—for example, the mystic has "renounced" the body. This view is, I think, wrong; for the mystic has achieved a state characterized not by a repudiation of the flesh, but one in which he experiences the implicate union of opposites: body and nonbody, spirit and matter, health and illness, birth and death.

If we begin to *experience* the domain in which the issues of health and disease cease to appear as absolutes, our ordinary health strategies can be seen in a different perspective. Health care becomes an arbitrary participation in only one level of reality, the explicate order. The grim urgency of health care imperatives ("Perform a death-defying act: have your blood pressure taken!") changes. Not that health, if neglected, *won't* evolve into illness, but that this evolution describes events only on the explicate level.

This is no endorsement of self-abuse and neglect of health. On the contrary, my suspicion is that an experiential understanding of the relativity of health and disease will lead to an increasing respect for one's material body, and that a fuller flowering of health will ensue. To transcend health care, to experience health as irrelevant, is not to neglect it. It is rather to regard all matter, including one's physical body, as alive and beyond health, grounded with conscious thought in the implicate domain. Rather than engendering an abusive disregard for the flesh, this point of view is more likely to promote sound health care—but not out of a fear of dissolution and death, but from respect born of an awareness (as Bohm states) that death is a mere abstraction, and that all is alive.[5]

The application of Bohm's cosmology to considerations of health care present an immediate problem. If Bohm's proposals for an implicate and explicate order are correct, it is clear that the efforts of modern medicine are wide of the mark. They focus only on the reality of the explicate order, the realm of our habitation, where the world is one of separate objects and events. The implicate domain, where the very *meaning* of health, disease, and death radically changes, is currently of no concern to medicine. The totality that enfolds everything is ignored.

This dilemma is illusory if Bohm is wrong. Is he? We do not know. Bohm's proposals are made in utter seriousness, but he is explicit in saying they are only proposals, as he views any suggestion in science. Not only is he willing to admit that his proposal cannot be proved, he points out that *no* scientific "proof" is absolute. We know, for example, that scientific proofs apply to only certain areas of the universe, and that they rest on the assumption that all the territory in the universe works the same as it does in our local sphere. Moreover, says Bohm, Gödel's theorem alone (Part IV, Chapter 3) suggests that for every assumption we are aware of, there must be countless others we do not recognize. Some of these are sure to be true, some false. So in some sense the criticisms we would apply to the tentative proposals of Bohm must also be leveled at the hardest scientific data we have.

Perhaps the physicist Shimony is correct in his appraisal of Bohm's ideas of the implicate order. He observes that Bohm has for thirty years made significant contributions to the foundations of modern physics. Thus, he should be listened to.[6]

How could medicine redirect its course? Instead of "keeping the parts running" ("explicate therapy"), how would it implement an "implicate therapy"?

I do not believe the task is a hopeless one. Indeed, there are indications of an emerging paradigm in medicine that will foster an experiential awareness of the implicate order. These methodologies are mentioned throughout this book. They have as their foundation this underlying understanding: mind and body are intrinsically united, and consciousness is the fulcrum of health.

CHAPTER THREE

IMPLICATIONS FOR UNITY: SCIENCE, LOGIC, AND MYTH

. . . Nature herself reveals little of her secret to those who only look and listen with the outward ear or eye. The condition of all valid seeing, upon every plane of consciousness, lies not in the sharpening of the senses, but in a peculiar attitude of the whole personality: in a self-forgetting attentiveness, a profound concentration, a self-merging, which operates a real communion between the seer and the seen. . . .

—EVELYN UNDERHILL
MYSTICISM[1]

PHYSICIANS AND MEDICAL SCIENTISTS have been loathe to address the issues raised by the foregoing considerations. It is almost a modern embarrassment to have to admit to the importance of human factors in disease causation when all along the answers had been expected to arise from the cryptic depths of molecular biology. But the paradox that has arisen is that dispassionate scientists who have insisted on a value-free, emotionless science have unearthed compelling evidence that in disease causation human emotions are of paramount importance!

In many prestigious scientific circles it is still considered a down right ignoble endeavor to leave the objective world of molecular biology to dabble in mind-body investigations. This attitude reflects a prejudice that "real science" should be purged of all matters of the mind. "Mentalism" and values in science are regarded as an equal curse. This attitude is expressed by the great French molecular biologist Jacques Monod, who was acrimonious in his insistence that an objective science cannot cohabit with values of any sort.[2]

But for all the vitriolic insistence that science has no place for human values, the evidence that human values are important in disease causation will not go away. This conflict in bioscience is reminiscent of the monumental struggles that characterized the revolutionary expansion from classical mechanics to quantum mechanics. At the turn of the century, physicists were comfortable with an objective description of the world. But by the late 1920s, when a comprehensive theory of quantum physics had been worked out, pure objectivism had been discarded in favor of a view of the world in which the observer could not completely separate himself from his observations. New conceptualizations of how physical observations came about were necessary, which in certain cases invoked explanations that were totally contrary to common sense. Though seemingly illogical, these new ideas *were necessary to explain the data* arising from atomic experiments of increasing refinement.

Today our investigations of disease causation are becoming increasingly refined. As a result we are unearthing data that conflict with entrenched ideas of how disease occurs. What are the origins of this conflict?

We shall examine its roots and attempt to point to an eventual solution to the disputes between the orthodox "molecular biologist-objectivists" and the emerging "mind-body bioscientists." We shall look at some crucial questions that are ordinarily skirted in these disagreements: What do we mean by scientific methodology? Can we demand a stringent objectivity in the biosciences when this demand has already been relinquished in modern physics? Is human logic unbounded in its capacities—i.e., how much *can* we know? Is the interaction of consciousness and the physical world real or imagined?

Finally, is there any basis for a reconciliation between bioscientists who freely flirt with "human factors"—including emotions, feelings, and values—and those scientists who regard such flirtations as a ruination of traditional science?

I believe a union of these points of view is possible. I believe it is possible to show that not only does evidence for mind-body unity and a central role for human consciousness arise quite naturally from science as we know it, but there is a pervasive principle of unity that is implied in *all* human thought and perception.

The observations that follow are drawn from extremely diverse sources. If these sources seem immiscible, I offer Heisenberg's comment:

> It is probably true quite generally that in the history of human thinking the most fruitful developments frequently take place at those points where two different lines of thought meet. These lines may

have their roots in quite different parts of human culture, in different times or different cultural environments or different religious traditions: hence if they actually meet, that is, if they are at least so much related to each other that a real interaction can take place, then one may hope that new and interesting developments may follow.[3]

THE METHOD OF SCIENCE

The modern scientific approach to understanding relies overwhelmingly on rational thought. Indeed, scientific thinking is rational by definition. We believe that science is our most powerful tool in understanding nature, and underlying this pervasive notion is the assumption that rational thinking is itself powerful. Where science gives us an incomplete view of the world, we feel it is not the process of rational thought itself that is flawed, but science, which has gathered insufficient data against which we can apply the methods of logical analysis.

In science we make observations, form hypotheses, and test these hypotheses by constantly fitting them against ongoing observations. In the case of a misfit between repeated observations and hypotheses, the hypothesis is revised, leading to a more perfect world view. By and large, the faith of the scientist is that this process, if unimpeded, will lead to a perfect view of the universe.

It is little wonder that observations that call this faith into question seem to cast despair on the whole scientific endeavor. Such is the case with Gödel's theorem, which is virtually ignored in the scientific community.

Gödel's Theorem

In 1931 a young Austrian mathematician, Kurt Gödel, proved two astonishing theorems. "The first theorem says that any logical system which is complex enough to include, at least, simple arithmetic, can express true assertions which cannot, nevertheless, be deduced from its axioms. And the second theorem which Gödel deduced says that the axioms in such a system, with or without additional truths, cannot be shown in advance to be free from hidden contradictions."[4] In short, a logical system that has any richness can never be complete, and it cannot even be guaranteed to be consistent.

In the years that followed, other disconcerting theorems were established. Turing in England and Church in the U.S.A. showed that "no mechanical procedure can be devised which could test every assertion in a logical system and in a finite number of steps demonstrate it to be either true or false."[5] In other words, one simply could not test a logical system in exacting ways. "And Alfred Tarski in Poland proved in 1936 an even deeper limitation to logic than Gödel showed. Tarski proved that there can be no precise language which is universal; every formal language which is at least as rich as arithmetic contains meaningful sentences that cannot be asserted to be either true or false."[6]

For those who are not logicians and mathematicians, these logical proofs may seem impossibly complex. But they have been scrutinized now for almost half a century by mathematicians and logicians of the highest caliber, and have not been shown to contain any inconsistencies.

What do these extraordinary statements mean? All of science, as Bronowski has observed, hopes to set up a basis of fundamental axioms and then to test them by matching them up against observations in the world, and to make deductions in an exact language—the language of physics, for example, or the language of neurophysiology. This is the scientific ideal. The results of Gödel, Tarski, Turing, and Church show that *this ideal is hopeless.*

These theorems show that the aim of the physical sciences since Newton cannot be realized. The laws of nature cannot be put down in a deductive, axiomatic, and formal way, a way that is simultaneously both unambiguous and complete. They also go farther: if we ever were to find ourselves at a stage of scientific inquiry where we felt that the laws of nature did make a complete and unambiguous system, we would have to conclude that we had made errors in our thinking, that we had somehow made mistakes. For these theorems tell us that it is impossible to perfectly describe the world, even in the abstract, using an axiomatic and deductive system.

Yet we go about our business in science supposing that nature does obey a set of laws of her own that are complete, precise, and consistent. After all, nature works. But if the laws of nature are consistent, then "their inner formulation must be of some kind which is quite different from any that we know; and at present, we have no idea how to conceive it."[7]

Every scientific system is, then, incomplete.

The theorems of Gödel, Turing, Tarski, and Church form a common family of limitations. What do they have in common? They all refer to intrinsic difficulties in all symbolic language. The problem is this: language is used not only to describe parts of the world, it is used to describe itself. In each of these theorems, "the proof hinges on a construction by which a proposition *about* arithmetic is expressed as a proposition *in* arithmetic."[8] This leads to statements of self-reference, perhaps the most famous of which is the comment of Epimenides the Cretan, "All Cretans are liars." If this statement is true, it is false; and if it is false, it is true.

All formalized systems in science are dogged by this problem. In science we wish to do more than merely describe what we observe. We wish to know if the descriptions are true or false. But the proofs above tell us that anytime we say "is true" or "is false," the logical system has begun to talk about itself—and in making self-reflective statements, it becomes victim to the limitations we have seen.

Consciousness, the Brain, and Gödel's Theorem

It may be that the problems attendant to self-reflective statements are pervasive in nature, cropping up anytime human thought and language are involved. Consider, for example, the stickiest problem of all of philosophy and neurophysiology, the relationship of consciousness and the brain. How does consciousness arise from the brain? We can safely assert that no one knows. And it may be that the answer will always be shrouded; for in thinking about this problem, we are immediately put in the position of thinking about our own thoughts. In so doing, we make statements about ourselves. Man, thinking about his own thoughts, his own brain, is subject, perhaps, to Gödel's dilemma, of being plagued by making self-referential statements, of talking about himself. Perhaps we can never understand our own consciousness fully because we can never step outside our own minds.

SCIENTIFIC OBSERVATION: THE MODERN VIEW

The scientific position has been stated succinctly by Jacques Monod: "The cornerstone of the scientific method is the postulate that nature is objective."[9] Any other possibility is, for the average scientist, quite unthinkable. Most of us agree. We find natural the idea that the world exists apart from us, that it occupies an independent existence in its own right. Scientists are able to approach this kind of world, make observations from it at a distance, extract valid and meaningful data, and then retreat to make sense out of these observations. The objective world is what makes science possible.

This idea of doing science, however, belongs to the eighteenth century, not to our own. This belief has been challenged in our time by quantum physics. The notion of science as an objective endeavor was most forcefully shaken by Heisenberg's Uncertainty Principle. Heisenberg showed that the very attempt to gain knowledge at the atomic level involved inevitable changes in what was observed. He demonstrated, moreover, that this uncertainty was not due to the clumsiness of the scientist's instruments, but came about as a result of intrinsic properties of matter. It was not possible, even in principle, to view the smallest material realms with completeness and certainty.

This situation is described by the physicist John A. Wheeler:

> Nothing is more important about the quantum principle than this, that it destroys the concept of the world as "sitting out there," with the observer safely separated from it. . . . To describe what has happened, one has to cross out that old word "observer," and put in its place the new word "participator." In some strange sense the universe is a participatory universe.[10]

Intuitively, it seems that the deeper one penetrates nature, the more mechanical things should become.[11] For example, in going from organs to cells, events seem more mechanical, as they do in going from cells to molecules. But there is a point at which this approach to understanding nature begins to backfire. It is at the level of the molecule that the reductionistic method fails us. Twentieth-century physics has shown that if one subdivides a DNA molecule—or any molecule—further reductions in size begin to reveal unpredictable effects. Beyond the level of the molecule, diminutions in size do not reveal an increase in mechanical behavior. At this level things begin to become *less* mechanical. For one has entered the world of the quantum, a world governed by sheer probability and by nondeterminism.

Where does this leave us?

(1) Modern physics puts limits on what we can observe. We cannot get, even in principle, all the data, for the process of data collection and observation is not purely objective. The data cannot be isolated and extracted. We interfere. Experiments show that our own conscious efforts function in strange ways to bring about, to some extent, what we call the external world (as we shall later see). Thus, peculiarly, we *become* the very data we try to observe. Nature is not objective because we are not separate from it.

(2) The theories of logical limitations tell us that not only are we unable to get the data we wish, there are limitations on how we can

handle the information we *can* get. It is not possible to think about the data we have in a logically consistent and completely unambiguous way.

Bell's Theorem

We have examined Bell's theorem in Part III, and only a brief restatement will be given here.

In 1964 the physicist John S. Bell, in a landmark paper, proved a revolutionary theorem. It has been subjected to several refinements since its elaboration, one of the clearest of which is given by Henry S. Stapp: "If the statistical predictions of quantum theory are true, an objective universe is incompatible with the law of local causes."

An objective universe is simply one that exists apart from our consciousness. It is there when we are not looking, when we are not measuring it.

The law of local causes implies that things happen "locally"—i.e., that nothing can happen faster than the speed of light, that energy cannot travel faster than the speed of light.

In order to test Bell's theorem, John Clauser performed an experiment, which has by now been run many times with the same consistent results. It is said to prove that the statistical predictions of quantum mechanics are indeed true, and at present Bell's theorem stands true.

The implications of Bell's theorem are astonishing, and are called by Stapp the most important result in the history of science. Quite simply, as stated by the French physicist d'Espagnat, Bell's theorem proves that the ordinary idea of an objective world unaffected by consciousness lies in opposition not only to quantum theory but to facts established by experiment.[12]

These conclusions are an affront to any scientist who wishes to cling to a strict objective view of the external world. Experiments such as Clauser's tell us that what we consider the objective world depends in some measure on our own conscious processes. There is no fixed external reality.

TRANSCENDENCE RECONSIDERED

Through the ages the mystical traditions have valued the spiritual qualities of man over the physical. Emphasis has been placed on transcending the physical. In the background of most mystical traditions is the idea that the body somehow is at odds with the spirit. A war is going on. One must purify the soul, and achieve an enlightened status by going beyond the physical.

In a sense, all "transcendent philosophies" seem dubious. They appear to embody a violation of Gödel's theorem. They ask one to step outside one's self, to leave the system one is in; and thus they lead, it seems, to an infinite progression of having to continue to invent ever larger systems which must be transcended themselves. This may lead to analytical or spiritual progress, but it also leads to infinity, as Gödel has shown. Enlightenment comes, perhaps, when one realizes that the attempt to transcend one's self is not only unnecessary but impossible—not only for the reason that one cannot pull oneself up by one's bootstraps, but for the reasons Gödel has shown, as well.

This is a central lesson of Zen Buddhism. It is the job of the Zen master to guide the student to the point where he gives up. The student realizes that he cannot think himself out of his predicament, and that his predicament is, indeed, in some sense illusory. The famous Zen koans, or puzzles, that are given to students to solve as an aid to enlightenment, are perfect examples of Gödel's theorem in action—the discursive mind, thinking about itself, frustrating itself in its incessant attempt to figure things out. The role of the Zen master is to help in this process, assisting the student in realizing that true understanding is not to be achieved with the rational mind.

Perhaps the spiritual goal of transcending the physical can be rethought. Our greatest spiritual achievement may lie in total integration of the spiritual and the physical—in realizing that the spiritual and the physical are not two aspects of ourselves, but one. Perhaps the ultimate spiritual goal is to transcend *nothing*, but to realize the oneness of our own being, which is implied by Gödel.

We have traditionally built our systems of religious thought along the classical view of an objective universe. We pursue our spiritual search according to a model that we make along classical lines. This is done unconsciously, of course. We build a model in which we are an individual unit in a particular place at a particular time, pursuing a particular future goal which is "out there"—be it salvation, satori, enlightenment, self-actualization, or being born again—and we are influenced in this process by outside forces in typical cause-and-effect ways. What have we here? We have designed a model of a spiritual quest along seventeenth-century lines, along the lines of a clockwork view of the universe.

But one by one, these characteristics of an objective world have been overturned by the modern physical view. A fixed space and time is now rejected in favor of a relativistic notion of spacetime. There are now no fundamental units, and all the "bits" of the universe stand in dynamical relation to all others. The very notion of a particle has become diluted to the point of metaphor. And the traditional idea of causality has been abandoned in modern physics; a probabilistic, not a causal, view is now accepted as the only explanation of subatomic occurrences that is consistent with experiment.

The classical modeling that we ordinarily use in our models may be a great hindrance to the eternal spiritual goal. This kind of modeling denies the organicity, the sense of unity and belonging, which is at the heart of the mystical experiences of practically every culture that has left any written record of its spiritual tradition.

The records of many of the great religious traditions, including the mystical traditions of the Christian church, Taoism, Hinduism, and Buddhism, give the very strong impression that enlightenment comes when one begins to think in nonclassical ways, using models built according to modern physical views; when one is free to sense the dynamical qualities of interrelation and interconnection that are a part of the new physical view of the world.

The view of Plotinus, from the third century, reflects this view:

> See all things, not in process of becoming, but in being, and see themselves in the other. Each being contains in itself the whole intelligible world. Therefore All is everywhere. Each is there All, and All is each. Man as he now is has ceased to be the All. But when he ceases to be an individual, he raises himself again and penetrates the whole world.[13]

ON BEING STUCK

Some persons are stricken with a sense of despair when they discover Bell's theorem because it suggests a kind of "superdeterminism"—that what occurs in you is influenced by every other occurrence in the entire universe.* If this is so, how can one be in control? And, thus, everything seems determined, and there is nothing to be done about it. There is more: Gödel's theorem tells us that

---

*This nuance of Bell's theorem relates to an earlier thought experiment suggested by Einstein, Rosen, and Podolsky. This experiment, originally developed as a reductio ad absurdum to quantum mechanics, provided for occurrences of the most peculiar sort, such as simultaneous and instantaneous changes in distant objects. See Part III, Chapter 4.

there isn't any way we can *think* our way out of these things, no matter how hard we try.

Determinism suggests that I am embedded in this world, this universe; that I am stuck in it; that I cannot possibly get out; that what I think and do and struggle against makes absolutely no difference at all. In our own time this view has given rise to a burdensome sense of defeat.

The mystical record tells us, however, that there are other legitimate human emotional responses to this situation. It suggests that when one realizes this "predicament," the realization can become a cause for unspeakable ecstasy. A sense of belonging may ensue—a feeling of wholeness, of not needing *to do* anything or *to think* anything. I am in the universe, and the universe is in me. *That is enough!*

Rather than casting a pall on the spiritual aspirations of man, the theorems of Gödel and Bell do much to affirm the experiences of the great mystics of recorded history.

The modern view of science, however, rejects these kinds of comparisons. Mixing science and spiritual values is an abomination of the highest order. A dispassionate and value-free science is the traditional ideal. But one must design one's philosophy along the lines of *some* physics, be it modern physics, classical physics, or physics of a different kind. One cannot employ no physics at all. It may be a part of the scientific philosophy to say that scientific and spiritual values should not be mixed, but that in itself is not a scientific statement. As Huston Smith has pointed out, it is a statement *about* science, but it is not science.[14] (Probably the most compelling reason why most scientists resist mixing scientific and spiritual values is simply the fear that other scientists would think poorly of them if they did.)

Perhaps the view of Einstein is to be preferred: "Science without religion is lame; religion without science is blind."[15]

The making of myths, like the making of spiritual philosophies, borrows a world view of some sort. Along what lines do we make our myths? Along common sense notions of a view belonging to the seventeenth century, or along the disconcerting descriptions of modern physics? The mythmaker cannot hide. He/she invokes *some* view of the universe.

MYTH AND SCIENCE

The theories of logical limitations imply a psychological correlate: we cannot get outside our minds any more than we can step outside an axiomatic and deductive system of thought. Self-transcendence, as well as an ultimately complete and unambiguous rational system, may be impossible. The pessimistic and despairing conclusion to this turn of events is that I am "stuck." The conclusion most compatible with the mystical record, however, is that I am One.

This finds an eerie echo in the modern physical view that I cannot step outside nature, that there is no pure objectivity possible in science. The pessimistic and despairing conclusion here is that my science is limited, that I am drowned by uncertainty. But the conclusion most compatible with the mystical record is that nature and I are One.

Therefore, from this point of view we see an interaction of mysticism, myth, and science. But what comes of mysticism and myth suffused with science? Those who see myth and symbol as one of mankind's most vivifying life forces may shudder at the flirtation of myth with science: myth debased to the level of science is myth emasculated, myth profaned. This conclusion is as wrong as it is unnecessary. *For it is science, not myth, which is redefined.*

What is science? We have perhaps had it wrong all along. It is likely that we shall never henceforth be able to legitimately regard science as the queen of the intellect, for the traditional scientific view of the world has been scuttled in favor of a view *that cannot be comprehended by rational thought.* Moreover, the theorems dealing with the limits of logical thought have hinted at a quality of oneness in our own minds. *Hence, both the modern view of science and the aspect of consciousness that sustains it, rational thought, have themselves come to seem almost mythical.*

As a demythologizing power, modern science is effete. It is as if the Mythmaker has transformed science, turning science into myth. Bohr intimated as much:

> . . . when it comes to atoms, language can be used only as in poetry. The poet too is not nearly so concerned with describing facts as with creating images and establishing mental connections. . . . Quantum theory . . . provides us with a striking illustration of the fact that we *can* fully understand a connection though we can only speak of it in images and parables. . . .[16]

The hallmark of modern science is that it has outrun common sense; and in so doing it has run headlong into our metaphorical, poetic self, the same part of our self which mythologizes. Science in our time has come to myth, and myth has come to life.

Science and myth, like lion and lamb, may one day lie together in peace. Then we shall find ourselves free of the terrible historic necessity of having to mythologize the unity of the universe.

Coleridge said,

> What if you slept, and what if in your sleep you dreamed, and what if in your dream you went to heaven and there plucked a strange and beautiful flower, and what if when you awoke you had the flower in your hand? Ah, what then?

The Myth of Unity is alive. It is Coleridge's rose, and it is in our hand.

CHAPTER FOUR

UNITY, LANGUAGE, AND DISCOVERY

But what are concepts save formulations and creations of thought, which, instead of giving us the true forms of objects, show us rather the forms of thought itself? Consequently all schemata which science evolves in order to classify and organize and summarize the phenomena of the real world turn out to be nothing but arbitrary schemes— airy fabrics of the mind, which express not the nature of things, but the nature of mind.

—ERNST CASSIRER[1]

IN PART III WE HAVE EXAMINED EVIDENCE of our oneness with nature. From several perspectives we have seen that the view of ourselves as independent objects that are isolated from the universe we inhabit is erroneous. We have looked to science for this evidence, and not to the intuition of the poet and mystic.

Yet it may turn out that even the "hardest" data we can marshal in the description of our oneness with the universe is "contaminated" with an inescapable subjectivity. A curious turn of events has occurred: in using a presumedly *objective* method of distancing ourselves from the universe we are observing (the traditional approach of science), we have found data that shows us that we *cannot* distance ourselves from the universe because of our oneness with it.

We have encountered a prime feature of modern science. As Bronowski has asserted, a hallmark that distinguishes the science of our century from that of the last is the discovery that the scientist cannot dissociate himself from what he is measuring. He is trapped in nature *as part of it*. Any attempt to measure nature results in a measurement of one's self—just as surely as if the scientist had turned his microscope or telescope in his own face.

Perhaps the most stunning expression of this characteristic of modern science surfaced in modern physics through the famous uncertainty relationship of Heisenberg, who showed that even the most refined attempt to gain knowledge at the subatomic level was bound to be limited by the changes brought about by the fact of observation itself. Observation changed things—and the measurer thus became part of the measurement. Slowly the recognition evolved that the quest for "reality" was a convoluted maze turning inwardly at some point on consciousness itself. As Heisenberg put it, what we are observing is not nature itself, but nature exposed to our method of questioning.

And how do we question? All of our methods of interrogating nature depend upon language—and it is the very nature of language to refer to things. We therefore think in terms of things. How can we possibly think about nonthings, no-things, nothing? In our very *forms* of thought we instinctively divide the world into subjects and objects, thinkers and things, mind and matter. This division seems so natural that it has been presumed a basic maxim of objective science.

Resoundingly, however, modern physics tells us that the dichotomy of mind and matter violates the wholeness of the world. In expressing this wholeness, John A. Wheeler states that the universe is "participatory." As Professor Henry Margenau puts it, the physicist "creates his world"; and in Sir Arthur Eddington's description, "the stuff of the world is mind-stuff."

Ordinary language is inadequate in expressing the oneness of mind and matter because it conveys the idea of a correspondence between thoughts and things, between subjects and objects. But as these statements by modern physicists illustrate, language has run headlong into modern physics, which suggests that there is nothing to refer to outside of oneself.

If there is nothing to measure outside of one's immeasurable self, then what is it that science measures? This is the root of the so-called "measurement problem" of modern physics. The genesis of this apparent futility, according to physicist David Bohm, is the imprisonment we experience within our language. Through our language we express our belief that if, in attempting to measure the world objectively we wind up measuring ourselves, a measurement problem arises. Yet the "problem" lies rooted in our language—which forces us in subject-object terms to suppose that we stand apart from nature in the first place. The problem depends for its existence on the language we choose to use.

Just as the observer was supposed to be independent from what was observed, we have traditionally believed that science too was independent from the language it used. Both presumptions have been questioned in our own time by modern physicists. Early on Einstein perceived that the *content* of traditional Newtonian physics was tied to the older language it used; and he was instrumental in devising a new language form which allowed, for example, new descriptions such as the mutual interrelatedness of space and time. Without new language forms such as "signal" and "field" the new concepts might not have taken root.

Niels Bohr's principle of complementarity also challenged the language, which presumed that a thing must have one identity or another. Bohr asserted that a thing could have multiple identities (e.g., an electron could be a particle *and* a wave), in spite of the violence this form of thought did to a language rooted in common sense. Bohr fully recognized the insults that were dealt the traditional language forms by the new descriptions of physical events, and in attempting to escape the constraints of ordinary language he proposed that, in describing atoms, it was not only permissible but *necessary* to use language as in poetry.[2]

In the rich interplay between language and discovery, it is important to recall that language frequently precedes discovery. Or perhaps we can say that new discoveries in language stimulate new discoveries in the natural world. As Barfield points out, our *selection* of experiments and our design of the machines to execute them are imbedded in the language form.[3] Thus, new forms of language lead to new forms of discovery, which in turn may lead to new views of the world.

To what extent, then, are we justified in looking to science for evidence for our oneness in the world? Are we inevitably doomed to peer into our own minds, deflected there by the mirror of language? Perhaps not. Perhaps there are forms of language that permit a more complete recognition of the relationship of subject and object, of "thing and think." David Bohm has proposed that we *can* go beyond ordinary language whose subject-object structure is inadequate to convey the "holistic and process character of reality."[4] Bohm has proposed a new model of language called the "rheomode," emphasizing the Greek word that means "to flow." He suggests that a primary role be given the verb instead of the noun, thus reducing the emphasis on subject and object. This suggestion recalls an earlier observation by Buckminster Fuller. Sensing the same deficiency of ordinary language forms in conveying a true relationship with the world, Fuller once announced, "I seem to be a verb!"

William Carlos Williams once wrote, "A new world is only a new mind!" There is on the surface little difference in his view and that of Henry Margenau:

> I am perfectly willing to admit that reality does change as discovery proceeds. I can see nothing basically wrong with a real world which undergoes modification along with the flux of experience.[5]

Yet scientists for the most part have always been leery of admitting to the flux of thought, language, discovery, and "reality." For most persons in science, a changing reality is a contradiction in terms. How can science remain on its preferred ground of objective measurement and observation and at the same time admit to Eddington's "mind-stuff" as the stuff of the world?

These are the concerns of Bohm. In spite of his belief that it is a fundamental error to disturb the "unanalyzable wholeness" of the world by insisting on observers and observables, he nonetheless asserts that the Western way of measuring the world does contribute significantly to our wisdom about it. But, says Bohm, although this wisdom is insight into a necessary aspect of reality, it is an aspect which is both secondary and dependent.[6] With his concepts of "implicate" and "explicate" order, Bohm has attempted to use new forms of language to stimulate an understanding of his proposed multiple levels of reality.

The previous chapters dealing with various ideas of science—dissipative structure theory, hologram theory, the biodance—are offered, therefore, with a caveat. To the extent that they are taken as evidence drawn from an older science, their message is bound to be distorted. For no subject-object science can authentically and convincingly contribute to a concept of unity within nature, since its very modus operandi assumes a *separateness* of the observer from the rest of the world.

It remains a future task for science to complete the descriptions of the relationships of thought and form, of subjects and objects. For now, in our search for evidence of unity in nature, we shall do well to recall Niels Bohr's words:

> . . . when searching for harmony in life we must never forget that in the drama of existence we are ourselves both actors and spectators.[7]

CHAPTER FIVE

CONSCIOUSNESS AND MEDICINE: WHAT LIES AHEAD?

. . . science has been affected by a point of view which tries to be value-free. This is of course mere prejudice.

—DAVID BOHM[1]

CONSCIOUSNESS, MEDICINE, AND THE PHYSICAL WORLD

The role of conscious mental activity in the evolution of health and disease has been seriously undervalued. The reasons underlying this rest primarily on the traditional belief that human consciousness is a secondary phenomenon, a derivative of physiological processes—i.e., it is purely a function of what occurs in the body. This view is succinctly stated by Carl Sagan: "[The brain's] workings—what we sometimes call mind—are a consequence of its anatomy and physiology, and nothing more."[2]

This view is in effect a definitional strait-jacket because it will not accommodate certain results that point to some odd characteristics of mind. For example, Robert Jahn, Dean of the School of Engineering at Princeton, has demonstrated that a subject watching an optical interference pattern on a Fabry-Perot interferometer can change the spacing of two parallel images. Similarly, subjects have shown the ability to change the magnetic field intensity registered on a magnetometer that is shielded from all external physical influences.[3] Impossible? Yes, if one holds to a strict definition of consciousness such as the reductionistic model espoused by Sagan and most working scientists.

In the jargon of parapsychology these are examples of psychokinesis. These phenomena, commonly called "mind over matter," have traditionally been regarded by orthodox science as fraudulent.

206

The modern evidence for such events, however, is mounting, and it is different in kind from such stage events as table rappings, levitation, and spoon bending. It is perhaps prophetic that first-rate scientists such as Jahn are venturing into the murky waters of parapsychology, an excursion that in an earlier day would have spelled doom for a career in academic science. Now the climate is changing.

What is human consciousness actually capable of? Consider the studies by Ullman and Krippner at the Dream Research Laboratory of New York City's Maimonides Hospital.[4] A subject, while sleeping soundly in a distant room, was "sent" specific images by a "sender" at a particular stage of sleep. The subject was then awakened and was asked to record his dream content. His description was then compared by an independent panel of judges to the material being sent to him. The correlation in many instances was astonishing, and in the opinion of the panel of judges could not possibly have been explained by mere coincidence.

Experiments in "remote viewing" have been conducted by the physicists Puthoff and Targ at the Stanford Research Institute, wherein a subject tries to envision a preselected distant target. The results? Again, gifted subjects appear to be extraordinarily accurate in their descriptions.

In modern medicine events that are equally unbelievable have actually become commonplace. Such happenings occur with regularity, for instance, in biofeedback laboratories. In a biofeedback laboratory subjects are attached to various feedback devices—usually solid state electronic instruments—that measure body events of which one is usually unaware, and that feed back this information to the subject by way of a moving meter, a blinking light, or a variable sound. The subject then uses this information to create further change in what is being measured. For example, he may learn to lower or increase his heart rate or blood pressure, increase the blood flow to specific body regions, or increase or decrease the electrical activity in certain muscle groups. The control and specificity of these skills is quite remarkable: many subjects can learn to increase blood flow to a single finger or to a particular circumscribed area on the forearm. Or they can learn to control the activity in the muscle cells supplied by a single motor nerve!

What goes on in biofeedback laboratories can hardly be accounted for by traditional learning theory. Most subjects have never had previous experiences to which these events can be contrasted and compared. Yet they are capable of exercising control over certain body processes to a degree regarded as impossible only a decade ago.

Control of shielded magnetometers and interferometer patterns, dream telepathy, remote viewing, biofeedback accomplishments—these events force us to reconsider how human conscious mental activity interacts with the physical world. The traditional way of dealing with these findings has been to dismiss them as either downright deceptive or as the products of research by well-meaning but naive and misguided scientists—an attitude that is indeed mandated *if* one holds to the traditional notion that consciousness is derived *from* the physical world, but cannot itself influence it.

It is becoming extremely difficult to dismiss the evidence suggesting that conscious mental activity can exert change in the world. It is true that some scientists may still be willing to ignore objective findings in order to salvage precious theories when collisions occur between what is observed and what is expected; but many thoughtful scientists are looking beyond the extant ideas of how mind and matter relate, attempting to formulate new theories to account for the kind of observations mentioned above.

It is ironic that impetus for a new view is emerging from neuroscience itself, long the stronghold of stringent reductionism. The eminent neurophysiologist Roger Sperry, the discoverer of the differential function of the brain's cerebral hemispheres, has been outspoken in this regard. In addressing the question, what is mind? Sperry has stated, "[It is something which] moves matter in the brain."[5] Sperry is attributing an independent potency to human mental activity, a position that has always been an anathema to mind-body reductionists who view consciousness as nothing more than the outcome of physiologic events in the body.

Perhaps most importantly, this position is also to be found in the views expressed by many quantum physicists. In commenting on the relationship between human consciousness and the physical world, the Nobel-winning physicist Eugene Wigner states that if mind could *not* affect the physical world but was only affected by it, this would be the only known example in modern physics of such a one-way interaction. For in modern physics, one-way interactions are not known to occur.

In recent years physicists have had to address the interplay of consciousness and the physical world. In quantum physics much has been made over Bell's theorem. The implications of this theorem and the experimental findings that flow from it are staggering. They force us to consider that the entire notion of a purely objective world is in conflict not only with the *theory* of quantum mechanics, but with the facts drawn from actual experiments.[6] These findings point insistently to a profound interaction between conscious mental activity and the physical world itself.

Because of the accumulating evidence of a fundamental interaction between mind and matter, the American Association for the Advancement of Science addressed this issue formally at its annual meeting in 1979 in a symposium entitled "The Role of Consciousness in the Physical World." Even though a storm of controversy predictably followed, it was perhaps prophetic that the most prestigious group of physical scientists in our society agreed to acknowledge these vital issues. One of the spokesmen for the necessity of a new attitude toward conscious human mental activity was Willis Harman of the Stanford Research Institute. In formulating a new approach, Harman described what he considered the qualities of human consciousness that are required to explain known observations:

1. mind is spatially extended
2. mind is temporally extended
3. ultimately mind is predominant over the physical
4. minds are joined

The qualities of consciousness characterize a view which is fundamentally different from the reductionistic approach described previously by Sagan and which is acknowledged by most medical scientists today. What do these new ideas portend for medicine?

The new view of consciousness asserts unabashedly that conscious mental activity exerts measurable effects on the physical world—a world that includes human bodies, organs, tissues, and cells. Mind becomes a legitimate factor in the unfolding of health and disease.

IS OBJECTIVITY POSSIBLE IN MEDICINE?

The attribution of physical potency to human consciousness generates an unexpected possibility: all of medical research—past and present—may be hopelessly flawed. Why? Because it has been conducted with a fundamental assumption that may be in error: that the effects of the experimenter, such as conscious attitudes and biases, could be eliminated from the experiment. Medical scientists have believed that scientific experiments when properly conceived and executed could render the intrusions of human consciousness inconsequential. Mind could be managed; it could be rendered effete in the experimental design. Thus, objectivity in medical research could be guaranteed.

This assumption is in doubt. We face the possibility that pure objectivity is indeed impossible. For if an objective world is an illusion, as quantum physicists such as d'Espagnat tell us, then all in it—including experiments, experimenters, and experimental subjects—participate in this nonobjective reality. Thus, objective medicine may be an illusion.

We have perhaps had hints all along that point to this state of affairs, which we have tried to ignore and explain away in medicine. Consider, for example, that clinical factor which we physicians call "the will to live." Most doctors have cared for patients who seem to defy their illness. Frequently these patients are difficult to care for, for they may be tenacious, truculent, aggressive individuals who have a mind of their own (which is the issue at hand!). They typically form poor relationships with physicians and nurses, may follow instructions poorly, and are a sharp contrast to the passive, meek, compliant person who is typically referred to as a good patient. The patient with the will to live frequently outlives his prognosis. He doesn't die on time.

Is the will to live evidence of an effect of consciousness on the physical world? Is it an event portended by Bell's theorem and the nonobjective reality of quantum physics? We must at least be open to the idea.

An admission of the role of consciousness in our world view will force radical changes in the way we view even the most mundane transactions between doctors and patients. Consider our prevalent attitude about the ordinary physical examination. An expanded view of consciousness leads us to the conclusion that there is no such thing as a *physical* examination; and the error of the patient who thinks he is *getting* one is exceeded, perhaps, only by that of the physician who believes he is *performing* one. It is impossible, even in principle, to examine only the physical body, for the reason of the body-mind continuum we have examined. To touch the body is to touch the spirit—and all examinations, laboratory tests, and diagnostic studies are a window to the psyche as well as to the soma.

A clinical phenomenon commonplace in medicine is the placebo effect. It has long been recognized that many patients will respond to any therapy—even if it is an inert medication such as a "sugar pill." This response has always been unwanted by medical researchers, since it is a real nuisance. One never knows when a "real" medicine is given whether the response of the patient is due to the effect of the medication or if it is simply evidence of the "placebo response." In conducting medical research, therefore, ingenious ways have been devised to somehow annul this event.

The guiding assumption has been that any response on the patient's part that is due to the placebo effect is evidence that the problem being treated was somehow not real. It existed in the patient's imagination and did not occupy true importance in his overall health. Otherwise, it is said, it would not have responded to the placebo. What can be cured *by* mind must only exist *in* the mind.

When seen from the perspective of a nonobjective reality, though, the placebo effect assumes new stature. The emerging reality asserts that consciousness can intervene in the physical world. Thus, its effects can be as real as those of any pill; and the fact that a symptom responds to the play of conscious attitudes on the part of the patient is no reason to ascribe to it an imaginary status. We must consider that the placebo response may represent clinical evidence, therefore, of a nonobjective reality which is determined by the interplay of consciousness and the physical world.*

Another euphemism that has long been popular in medicine is the term "the natural course of the disease." Given a specific disease—say cancer of the breast, which has spread throughout the body—a wide spectrum of survival time is known to occur. Some patients will die of this disease in a few weeks, while others may live for years. Cases are reported, even, of metastatic cancer completely regressing, disappearing beyond the ability of diagnostic tests to demonstrate it, and never to return. These so-called spontaneous cures are rare, but are certainly not unheard of. Physicians and medical scientists speak of these events collectively when they talk about the natural history of the disease. All diseases are described in this way in modern medicine.

Moreover, this general interpretive approach is used in assessing the response of patients to any therapeutic intervention. Again, there is a spectrum of response to any and all therapies. If, for example, a potent antitumor drug is given for disseminated breast cancer, some patients will show no response, some will show a

---

*The mediation of this particular interplay may be due to the brain's chemicals, the endorphins, since the effect of placebo pain medication can be blocked by the prior administration of naloxone, a substance that is known to inhibit the action of the endorphins.

marked response, while most will demonstrate a therapeutic response somewhere in between these extremes. All therapies—even placebos—evoke this spectrum of response in large populations of patients. This is the famous Gaussian distribution of the medical statistician, the famous bell-shaped curve.

It may be only coincidental that Bell's theorem in quantum physics and the bell-shaped curve of the medical scientist are identically named, but the statistical skewing seen in the course of all human illnesses, as well as their response to therapy, may possibly be accounted for by the nonobjective reality foreshadowed by Bell's theorem.

"The natural course of the disease" is a wastebasket term in medicine, with primarily statistical meaning. It is assumed that it occurs because of the physiological variability of human beings—yet this explanation is itself a gigantic wastebasket with little explanatory power. Merely ascribing the scattering of human therapeutic responses and the variable course of human disease to the fact that patients simply vary in their physiology dodges the issue. This explanation neglects, for example, the fact that variability in many human physiological responses is known to be highly susceptible to the impact of consciousness, a conclusion that is obvious to anyone who is familiar with day-to-day occurrences in a biofeedback laboratory.

In the light of Bell's theorem and the irreducible characteristics of consciousness described by Harman, we must look beyond the blinding euphemisms of "human variability", "the placebo response" and "the natural course of the disease" and attempt to dissect the effect of human consciousness on specific disease processes. The possibility that patients actually influence the course of their own illness as well as their response to therapy through the impact of their consciousness on the physical world—which contains their own bodies—must be seriously considered, unless we wish to ignore the theoretical considerations and the experimental data of quantum physics.

HOLISTIC HEALTH CARE: SOME GENTLE ADMONITIONS

Consider the impact the new views may have on our concept of self-responsibility in health care. Self-responsibility has become the clarion call of the so-called holistic health care movement. More than any other single factor, perhaps, the reliance on self and the de-emphasis of authoritarian medical care distinguishes the holistic endeavor. The holistic movement has rightfully criticized the traditional role of the patient as a supplicating, childlike figure. And the costly, depersonalized, technological approach of modern medicine has received sharp fire. But the new self-care methodologies have arisen primarily not because of these objections to the present system, but because new concepts of self-responsibility have evolved. However fertile the influence of the holistic movement may prove to be, in its shrill insistence on the concept of *self*, the holistic health care movement is inconsistent with the deepest meaning of the word.

In the foregoing chapters we have seen that the concept of an isolated self is illusory. Interaction of selves is not merely optional, but obligatory. No matter the level of scrutiny of the self—whether at the macroscopic level of the interpersonal, at the microscopic level of the biological-chemical self, or at the subatomic level—the noninteracting, isolated self is an indefensible construct, at best (like the flow of time) a psychological illusion.

For all its attributes, the holistic health care movement in its present philosophical form will never achieve true transcendence of the present system of health care because it invokes the same world model: human beings are seen primarily as distinct entities who exist quite apart from other selves and from other physicians. The holistic health care model is thus distinguished not in kind, but in degree, from the orthodox world view of traditional medicine. The question is not who wields authority in the health care game, nor even what the rules of the game might be. The crucial distinctions have to do not with authority but with no less than how the universe behaves—and, thus, as the preceding chapters have attempted to make clear, what is meant by self.

The confusion over "self" and "other" pervades the holistic movement. For example, in some circles it is judged a sign of weakness or failure to "take a pill" or to submit to any therapeutic maneuver that is purveyed by the medical establishment. Ideally, it is claimed, one should stay healthy through one's own strategies, relying on orthodox medicine only as a last resort (if even then). Certain health aids, thus, become acceptable while others are condemnable. The credo has become chaotic. For instance, vitamins are not of themselves valuable—it depends on their source, whether "organic" or not. Moreover, the dosage is crucial. A complex system of beliefs has arisen regarding *all* chemicals, including the water and food we ingest and the very air we breathe.

Many such admonitions will undoubtedly prove of value, while others will not. Yet regardless of the future validation or failure of the therapeutic principles that are espoused by the holistic health care movement, the entire emphasis seems flawed in the light of the new views we have examined, because the foundation of the credo of the holistic movement is, after all, that therapy is an object— something to be taken, ingested, or participated in. But an herb tea (a holistic acceptability) is as real an object as is a pencillin injection or an x-ray beam. An organically extracted vitamin is as real an object as one that is mass-produced from basic chemical components. Naturally grown foods are objects in the same sense that a pesticide is an object.

The holistic movement commits the same failure as the traditional system of medical care by placing primacy on the *objectivity* of health care. Whether one prefers to be called a "client" rather than a "patient" (a bone of contention in some holistic circles), both patient and client remain objects—objects *to* whom and *for* whom acts are done. Regardless of whether pills are eschewed, or whether naturally derived medication is preferred, both are objects still. From the perspective of the new view, no fundamental distinctions have been made, for both systems remain anchored in a similar world view characterized by a floundering multitude of separate selves surrounded by a sea of objects, all engulfed by a typically Newtonian universe of cause and effect, of push and pull.

In spite of a profound personal sympathy for many of the leavening influences wrought by the holistic health care movement, I must lovingly chastise it and wish upon it a philosophical maturity it has yet to attain. In many ways it has strained at a gnat and swallowed a camel. Its opportunity as a truly transformative power will wither as long as it recreates the same basic philosophical errors of the present system.

The fundamental issues do not, after all, hinge on pills, pesticides, x-rays, or who does what to whom. I trust it is clear from earlier chapters that we all have roots in the universe; that interpenetration of all matter is the rule; and that the dividing line between life and nonlife is illusory and arbitrary. There is only one valid way, thus, to partake of the universe—whether the partaking is of food, water, the love of another, or, indeed, a pill. That way is characterized by reverence—a reverence born of a felt sense of participation in the universe, of a kinship with all others and with all matter. Seen against the scope of a universal interpenetration, arguments over pills and herb teas, or about organic versus artificial therapies, begin to sound like the banter of children.

A reverential attitude that bespeaks a oneness with the universe can transform the commonest act. In certain holistic circles the ingestion of caffeine is decried. Yet the Japanese have for centuries elevated the simple act of caffeine consumption to the status of the tea ceremony, which has evolved into an astonishingly beautiful expression of spirituality. In the tea ceremony the meaning of space, time, and person are altered in ways we have previously examined. In the tea ceremony, no one quibbles about caffeine.

Is this analogy strained? What does the Japanese tea ceremony have to do with the legitimacy of medical acts of various sorts? In my view the comparison is valid—for any medication or therapeutic act can be partaken of in the same way. The great shamans have always known this. We have come full circle to my fellow intern, Jim, who ceremoniously used a simple act—clipping and burning a lock of hair—to save a dying man. It is not the act itself that is crucial, but the conscious attitudes that surround it. As the study of the petted and loved rabbits demonstrated, what is ingested is not as important as we usually believe; for the petted, loved rabbits were largely spared the deposition of cholesterol in their hearts' arteries, even though they ate the same cholesterol-rich diet as an unloved and unpetted group, a group that was ravaged by the disease. Giving medication, whatever the type, like drinking tea or partaking of food—or like clipping a lock of hair from a bewitched and dying man—can be done reverently. It is the sense of reverence, oneness, and unity that allows the power of healing to flower. This is power which, I feel, all true healers evoke. It is the power we have lost in our age, and which we may yet regain through a new understanding of space, time, matter, and self.

THE TOTAL-BODY-AS-MIND

Where in the body is our consciousness located? Almost no one seriously doubts its association with the brain. Our sense of "I" rests somewhere above the clavicles, and the rest of the body is relegated to an inferior, nonthinking category.

It is not true, however, that all humans assume the brain to be the seat of consciousness. Cultural differences profoundly influence these associations. Various cultures are known to confer the sense of "I" to sundry body parts—for instance, to the heart or to the central abdomen. Even within our own culture the idea of the locus of consciousness sometimes varies. Once when asked where her consciousness was located within her body, anthropologist Margaret Mead thought briefly and replied, "Why, all over!"

The most disturbing data bearing on our locus of consciousness, and what we mean by intelligence in general, comes from the well-known "split brain" work of neurophysiologist Roger Sperry. As part of a therapy for patients with intractable epilepsy, the communication between the right and left cerebral hemispheres of the brain (the corpus callosum) was interrupted surgically. Sperry found afterwards that these patients made different use of the two halves of the brain, a fact that is obscured in persons in whom the anatomic bridge between the brain's hemispheres is intact. He was able to demonstrate that the left cerebral hemisphere processed information in logical, verbal, and linear ways. The right hemisphere, however, functioned in nonlogical, nonlinear ways. It could process entire patterns and processes in nonverbal, intuitive modes. And, astonishingly, when only the right hemisphere was presented with (visual) information, it could process the stimuli and respond in highly complex and intelligent ways *without the occurrence of any conscious awareness*.

In the wake of Sperry's findings (for which he shared a Nobel Prize in medicine in 1981), an immediate problem presents itself. Our customary ways of equating conscious awareness and intelligence seem to be wrong. Our brain can think and perform intelligently without a shred of accompanying conscious experience. Quite obviously, then, intelligence, thought, and conscious awareness are not equatable.

But a curious problem arises. If an entire cerebral hemisphere can function outside our awareness, how can we know that other organs in the body that also function without any input into our conscious experience *do not also think*? Take, for example, the basic functional unit of the kidney, the nephron. We ordinarily conceive it to be a passive microscopic filter through which our blood flows. Metabolic wastes are cleansed from the filtered blood and are eventually excreted into the urine. An overtly simple process, the nephron's physiological feats are of astonishing complexity. It responds to an array of ever-changing signals with silent precision. Hormonal, neural, and osmotic events bring homeostatic mechanisms into play within the kidney without triggering even a glimmer of conscious awareness.

What is the difference between the behavior of the nephron mass in the human kidney and the right cerebral hemisphere in the human brain? We are conscious of neither. Both process information beneath our threshold of awareness. Yet we ascribe a "mental" quality to one and not the other. Why?

Do the acid-secreting parietal cells in the stomach think? Do the formed elements in our blood such as red cells, leukocytes, and platelets possess mental qualities? We must be open to the idea. If we ascribe the qualities of thought and mentation to our right brain, whose "thinking" frequently is completely unconscious, perhaps we should be reluctant to relegate all of our nonbrain body parts to the status of "dumb organs" simply because we are also unconscious of their function.

Biologists have, of course, long proposed that the automatic function of body parts was a survival mechanism for our species during our long evolutionary ascendency. If we had to consciously attend to the incredible variety of chemical, neural, and mechanical stimuli impacting on each of the millions of absorptive villi which line our intestinal tract we would likely be overwhelmed with information. Most of the events occurring in our body we do not know, nor do we need to know.

But maybe, just maybe, our skin *does* think—and our muscle cells and sweat glands and ear drums, too. Because we realize now that complex thought forms thrive in our unconscious "right brain," the possibility cannot be dismissed that the entire human organism is alive with thought.

Our concept of our brain as the center of thought may be utterly spurious, a kind of chauvinistic cerebralism which will not bear the scrutiny of our new knowledge. Far better, perhaps, to regard the entire body as a brain—if by brain we mean the site of human thought.

How do I retrieve information from my left fifth finger? How can I begin to perceive the amount of blood flowing to my foot? (These skills are routinely cultivated by subjects in biofeedback training.) There are, of course, actual anatomic bridges between these body parts and the brain—the network of peripheral nerves that ascend via the spinal cord to the cerebral hemispheres. The neurochemical events characterizing the transmission of information from distant body parts to the brain are well known.

But electrochemistry is not thought. And as we have seen, thought is not always conscious. What is the bridge between the electrochemical events in the body and human conscious experience? We do not know. This is the domain of the ancient "mind-body problem," a problem which, according to Brown, may be insuperable:

> There are two gigantic questions about consciousness and thought that may never be answered. The first is how the physical processes of the body, from the receptors of sensations in the toes to the labyrinthine exchange of information within the brain during thought, are translated into conscious experience. The second question that may forever defy explanation is how the electrochemical changes in the nerve cells transmit meaningful information, i.e., how information sensed by the nerve receptors of the body converge in brain substance to become the content of thought.[7]

How does the stimulus from my right hand become the content of my conscious awareness? How do I account for my sense of "I"? These are Brown's unanswerables. If there are questions in science that should be examined periodically simply for the purpose of stimulating a proper humility in scientists, these are surely they.

We know that the boundary between the conscious and unconscious is a dynamic one, one that is constantly shifting and always in motion. I may not remember what I had for dinner last Wednesday, but with some effort I might recall it. I may have no awareness of what the sole of my left foot feels like at this moment, but if I pay attention I begin to perceive signals from this part of my body. Conscious and unconscious information is always in a state of flux.

But how dynamic *is* the boundary between the conscious and unconscious? To what extent can body processes be brought into conscious *awareness*, and to what degree can they be brought under conscious *control*? Limits do seem to exist. For example, the unconscious mind can be shown to have abilities that *never* enter conscious awareness.[8] But for most physiologic events in the body we must profess a profound ignorance as to the limits of awareness and conscious control. It is an open question. In biofeedback laboratories subjects routinely develop conscious control of specific brain-wave patterns, sphincter contraction, and stomach acid secretion—body functions that have traditionally been regarded as beyond conscious control. Yet these events reveal that a rigid fixity is not a quality of the boundary between body and mind.

In one physiological function after another we have seen human subjects develop conscious awareness and control. Many body functions, therefore, behave just the same as a bimodal brain: although they ordinarily respond intelligently to complex stimuli without ever triggering our conscious awareness (as does the right cerebral hemisphere), they are capable of being "captured" and intentionally directed through logical, volitional, and conscious effort (the left hemispheric mode).

A new view of the body begins to emerge. Far from being comprised of dumb organs, body parts can be said to unconsciously think—*if* we wish to continue to insist that the right cerebral hemisphere thinks. Moreover, the function of many (perhaps all) of them can be influenced by conscious awareness. The interplay between autonomous control and control by the higher brain centers is so intimate that the very concept of body "part" is tenuous; and the attempt to conjure an image of the body made from bits and pieces automatically introduces inaccuracies into the way it functions. What view is more accurate? Perhaps that of a nonsegmented, indivisible process; or perhaps the view of "total-body-as-mind."

Yet we stubbornly resist the idea that other organs could occupy a co-equal status with the brain. After all, *something* must be in charge! We attribute a primacy to the brain, the presumed seat of consciousness, out of an assumption that the body's processes would run amok without some ultimate hierarchical restraint.

Our tendency to think in such terms reflects our prejudice in constructing our world along the lines of cause-and-effect. Nothing in the universe—nor in the body—happens without a cause, so we presume. Everywhere we look in the body we see evidence that we interpret in this way. For example, the hypothalamic region in the brain secretes a thyrotropin releasing factor that *causes* the pituitary gland to release thyrotropin, which in turn *causes* the thyroid gland to release thyroxin, which *causes* the metabolic rate of the body to be set at a certain level—the domino theory applied to the physiology.

Yet interpretations other than those that emphasize cause-and-effect are possible. As the French mathematician Henri Poincaré observed,

> Modern man has used cause-and-effect as ancient man used the gods, to give order to the universe. This is not because it was the truest system, but because it was the most convenient.[9]

Why is our cause-and-effect model of how the body works convenient? Simply because this explanation does for us what the belief in the gods did for ancient man: it confirms our world view. Our view of the universe dictates our view of the body; nothing, thus, happens without prior cause. We are blind to the fact that our view of the world and our view of the body are elected for reasons having more to do with convenience than with truth.

Our preference for a cause-and-effect view of body function is a result of what Koestler has called "the greatest superstition of our age—the materialistic clockwork universe of early nineteenth-century physics."[10] The superstition is so pervasive that we are blind to schemes of greater explanatory power.

Night invariably follows day, yet we do not believe that night causes day. Summer invariably follows spring, yet we know there is no causality involved. Why? After all, no exceptions to this sequence have ever been observed. We simply have more comprehensive models that deal with larger perspectives—those of planetary motion and solar system dynamics. We sense patterns rooted in universal processes. It simply has become *inconvenient* to use cause-and-effect to explain the day-night and spring-summer sequences.

Can we go beyond our traditional cause-and-effect habits in assessing our body function? Can we transcend our tendency to put the brain in charge, to impute intelligence only to the brain, and to relegate the rest of the body to the status of dumb organs? Unless we do so we shall continue to find ourselves believing such awkward fables as, "My brain caused my hand to write this word"—a construction no less absurd than the ancient notion that night invariably causes day.

We will begin to fathom the potential of the human body when we allow ourselves the larger view, a view which transcends cause-and-effect by emphasizing patterns, processes, and wholes; and when we free ourselves to taste the unity and oneness that interlocks the universe.

MEDICINE AND THE SECOND REVOLUTION

The possibility that human consciousness can exert measurable effects in the world may leave most medical scientists aghast. They may suggest a position of helplessness on the part of researchers— for if the world of the laboratory, the world of controlled medical investigation, is not objective but is subject to the caprice of mental activity, the entire scientific endeavor is hopeless. A reality that shifts according to the conscious whims of the experimenter or the subject is no reality at all. It is an unstable panoply of events against which the techniques of science cannot possibly be applied. An objective world is required by science.

Yet this conclusion is surely false. In spite of the agreement by many quantum physicists that there are profound nonobjective facets to reality, quantum mechanics is alive and well and flourishing. It did not cease to exist with the recognition of a nonobjective world. Rockets still go to the moon, and prediction is still possible. By analogy, the insistence by modern bioscience that medical reality is not and cannot be affected by factors of consciousness reflects an unfounded fear. There is no reason to suppose that medicine as a scientific discipline will cease to exist if it admits consciousness to be an important factor in the investigation of health and disease.

Indeed, it would be the richer for it. If all the medical experimentation ever done contained concealed effects of the conscious activity of the experimenter and of the subject; if response to all therapeutic endeavors was shown to be nonobjective in principle; and if the natural course of all human illness were influenced by factors of consciousness, we would have thereby discovered a force in medicine potentially powerful enough to dwarf any achievement of the modern scientific era. There is no cause for a forlorn sense of loss on seeing the departure of a sheer objectivity from medicine. Rather, a celebration is in order, a joy born of a clearer vision.

The rejection of belief in a principle that never existed and that was never really needed has always been a milestone in the growth of science. The belief in the ether, in the existence of caloric, and in phlogiston were painfully discarded in an earlier day, all to the greater health of science. But these revisions dealt with the *content* of science only; and if they were painfully discarded, the redefinition of the character and essence of science will be even more agonizing for those involved. No matter how chaotic these changes prove to be in medicine, however, the loss of the illusion of objectivity will be no less than the loss of fetters and chains. The requirement that medical science be objective has forced the virtual denial of a potent factor in health and disease, that of conscious mental activity. We now face the prospect of utilizing conscious intervention in admissible and intelligent ways. Entirely new therapies stand to be developed, freeing us from forms of treatment based solely on an inhumane reductionism.

The rules that will guide the new nonobjective medicine may be different in kind from the old rules, but can nevertheless be implemented and formulated according to a strict discipline. All is not lost. There are no directions in the cosmos, yet astronomers can still find their way around with great precision. And in a nonobjective reality the discipline of medicine will remain; but in it we will find our way according to a new sense of direction, the power of which we are at last beginning to fathom.

In *A Sense of the Future*, Bronowski stated,

> So the second scientific revolution has abandoned the hidden tenets of the first. Its model of nature no longer assumes that she must be causal, continuous, and independent. These assumptions were idealized from everyday experience, and they were right, and splendidly successful, during two centuries when physics worked and measured on the everyday scale. They have turned out to be false on the small scale of the atom and on the large scale of the nebulas, and at least inappropriate to studies of the living.[11]

Our orthodox models in medicine have come to the same fate as the models of the first scientific revolution: they are sadly inappropriate to studies of the living. Just as the older physical models of the universe wrongly attributed causal and independent qualities to the universe, the current medical models impart the same qualities to man. And just as the clockwork picture of the universe that was dictated by these attributes was abandoned in the onslaught of new data, our mechanistic views of health and illness will give way to new models which, too, will be more consistent with the true face of the universe.

The second scientific revolution has finally begun to stir medicine. We can hope that it brings with it what we have never had: a medical model which at last is appropriate to the study of the living.

REDUCTIONISM: A LAST AND FUTURE LOOK

A feature of such a new model will be its ability to span the heretofore unbridgeable chasm separating a humanistic medicine and a reductionistic bioscience. Any new model must deal squarely with the assertions that we are nothing more than the consequence of our anatomy and physiology, the traditional contention of mechanistic, reductionistic science. The reflex action of most humanists and holists in medicine has been to search for clever reasons and evidence to contradict this doleful possibility—without having been able, however, to convince the reductionists of their errors. No future prospect for medicine could be headier than the potential resolution of this ageless debate.

Perhaps these well-worn, stalemated arguments can now be steered in a fresh direction. Both sides—those who fight for a primacy for human consciousness and those who maintain that our blind cellular chemistry is dominant—have yet to deal with key assertions that are now beginning to flow from certain areas of modern science. In surmising how the debate might turn, consider some of the issues we have observed:

(1) Matter has become "de-materialized" by modern physics. The emphasis is no longer on objects, but on processes, fields, and wholes.

(2) Cause and effect are not identifiable at the most fundamental levels in nature where individual events take place.

(3) Dividing lines in nature between the microscopic/macroscopic, living/nonliving, and conscious/unconscious appear increasingly arbitrary, if not impossible to define.

Now we can ask: if the reductionists *are* right, and if mind, consciousness, and all human activity can be reduced to the behavior of matter, *where for the humanist does the tragedy lie?* For with the modern redefinition of matter the tragedy vanishes. The debate is turned on its head, and it is just possible that *the humanist wins the argument by losing it.* For matter is not matter in the old sense, the sense in which the humanist-reductionist debate was born, but is something altogether different.

What is matter? Not the isolated, fragmented, dead pieces of mere "stuff" whose behavior is governed by nature's ironclad laws, but something which in the modern sense has been utterly transformed. *It is that in which is included the whole* (Bohm). *It is that whose movement shakes the entire universe* (Eddington). *It is that in which can be found the rudiments of mind itself* (Delbrück, Walker). *It is that whose very nature depends on the consciousness of the human who is observing it* (Heisenberg, Wheeler). *It is that to which death cannot be attributed* (Bohm). *It is that which defies entropic decay and disorganization* (Prigogine). *And it is that which shares with spiritual values a similar kind of reality* (Wigner).

What, thus, is tragic about our reduction to matter? Is not such a fate surely more an elevation that a reduction or a debasement? How can we continue to use words such as "nothing but" and "mere" in describing matter?

I feel, even as I write these words, a genuine amusement in considering the possibility that reductionism may turn out to be correct after all, but for all the wrong reasons, for reasons never predicted by a classical, reductionistic science. Or can we say that the reductionists have provided the humanists a victory by showing that we are "no more" than "mere" matter? If so, it will have been a strange struggle between humanism and reductionism, one which both opponents have ironically won.

If the nature of matter proves to resemble the presentiments of the above scientists, then *it is precisely matter that we should wish to be, for the reason that matter has become ourselves*. Prigogine's words are again appropriate:

> Nature is part of us, as we are part of it. We can recognize ourselves in the description we give to it.[12]

If the debate over reductionism were to prove tractable along these or similar lines, the resolution would itself suggest a strange self-reflective loop: reductionism becoming one with the opposing view, for reasons which themselves hinge on unity, on oneness.

We cannot know, of course, which future directions the humanist-reductionist debate may take for the reason that we have as yet no complete knowledge of the qualities of mind *or* matter. Perhaps we shall see the debate sharpen in future times as never before, as new knowledge arises. But for my part, I think this would be quite unlikely—for the signposts in nature pointing to a unity between man and the world, and between mind and matter, are simply too numerous to ignore. The future thus points, I feel, toward a rapprochement between humanistic medicine and scientific reductionism.

CONCLUSION

No attempts to refine our present medical system will prove ultimately successful unless they address the deficiencies of the most basic assumptions on which the system rests. We have examined these assumptions in the preceding chapters, looking to science for fresh approaches to the fundamental meanings of time, space, birth, death, health, and illness. The resulting models exhibited the salient feature of oneness and unity between man and nature.

The physicist Paul Dirac once remarked,

> It is more important to have beauty in one's equations than to have them fit experiment.[13]

The same requirement holds, I feel, for medical models as well as for equations. And when medical models embody beauty—the beauty of oneness and unity—*and* fit experiment, there is cause for delight.

But the new models proposed herein, though perhaps more beautiful and delightful to some than are the old ones, are not yet quite right, either: no scientific theory has ever escaped eventual revision and modification, and the proposed models will be no exception. Newer models will emerge. What form they will take remains to be seen. We can fathom, however, that to the extent that they have beauty and simplicity, and to the degree, perhaps, that they increase our delight, they are correct; and that to the extent that they embody unnecessary complexity and ugliness, and add to our dread of dissolution and death as do the old models, they are to be eschewed.

Sit down before fact like a little child, and be prepared to give up every preconceived notion, follow humbly wherever and to whatever abyss Nature leads, or you shall learn nothing.

—T. H. HUXLEY

POSTSCRIPT: MYOCARDIAL INFARCTION 2000 A.D.

SAM PLATTE, NOW IN HIS 50s, had looked forward for years to fishing these high mountain lakes once again. He first discovered them thirty years ago, and they still teemed with cutthroat and brook trout. For Sam these alpine meadows and jewelled lakes were paradise incarnate.

Yet he was unaccountably tired. Ordinarily robust, he experienced a fatigue he simply could not explain in view of a morning of leisurely fishing. Gradually his tiredness became oppressive. He became perceptibly short of breath and slightly nauseated. Strangely, though the air was crisp, he had begun to sweat. When the heavy sensation in his chest evolved into a gnawing, dull ache he knew something was wrong. As the ache spread to his neck and left arm, Sam activated the cardiovascular monitoring device built into his wrist watch, which gathered information by sensing the dynamics of the pulsation of the radial artery in the wrist. Within thirty seconds the digital display had given him serial readings of his blood pressure and heart rate. The information was alarming: his blood pressure was subnormal and was falling, and his pulse rate was slow and erratic. Sam Platte knew he was experiencing a heart attack.[1]

He weighed his options. He knew the first hour following the onset of symptoms of a myocardial infarction was critical. Traditional outlets—the hospital emergency room and coronary care unit—simply were not available. Just as well, he thought; for in matters of health he preferred the new ways, his own ways.

Laying his fishing rod beside him, in full command of his senses, he slowly sank supine to the soft, green moss surrounding the lake. Another reading from the cardiovascular wrist monitor confirmed his earlier findings. He reasoned that his problem likely lay in an obstructed coronary artery in the heart, causing a deficit in the flow of blood and oxygen to a particular part of the heart muscle. The heart's main pumping chamber, the left ventricle, deprived thus of its necessary nutrients, was failing. The forward ejection of blood from the heart was diminishing, accounting for the fall in blood pressure and shortness of breath. The heart muscle responded to this insult by developing a slow, inefficient and chaotic rhythm. Sam Platte knew these events would likely terminate in death unless he acted quickly.

He first initiated constriction of the blood vessels in the periphery of his body, expertly using mental strategies to divert blood from certain body parts—skin, arms, legs—to the body core, thus raising the blood pressure.[2,3,4] During this process, and indeed since the initial recognition of his dilemma, he remained in intimate awareness of his psychological state. He knew of the potentially devastating effects of fear, anxiety, and terror in the setting of a myocardial infarction.[5,6] It was well known that these emotions greatly increased the likelihood of the development of malignant, fatal irregularities of the heartbeat. Sam Platte remained in control of his emotions.

Yet, ironically, it was not *control* for which he was now striving. In the years he had dedicated to learning these disciplines of self-regulation, he had learned that only through an ineffable, passive volition, a giving up, could control come about.[7] In his own mental strategy, Sam gave himself over to a greater wisdom—as he conceived it, the wisdom of the body, the wisdom of the universe. For him this was not an overt religious expression, but a recognition of the interrelatedness and oneness that he knew to be an accepted facet of the scientific world view.[8]

Lying on the soft, lush lake shore, Sam internalized his world view: he allowed the wisdom he believed in to flow through him and to become part of him, as he became part of it. Through years of disciplined practice he had learned that this commingling, this internalization, exerted real consequences—that his own attitudes about his relationship to the universe emerged physiologically, creating concrete, measurable bodily change. He knew that a world view that reflected isolation, fragmentation, and aloneness emerged as fear and anxiety, and generated in situations such as this a cascade of physiologically destructive concomitants. He had learned that the alternative stance of relatedness and oneness with the world annulled in large measure these malignant events and evinced an equilibrium of mind and body he sorely needed now. Yet this was no selfish strategy he was electing, as if to escape some dreadful fate; he merely set himself to the path which for him now seemed truest. In fact, he saw his present experience not as a crisis or plight, but merely an event in space and time which could be recognized as such and dealt with if he so elected. And it was his choice to deal with this event definitively and in his own way.

Still he could not say precisely why he was capable of maintaining an unmoved psychological equanimity, but he knew his world view was somehow fundamentally involved in the process. He disregarded the possibility of personal extinction because, quite simply, he could not confirm it as a reasonable possibility, since it fit neither with his experiential states nor with the most accurate scientific descriptions of the physical world he could lay hold of.[9] He knew that interrelatedness was a fundamental factor in the then-accepted version of reality;[10] that science had disregarded time as divisible into past, present, and future; and that modern molecular biology had unsuccessfully attempted to demarcate the world of the living from the nonliving.[11] Thus, for Sam Platte, mortality and immortality simply were not cogent issues.

He then began to dispatch his pain to the level of imperceptibility.[12,13,14] Here he *knew* the physiological events involved—the willful, conscious release of pain-relieving chemicals of astonishing potency which were endogenous in brain cells, and which had been known for a quarter of a century. Of all the feats he had learned to exercise volitionally, this was the easiest. Moreover, Sam *enjoyed* this exercise—not only for the relief of his pain, but because of the definite euphoria elicited by the chemicals themselves.

As his pain faded beyond perception, Sam took another reading from the cardiovascular monitor. He was pleased with the data. His blood pressure was higher, now near normal; and his heart rate and rhythm were stable at acceptable levels.[15]

Having dealt with immediacies, he put finer skills to work. Sam had learned that purposeful intent could be brought to bear on sophisticated hematological functions.[16] Particularly relevant in his present situation were factors involved in blood clotting: the "stickiness" of the blood particles called platelets; the stability of blood clots inside veins and arteries; and the spasm of blood vessels.[17] Although he had no clear idea of the precise mechanism he would use, he committed himself now to the task of reversing the pathological clotting process in the coronary artery, which was responsible for his present dilemma. He knew the affected heart muscle was likely to be still viable—the obstructing process had not been present long enough for significant damage to ensue. Sam Platte had seen the evidence for voluntary control of these phenomena. Although he had cultivated the commonplace skill of altering blood coagulability externally—e.g., stopping cuts from bleeding[18]—he had never set about to alter the clotting process inside his body.

For this task he used mental imagery and visualization which for him seemed natural and reasonable and with an intensity commensurate to the gravity of the situation. His strategy seemed to work well, for within minutes another reading from the monitor revealed data that were completely within the physiologically normal range.

Exhausted, he fell asleep.

Sam awoke hours later. He felt well, as calm and placid as this reflective mountain lake, whose surface was beginning now to be broken by trout in their evening feeding. A golden sun was setting, and it was time for evening camp chores. He lay quietly for a while longer, pondering the events of the afternoon. He had averted a heart attack. Would he be capable of doing so next time?

He let the words "again," "next," and "time" filter through his mind—meaningless words he now thought, belonging to an obsolete view of reality, which had once held time to be linear, composed of a past, present, and future. In his earlier years, Sam too had held such a view. Reflecting on his own transitions in thinking, he smiled.

Gently retrieving his fishing rod he rose, noticing the impression his body had left in the lush moss. Slowly, quietly, he turned toward camp.

CLASSICAL AND MODERN PHYSICS: AN OVERVIEW

SINCE PHYSICS ESTABLISHED ITS PREEMINENCE in the early dawn of the scientific era as the repository of precision and predictability, medicine has looked to it as a role model. The world view of classical Newtonian physics provided physicians a working view of health, illness, birth, and death. From the clockwork universe of traditional physics came the model of the clockwork body—ticking away in perfect deterministic fashion unless perturbed, of course, by mechanical breakdowns we have learned to call disease.

A search for new models demands an examination of the models now in vogue—entailing, thus, a consideration of classical physics and its relationships to modern physical views.*

Perhaps the most abrupt turn in the history of the advance of science has been the revolutionary transitions that occurred in physics in this century. Every basic tenet of the older Newtonian view of how the world behaves has been abandoned in our century in favor of a radically new model. One of the primary contentions of this book is that medicine, if it is to command credence as a modern scientific discipline, must now face the repercussions of these changes. We are beginning to realize that an awkward situation has arisen in medicine: its traditional role model has changed, but medicine has not changed with it. *Space, Time and Medicine* explores the radical and inevitable changes faced by medicine.

---

*For fuller discussions of classical and modern physics, the following sources are recommended for the layman: Fritjof Capra, *The Tao of Physics* (Boulder: Shambhala, 1975), Fred Alan Wolf, *Taking the Quantum Leap* (San Francisco: Harper and Row, 1981), Gary Zukav, *The Dancing Wu Li Masters* (New York: William Morrow, 1979).

Physicists attempt to answer a fundamental question: how does the world behave? In the quest for answers, certain traits begin to stand out as irreducible features of the world itself. In the 1600s these features began to emerge primarily from the work of the great physicist Sir Isaac Newton.

Newton's universe can generally be regarded as behaving along the lines of common sense. Things went according to the way it seemed they *should* go. That this picture of the world survived almost unchallenged for nearly 300 years surely had to do with the fact that it was *so* compatible with human experience there was little room to doubt it.

Newton's universe was felt to be built of constituent parts, the atoms. These fundamental units were the bit pieces and building blocks that had early been postulated by Democritus and others. Nature was seen to be an assemblage of parts that behaved dynamically much like pellets or miniaturized billiard balls. These units of matter were fundamentally distinguishable from the empty space surrounding them, and they existed in a time that was axiomatically linear, consisting of a past, present, and future. Time flowed, much like a stream, and events occurred in the present moment linking past and future. Moreover, all events had distinct causes, although one might not know the cause at the time; and the proof that a cause existed was quite simply the observation that an event had indeed occurred.

Using these basic features of the world, Newton devised laws to describe how events unfolded in nature. These laws were magnificent not only for their elegant simplicity, but in their awesome power to predict. This powerful quality of prediction gave rise to the notion that if one had certain information about the universe—such as the position, velocity, and mass of all the particles comprising it—one could, using Newton's few simple laws, predict forever what would occur. Moreover, one could infer what had already happened into the infinite past as well. For this reason it is said that Newton's universe was one which could as easily run backward as forward.

The concept arose, thus, of the "ironclad laws of nature," which held the universe in a tight, mechanical grasp. As a consequence of Newton's laws, all seemed utterly determined and knowable.

It was against this background of certainty that a cascade of transformative events began to occur at the turn of this century. In 1887 the Michelson-Morley experiment cast grave doubts on the classical concept of the ether as the transport medium for energetic events in nature. Sir J.J. Thompson's discovery of the electron in 1896 destroyed the notion of the atom as the irreducible component of matter. And in 1900 Max Planck announced his "lucky guess," Planck's constant, showing that energy in nature was not smooth and continuous but lumpy and bumpy. Planck gave the name "quanta" to these packets of energy. His own attitude toward his monumental discovery reflected the power of the scientific dogma of the time: he was extremely reluctant to publish his findings, so poorly did they fit with anything which had come before.

Still, in 1900 the prevailing mood in physics was overwhelmingly one of self-assurance and confidence. In that year Lord Kelvin, one of the eminent physicists of the day, in an address to London's Royal Society stated that the mission of physics and physicists was almost done. There were only a few little "clouds" remaining to be cleared, and the job would then be completed. No one could have intuited what was to come.

In 1905, with the publication of Einstein's special theory of relativity, the sky fell on the secure, knowable, deterministic world of traditional physics. Einstein's stunning new views were so clearly presented and were so persuasive that within months they had been circulated and received by physicists around the world. After Einstein, physics would never be the same.

Today we recognize Einstein's special theory of relativity and the quantum theory as the two major cornerstones of modern physics. (Einstein's special theory of relativity has never elicited any experimental data to contradict it, and is on much firmer conceptual and experimental footing than his general theory.) These theories provide us with a world view that stands in stark contrast to the legacy of Newton, and their emergence is a superb example of what T. H. Huxley described as the most tragic event in science: the slaying of a beautiful theory by an ugly fact.

Today it is little appreciated that the movement from the sure, comfortable, traditional views in physics to the new ideas of the world was extraordinarily discomfiting for the central figures involved. One gets the picture of painful existential dilemmas being provoked in some of the protagonists by their confrontation with the findings of the "crazy atomic experiments," as Heisenberg called them. The recognition of this discomfiture is important, for it points to a crucial feature of this revolution in science. Those who were involved did not concoct the astonishing new views in any willful and arbitrary way; they did so out of necessity. They were faced with recurring, ineluctable data flowing from actual experiments. As scientists they had no choice.

What view has emerged from quantum theory? We have mentioned one aspect of the new picture, that of the discontinuous nature of energy. Moreover, the concept of building blocks in nature was abandoned. As Bohr continuously warned, "Electrons are not things." Nature's "particles" were shown to behave both as particles and waves, depending on the experimental design. Electrons exhibited curious behavior, appearing everywhere in their orbit at once, albeit more at one point than another, but everywhere present to some degree, ill fitting the earlier concept of discrete units. These characteristics forced an abandonment, thus, of Newton's earlier absolute distinctions between mass and empty space. In order to accommodate the strange features demonstrated by these "particles," the concept of the field arose. It was recognized that these fields were not independent in the way that particles were earlier presumed to be, but were fundamentally interconnected. The great English astronomer-physicist Sir Arthur Eddington epitomized this interrelatedness in his famous remark, "When the electron vibrates, the universe shakes."

A strict causality in quantum physics was jettisoned with the realization that single events at the subatomic level were unpredictable even in principle. There was an inherent randomness at nature's inner core. Heisenberg showed, moreover, that there were built-in limits to our ability to extract knowledge at this level. In his famous uncertainty principle, he demonstrated that one could not simultaneously determine the position and velocity of a particle. One had to choose what one wished to know, for one could not know both.

The view arose through quantum theory, therefore, that there simply was no physics in the modern sense for the individual subatomic event. Physics had to content itself with knowledge of large numbers of happenings before it could speak accurately. The old ironclad, deterministic view, therefore, gave way to one of a statistical and probabilistic nature. When collections of events were considered, however, the predictive capacity again surfaced with great accuracy—presenting, some said, merely another face of the older determinism; but the previous assurance of sheer knowability at all levels in nature had vanished.

No feature of quantum physics is more revolutionary that its acknowledgement of the subjective aspects of the world. The classical view held the world to be totally objective. It was "out there," depending in no way for human conscious activity to bring it into being. The world had a status that was completely independent from the way humans thought about it. In the modern view, however (according to the most widely held interpretation of quantum mechanics, the Copenhagen interpretation), human consciousness participates in the edition of reality that meets our eye. In fact, without an observer the concept of "reality" simply has no currency. For at the level of individual subatomic events, because of their inherent random, statistical, and probabilistic nature, several outcomes for each event are always theoretically possible. It is the act of actually observing that causes these possibilities to cohere into what we perceive as a single event in the world. Without the participation of an observer, what we refer to as reality simply does not unfold. Thus, the strictly objective status of the physical world has been transcended in the new view, and is replaced by a version of reality which attributes central importance to human consciousness.

From Einstein's special theory of relativity come ideas that are as revolutionary as any which emerged from quantum theory. Einstein asserted that the speed of light—not space and time, as Newton maintained—was absolute for every observer in the universe, regardless of his/her speed of travel. He proceeded to show how the notion of an absolute past, present, and future was indefensible; that "reality" could be ordered differently for different observers; how energy and mass were interconvertible; and how space and time necessarily fused experientially. The strength of the special theory of relativity was the same as that of the quantum theory: its predictions were repeatedly confirmed through the most rigorous experiments. Even the most audacious aspects of the theory, such as the slowing of time as the velocity of a particle increased; the slowing of clocks as they approached the speed of light; the contraction of measuring rods as their velocity increased; and the increase in the mass of an object with increasing velocity were born out experimentally time after time.

How can the view of nature portrayed in modern physics possibly be correct when it is so dissonant with our common sense ideas of how the world behaves? Alas, modern physics cannot help us with such questions; for physicists are concerned only with how well a theory succeeds in predicting events, not how compatible it may be with our expectations and prejudices. And in terms of their predictive power, the quantum theory and the theory of special relativity have no strong competitors. There simply are no compelling theoretical alternatives that could be used to restructure the Newtonian model of the world.

For the layman whose common sense is rudely trammeled by the modern point of view, perhaps there is the consolation that these bizarre notions are shocking and abrasive to physicists themselves. Their capacity to handily integrate the new ideas is, in fact, limited, and has given rise to the observation that physicists never really understand a new theory, they just get used to it.

NOTES

PART I

Chapter One

1. Alexandra David-Neel, *Magic and Mysticism in Tibet* (New York: Dover, 1971), p. 51.

Chapter Two

1. Willis Harman, *Symposium on Consciousness* (New York: Penguin, 1977), p. 3.
2. Lyall Watson, "Delusion: Collective Unconscious," in *Lifetide* (New York: Simon and Schuster, 1979), p. 206.
3. Thomas S. Kuhn, *The Structure of Scientific Revolutions* (Chicago: University of Chicago Press, 1962), p. 112.
4. Ibid., pp. 126–127.
5. Jacob Bronowski, *A Sense of the Future* (Cambridge: MIT Press, 1977), p. 42.
6. Werner Heisenberg, "Quantum Mechanics and a Talk with Einstein (1925– 1926)," in *Physics and Beyond* (New York: Harper and Row, 1971), pp. 59–69.
7. Jerome D. Frank, "Mind-Body Relationships in Illness and Healing," *Journal of the International Academy of Preventive Medicine*, vol. 2, No. 3, 1975, pp. 46–59.
8. H. Rasmussen, *Pharos* 38, 1975, p. 53.
9. George L. Engel, "The Need for a New, Medical Model: A Challenge For Biomedicine," *Science* 196, 1977, pp. 129– 136.
10. Ibid.

PART II

Chapter Two

1. G. J. Whitrow, *The Nature of Time* (London: Thames and Hudson, 1972), p. 11.
2. H. Nichols, "The Psychology of Time," *American Journal of Psychology*, vol. 3, 1891, pp. 453–529.
3. Robert E. Ornstein, *On the Experience of Time* (New York: Penguin, 1969), p. 101.
4. Ibid., p. 23.
5. Whitrow, *Nature of Time*, p. 15.
6. B. L. Whorf, *The Technology Review* 42: 229, 1940.
7. Whitrow, *Nature of Time*, p. 22.

Chapter Three

1. Mircea Eliade, *The Myth of the Eternal Return* (Princeton: Princeton University Press, 1954), p. 34.
2. Ibid., p. 35.
3. Ibid.
4. Ibid., pp. 85–86.
5. Ibid., p. 86.
6. C. Gottlieb, in the *Meaning of Death*, ed. H. Feifel (New York: McGraw-Hill, 1959), pp. 157–188.
7. Whitrow, *Nature of Time*, p. 14.
8. Ibid.

Chapter Four

1. Thomas Gold, "Relativity and Time" in *The Encyclopedia of Ignorance*, ed. R. Duncan and M. Weston-Smith (New York: Pergamon, 1977), p. 100.

2. A. S. Eddington, *The Mathematical Theory of Relativity* (Cambridge: Cambridge University Press, 1957), pp. 23–25.

3. Eliade, *Eternal Return*, pp. 89–90.

4. Louis de Broglie, in *Albert Einstein: Philosopher-Scientist*, ed. P. A. Schilpp (La Salle, Ill.: The Open Court Publishing Co., 1949), p. 113.

5. T. S. Eliot, "Tradition and the Individual Talent," in *the silent Zero, in search of Sound . . .*, trans. E. Sackheim (New York: Grossman, 1968), p. xiii.

6. R. H. Major, *Classic Descriptions of Disease* (Springfield: Charles C. Thomas, 1932), p. 534.

7. Bertrand Russell, *Mysticism and Logic and Other Essays* (London: Longmans Green, 1925), p. 21.

8. *Webster's New Collegiate Dictionary* (Springfield: Merriam, 1960).

9. Bertrand Russell, *Mysticism*, p. 21.

Chapter Five

1. K. Hamner, "Experimental Evidence for the Biological Clock," in *The Voices of Time*, ed. J. T. Fraser (New York: Braziller, 1966).

2. Gay G. Luce, *Biological Rhythms in Human and Animal Physiology* (New York: Dover, 1971).

3. Ornstein, *Experience of Time*, p. 31.

4. Ibid.

5. Ibid., p. 22.

6. Ibid.

7. Ibid., p. 34.

8. R.G.H. Siu, *Chi, A Neo-Taoist Approach to Life* (Cambridge: MIT Press, 1974), p. 154.

9. Ibid.

10. Ibid., p. 155.

11. Ibid.

12. Ibid.

13. Ibid.

14. Ibid.

15. Ornstein, *Experience of Time*, p. 32.

16. Siu, *Chi*, p. 156.

17. Ibid.

18. Ibid., p. 159.

19. O. Fenichel, *The Psychoanalytic Theory of Neuroses* (New York: Norton, 1945), p. 204.

20. Siu, *Chi*, p. 160.

21. Ornstein, *Experience of Time*, p. 103.

22. Lawrence LeShan, *How to Meditate* (Boston: Little, Brown, 1974).

Chapter Six

1. *Zen Buddhism* (Mount Vernon, N.Y.: The Peter Pauper Press, 1959), pp. 53–54.

2. Arthur Eddington, *The Nature of the Physical World* (New York: MacMillan, 1931), p. 419.

3. Ilse Rosenthal-Schneider, in *Albert Einstein: Philospher-Scientist* (La Salle, Ill: The Open Court Publishing Co., 1949), p. 132.

4. Ibid., p. 136.

5. Ibid., p. 137.

Chapter Eight

1. M. Friedman and R. H. Rosenman, *Type A Behavior and Your Heart* (New York: Alfred A. Knopf, 1974).

2. M. Cooper and M. Aygen, "Effect of Meditation on Blood Cholesterol and Blood Pressure," *Journal of the Israel Medical Association* 95:1, July 2, 1978.

3. N. H. Cassem, T. P. Hackett, and H. A. Wishnie, "The Coronary Care Unit: An Appraisal of its Psychological Hazards," *New England Journal of Medicine* 279:1365, 1968.

4. P. M. West, E. M. Blumberg, and F. W. Ellis, "An Observed Correlation Between Psychological Factors and Growth Rate of Cancer in Man, *Cancer Research* 12:306, 1952.

5. Cooper and Aygen, "Effect of Meditation."

6. O. Carl Simonton, Stephanie Matthews-Simonton, and James Creighton *Getting Well Again* (Los Angeles: J. P. Tarcher, 1978).

7. Jeanne Achterberg, and G. Frank Lawlis, *Imagery of Cancer* (Champaign, Illinois: Institute for Personality and Ability Testing, 1978).

PART III

Chapter One

1. Erich Jantsch, *The Self-Organizing Universe* (New York: Pergamon, 1980), p. 97.

2. S. Vaisrub, "Groping For Causation." *Journal of the American Medical Association* 241:8, 830, 1979.

3. Idries Shah, *The Sufis* (New York: Anchor, 1971), p. 63.

4. C. B. Thomas, "Precursors of Premature Disease and Death: The Predictive Potential of Habits and Family Attitudes," *Annals of Internal Medicine* 85:653–658, 1976.

5. Leonard R. Derogatis, M.D. Abeloff, and N. Melisaratos, "Psychological Coping Mechanisms and Survival Time in Metastatic Breast Cancer," *Journal of the American Medical Association* Vol. 242, No. 14, October 15, 1979, pp. 1504–1508.

6. *Work in America: Report of a Special Task Force to the Secretary of Health, Education, and Welfare* (Cambridge: MIT Press, 1973).

7. Cassem, Hackett, and Wishnie, "The Coronary Care Unit."

8. R. M. Nerem, M. J. Levesque, and J. F. Cornhill, "Social Environment As a Factor in Diet-Induced Atherosclerosis," *Science* 208:1475–1476, 1980.

9. Philip Slater, *The Wayward Gate* (Boston: Beacon Press, 1977), p. 106.

10. C. D. Jenkins, "Psychological and Social Precursors of Coronary Disease," *The New England Journal of Medicine* 284:244–255, 1971.

11. *Work in America*

12. Cooper and Aygen, "The Effect of Meditation."

13. Ibid.

14. R. A. Stone, and J. DeLeo, "Psychotherapeutic Control of Hypertension," *New England Journal of Medicine* 294:80, 1976.

15. Ron Jevning, A. F. Wilson, and J. M. Davidson, "Adrenocortical Activity During Meditation, *Hormones and Behavior* 10:54–60, 1978.

16. J. H. Medalie and U. Goldbourt, "Angina Pectoris Among 10,000 Men II: Psychosocial and Other Risk Factors as Evidenced by a Multivariate Analysis of Five-year Incidence Study," *American Journal of Medicine* 60:910–921, 1976.

17. G. W. Brown and T. Harris, *Social Origins of Depression: A Study of Psychiatric Disorder in Women* (New York: The Free Press, 1978).

18. S. J. Schleifer, "Bereavement and Lymphocyte Function," Presentation to American Psychiatric Association Annual Meeting, San Francisco, May 1980.

19. A. S. Kraus and A. M. Lilienfeld, "Some Epidemiological Aspects of the High Mortality Rate in the Young Widowed Group," *Journal of Chronic Disease* 10:207–217, 1959.

20. M. Young, B. Bernard, and G. Wallis, "The Mortality of Widowers," *Lancet* 1963; 454–456.

21. L. F. Berman, and S. L. Syme, "Social Networks, Host Resistance, and Mortality: A Nine-year Follow-up of Alameda County Residents," *American Journal of Epidemiology* 109:186–204, 1979.

22. L. Eisenberg, "What Makes Persons 'Patients' and 'Patients' Well?" *American Journal of Medicine* 69:277–286, 1980.

23. T. H. Holmes and R. H. Rahe, "The Social Readjustment Rating Scale," *Journal of Psychosomatic Medicine* 11:213–218, 1967.

24. T. Dobzhansky, *Genetics and the Origin of Species*, 3rd ed. (New York: Columbia University Press, 1951), pp. 78–79.

25. A. Montague, *On Being Human* (New York: Hawthorn, 1966), p. 30.

26. Ibid., p. 31.

27. Ibid., p. 32.

28. Ibid., p. 33.

29. G. G. Simpson, *Life of the Past* (New Haven: Yale University Press, 1953), p. 56.

30. R. Dawkins, *The Selfish Gene* (New York: Oxford University Press, 1976).

31. E. Schrödinger, "The Mystery of the Sensual Qualities," in *What Is Life?* and *Mind and Matter* (Cambridge: Cambridge University Press, 1967), pp. 166–178.

32. Ibid., p. 176.

Chapter Two

1. G. Murchie, *The Seven Mysteries of Life* (Boston: Houghton Mifflin, 1978), p. 321.

2. B. D. Davis, "Frontiers of the Biological Sciences," *Science* 209:88, 1980.

3. Murchie, *Seven Mysteries*, p. 320.

4. Colin Blakemore, *Mechanics of the Mind* (New York: Cambridge University Press, 1977), p. 22.

5. Schrödinger, "The Mystery," p. 172.

6. Fritjof Capra, *The Tao of Physics* (Boulder: Shambhala Publications, 1975), p. 209.

7. Ibid.

8. Ibid., p. 210.

9. G. Zukav, *The Dancing Wu Li Masters* (New York: William Morrow, 1979), p. 315.

Chapter Three

1. M. Lukas, "The World According to Ilya Prigogine," *Quest/80*, December, 1980, p. 88.

2. Ibid.

3. Jacques Monod, *Chance and Necessity* (New York: Alfred A. Knopf, 1971).

4. Lukas, "Ilya Prigogine."

5. M. Ferguson, *The Aquarian Conspiracy* (Los Angeles: J. P. Tarcher, 1980), pp. 165–166.

6. T. Merton, *The Way of Chuang Tzu* (New York: New Directions, 1969).

7. F. Barron, "The Psychology of Imagination," *Scientific American*, September, 1958.

8. L. Thomas, *The Lives of a Cell* (New York: Viking, 1974), p. 75.

Chapter Four

1. H. Margenau, "Metaphysical Elements in Physics," *Review of Modern Physics*, Vol. B, No. 3, July 1941, pp. 176–189.

2. J.S. Bell, *Physics* 1, 1965, p. 195.

3. H.S. Stapp, "Correlation Experiments and the Nonvalidity of Ordinary Ideas About the Physical World," *Physical Review*, D3, 1971, p. 1303.

4. A. Einstein, B. Podolsky, and Nathan Rosen, "Can Quantum Mechanical Description of Reality Be Considered Complete?" *Physical Review* 47, 1935, pp. 777ff.

5. Ferguson, *Aquarian Conspiracy*, p. 171.

6. J.F. Clauser and M.A. Horne, *Physical Review* D10, 1974, p. 526.

7. Zukav, *Wu Li Masters*, p. 320.

8. B. d'Espagnat, "The Quantum Theory and Reality," *Scientific American*, December, 1979, pp. 158–181

9. Zukav, *Wu Li Masters*, p. 313.

10. N. Herbert, "Scientists Explore Invisible Ocean of Glue," C-Life Institute Publication, February 1977, pp. 1–20.

11. Zukav, *Wu Li Masters*, p. 320.

Chapter Five

1. D. Bohm, *Wholeness and the Implicate Order* (London: Routledge and Kegan Paul, 1980), pp. 174–175.

2. Ibid., p. 174.

3. Ibid., p. 15.

4. Ibid., p. 174.

5. J. Lorber, "Is your brain really necessary?" *Science* 210:1232–1234.

6. R. Restak, *Science Digest*, March 1981, p. 18.

7. Aaron Smith and Oscar Sugar, "Development of above normal language and intelligence 21 years after left hemispherectomy," *Neurology* 25: 813–818, September, 1975.

8. Karl Pribram, interviewed by Daniel Goleman, "Holographic Memory," *Psychology Today*, February, 1979, pp. 71–84.

9. Bohm, *Wholeness*, p. 211.

10. B. Brown, *Supermind: The ultimate energy* (New York: Harper and Row, 1980), p. 274.
11. Ibid., p. 275.
12. Walt Whitman, "Locations and Times" in *Leaves of Grass* (New York: The Modern Library), p. 225.

Chapter Six

1. A.N. Whitehead, *Nature and Life* (London: Cambridge University Press, 1934), p. 30.
2. P.C.W. Davies, *Space and Time in the Modern Universe* (Cambridge: Cambridge University Press, 1977), p. 212.
3. G. Bateson, *Mind and Nature: A Necessary Unity* (New York: E. P. Dutton, 1979).
4. R. Davenport, *An Outline of Animal Development* (Reading, Mass.: Addison-Wesley, 1979), p. 353.
5. W. Heisenberg, *Daedalus* 87:99, 1958.
6. E. Wigner, *Symmetries and Reflections* (Woodbridge, Connecticut: Ox Bow Press, 1979), p. 192.
7. Ibid., p. 180.
8. F. Capra, "The physicist and the mystic—is a dialogue between them possible?" *ReVision* 4:1, 1981, p. 44.
9. J.P. Green, and H. Weinstein, "Quantum mechanics can account for the affinities of drugs and receptors," *The Sciences*, Sept. 1981, p. 27.
10. Ibid., p. 28.
11. Ibid., p. 29.
12. Wigner, *Symmetries*, p. 192.
13. M. Delbrück, "Mind from matter?" *The American Scholar*, June: 339–353, 1978.
14. David Bohm, "A Conversation with David Bohm," *ReVision* 4:1, 1981, p. 26.
15. C. Rustrum, *The Wilderness Life*
16. D'Espagnat, "Quantum Theory," p. 158.
17. Aldous Huxley, "The Perennial Philosophy," in *The Highest State of Consciousness*, John White, ed. (Garden City, N.Y.: Anchor, 1972), p. 65.

PART IV

Chapter One

1. Owen Barfield, *The Rediscovery of Meaning and Other Essays* (Middletown, Connecticut: Wesleyan University Press, 1977), p. 182.
2. J. A. Wheeler, "Is Physics Legislated by Cosmogeny?" in *The Encyclopedia of Ignorance*, ed. R. Duncan and M. Weston-Smith (New York: Pergamon, 1977), p. 23.
3. E. H. Walker, "Consciousness and Quantum Theory," in *Psychic Exploration, A Challenge for Science*, ed. E. D. Mitchell (New York: G. P. Putnam's Sons, 1976), p. 544.
4. K. Pelletier, *Toward a Science of Consciousness* (New York: Dell, 1978), p. 123.
5. H. S. Stapp, "S-Matrix Interpretation of Quantum Theory," *Physical Review*, D3, 1971, p. 1303ff.
6. P. C. W. Davies, *Space and Time in the Modern Universe* (Cambridge: Cambridge University Press, 1977), p. 221.
7. Hermann Weyl, *Philosophy of Mathematics and Natural Science* (New York: Athenium, 1963), p. 116.
8. L. Barnett, *The Universe and Dr. Einstein* (New York: Bantam, 1968), p. 58.
9. Alan Watts, *Tao: The Watercourse Way* (New York: Pantheon, 1975), p. 54.
10. L. Le Shan, "Human Survival of Biological Death," in *The Medium, the Mystic, and the Physicist* (New York: Viking, 1966), p. 232.
11. Capra, *Tao of Physics*, p. 307.
12. B. Hoffman, *Albert Einstein, Creator and Rebel* (New York: Plume, 1973), p. 257.
13. J. Schwartz and M. McGuinness, *Einstein for Beginners* (New York: Pantheon, 1979), p. 82.
14. Davies, *Space and Time*, p. 200.
15. Ibid., p. 201.

16. Russell, *Mysticism*, p. 21.

17. Davies, *Space and Time*, p. 56.

18. G. Leonard, *The Ultimate Athlete* (New York: Viking, 1974), p. 34.

19. M. Murphy, *Intellectual Digest*, January, 1973.

20. Pat Toomay, *The Crunch* (New York: Norton, 1975).

21. I am indebted for this image to O. C. Simonton, S. Matthews-Simonton, and J. Creighton, *Getting Well Again*, p. 205.

22. Capra, *Tao of Physics*.

Chapter Two

1. D. Bohm, "A Conversation with David Bohm," *ReVision* 4:1, 1981, p. 26.

2. M.H. Steinberg and B.J. Dreiling, "Glucose-6-phosphate dehydrogenase deficiency in sickle cell anemia," *Annals of Internal Medicine* 80:217, 1974.

3. Bohm, "A Conversation with," p. 31.

4. Ibid., p. 33.

5. Ibid., p. 26.

6. A. Shimony, "Meeting of physics and metaphysics," *Nature* 291: 435, June, 1981.

Chapter Three

1. Evelyn Underhill, *Mysticism* (New York: Dutton, 1961), p. 300.

2. Monod, *Chance and Necessity*, p. 176.

3. Capra, *Tao of Physics*, p. 10.

4. Bronowski, *A Sense of the Future*, pp. 56–73.

5. Ibid.

6. Ibid.

7. Ibid.

8. Ibid.

9. Monod, *Chance and Necessity*, p. 21.

10. John A. Wheeler, and J. Mehra, eds., *The Physicist's Conception of Nature*, p. 244.

11. Freeman Dyson, "The Argument From Design," in *Disturbing the Universe* (New York: Harper and Row, 1979).

12. D'Espagnat, "Quantum Theory," pp. 158–181.

13. Zukav, *Wu Li Masters*.

14. Huston Smith, "The Sacred Unconscious," *ReVision*, Summer-Fall, 1979, pp. 3–7.

15. A. Einstein, *Ideas and Opinions*, quoted in Edgar Mitchell, *Psychic Exploration, A Challenge for Science* (New York: Capricorn, 1976), p. 13.

16. Judith Wechsler, *On Aesthetics in Science* (Cambridge: MIT Press, 1979), p. 4.

Chapter Four

1. E. Cassirer, *Language and Myth* (New York: Dover, 1953), p. 7.

2. Wechsler, *On Aesthetics*, p. 4.

3. Barfield, *Rediscovery of Meaning*, p. 138.

4. Shimony, "Meeting of physics and metaphysics."

5. Henry Margenau, *The Nature of Physical Reality* (New York: McGraw-Hill, 1950), p. 295.

6. Bohm, *Wholeness*, p. 23.

7. P. Schilpp, ed., *Albert Einstein: philosopher-scientist* (La Salle, Ill.: The Open Court Publishing Co., 1949), p. 236.

Chapter Five

1. David Bohm, "A Conversation," p. 26.

2. Carl Sagan, quoted in *Brain-Mind Bulletin*, vol. 6, no. 5, Feb. 16, 1981, p. 1.

3. Willis Harman, Address to the Annual Meeting of the American Association for the Advancement of Science, Houston, Texas, 1979.

4. M. Ullman, and S. Krippner with A. Vaughan, *Dream Telepathy* (New York: MacMillan, 1972).

5. Brown, *Supermind*, pp. 122–123.

6. D'Espagnat, "Quantum Theory."

7. Brown, *Supermind*, pp. 121–122.

8. Ibid., p. 124.

9. L. LeShan, *The Medium, the Mystic, and the Physicist* (New York: Viking, 1974), p. 85.

10. A. Koestler, *The Roots of Coincidence* (New York: Random House, 1977), p. 77.

11. Bronowski, *A Sense of the Future*, p. 39.

12. Ilya Prigogine, in Lukas, "The World According to Ilya Prigogine," p. 88.

13. Timothy Ferris, "The Spectral Messenger," *Science 81*, October, 1981, p. 72.

POSTSCRIPT

1. M.M. Wintrobe et al., *Harrison's Principles of Internal Medicine* (New York: McGraw-Hill, 1974), pp. 1199–2000.

2. William A. Check, "Angiotensin in the Brain?" *Journal of the American Medical Association*, February 8, 1980, pp. 499–500.

3. Neal E. Miller et al., "Learned Modifications of Autonomic Functions: A Review and Some New Data," *Circulation Research* 27: Supplement 1: 3–11, 1970.

4. D. Shapiro, B. Tursky, and G. E. Schwartz, "Control of Blood Pressure in Man by Operant Conditioning," *Circulation Research* 27: Supplement 1: 27–32, 1970.

5. Q.R. Regestein, "Relationships Between Psychological Factors and Cardiac Rhythm and Electrical Disturbances," *Comprehensive Psychiatry* 16: 137, 1975.

6. Peter Reich et al., "Acute Psychological Disturbances Preceding Life-Threatening Ventricular Arrhythmias," *Journal of the American Medical Association*, July 17, 1981, pp. 233–235.

7. Herbert Benson et al., "Historical and Clinical Considerations of the Relaxation Response," *American Scientist*, July-August, 1977, pp. 441–445.

8. David Bohm, *Wholeness*, p. 174.

9. David Bohm, "A Conversation," p. 26.

10. David Bohm, *Wholeness*, p. 174.

11. Max Delbrück, "Mind From Matter?" pp. 339–353.

12. C.H. Hartman, 'Response of Anginal Pain to Handwarming," *Biofeedback and Self-Regulation*, December, 1979, pp. 355–357.

13. J.E. Adam, "Naloxone Reversal of Analgesia Produced by Brain Stimulation in the Human," *Pain* 2: 161–166, 1976.

14. A.V. Vogel, J.S. Goodwin, and J.M. Goodwin, "The Therapeutics of Placebo," *American Family Physician* 22: 105–109, 1980.

15. Theodore Weiss, "Biofeedback Training for Cardiovascular Dysfunction," *Medical Clinics of North America*, July, 1977, pp. 913–928.

16. Richard A. Kirkpatrick, "Witchcraft and Lupus Erythematosus," *Journal of the American Medical Association*, May 15, 1981, p. 1937.

17. E.R. Gonzalez, "Constricting Arteries Expand Views of Ischemic Heart Disease," *Journal of the American Medical Association*, January 25, 1980, pp. 309–316.

18. Elmer and Alyce Green, *Beyond Biofeedback* (New York: Delacorte, 1977), pp. 225–241.

INDEX